Medieval Justice

Medieval Justice

*Cases and Laws in France,
England and Germany, 500–1500*

HUNT JANIN

McFarland & Company, Inc., Publishers
Jefferson, North Carolina, and London

I will that just laws be established and every unjust law carefully suppressed and that every injustice be weeded out and rooted up with all possible diligence from this country. And let God's justice be exalted; and henceforth let everyman, both poor and rich, be esteemed worthy of folk-right and let just dooms [judgments] be doomed to him.[1]
— *Opening words of a law code ordained by Anglo-Saxon King Canute at Winchester in the eleventh century*

The present work is a reprint of the illustrated case bound edition of Medieval Justice: Cases and Laws in France, England, and Germany, 500–1500, *first published in 2004 by McFarland.*

LIBRARY OF CONGRESS CATALOGUING-IN-PUBLICATION DATA

Janin, Hunt, 1940–
Medieval justice : cases and laws in France, England, and Germany, 500–1500 / Hunt Janin.
p.   cm.
Includes bibliographical references and index.

ISBN 978-0-7864-4502-8
softcover : 50# alkaline paper ∞

1. Law, Medieval — History.   2. Justice, Administration of— France — History —
To 1500.   3. Justice, Administration of— England — History — To 1500.
4. Justice, Administration of— Germany — History — To 1500.   I. Title.
KJ147.J36   2009   340.5'5 — dc22   2004005502

British Library cataloguing data are available

Cover art: Illustration depicting the execution of Guillaume Sans in Bordeaux (*Chroniques de Froissart, No. 2644, Bibliothèque nationale de France, Paris*)

Manufactured in the United States of America

*McFarland & Company, Inc., Publishers
Box 611, Jefferson, North Carolina 28640
www.mcfarlandpub.com*

Contents

Acknowledgments

My special thanks are due, above all, to Dr. Paul Brand, senior research fellow, All Souls College, Oxford, who patiently rescued me from many pitfalls, large and small. Without his help this book simply could not have been written. He courageously read early drafts of each chapter. Not being content to leave well enough alone, however, I have added new material to many chapters after his corrections. Dr. Brand cannot be blamed, then, for any shortcomings in the final text.

I must also express my great appreciation to Dr. Marie-Charlotte Le Bailly of Leiden University in the Netherlands, who read much of the manuscript. She, too, must be held blameless for any errors herein. Thanks are due as well to J.L. Bolton, senior research fellow, History Department, University of London, who provided all of the information in Appendix II ("What Was One Penny Worth in the Middle Ages?").

I am also in the debt of Bruce Graham, a medievalist turned computer expert; Dr. Sue Dale Tunnicliffe, a British magistrate; Melanie Janin, a writer in Washington, D.C.; Dr. Benjamin Arnold, reader in medieval history at Reading University; Dr. Rosamond McKitterick, professor of history, University of Cambridge; Robert Laws, who gave me permission to use his excellent translations of François Villon's poems; and Emma Gormley of the Curatorial Office of the Palace of Westminster.

My Dutch editor, Petronella van Gorkom of Amsterdam, has done her usual fine job of producing a readable text from my rough drafts. I alone, however, am responsible for any mistakes, omissions or misjudgments which may remain in this book.

Hunt Janin
St. Urcisse, France
March 2004

Preface

This book is a survey of medieval justice, written for the general reader — that is, for someone with no special knowledge of this tangled subject. Its goals are clarity and simplicity, not academic hair-splitting. It covers the thousand years between the eclipse of the Roman world in Western Europe, which took place in the fourth and fifth centuries C.E., and the European Renaissance of the fourteenth and fifteenth centuries.

"Justice" has many meanings. According to the *Oxford English Dictionary*, one of them is "the exercise of authority or power or maintenance of right." A less abstract and more useful definition, however, is one put forward in the late fourteenth century by Jean Boutillier, a French medieval jurist. (A jurist is someone who, like a judge, has a thorough knowledge of the law.) In his book on customary law, entitled *Somme rurale* (*Overview of rural life*), Boutillier stated that "Justice, according to the written law, is a constant and perpetual determination to give everyone his due."[i]

SUBSTANCE AND FORMAT

A survey such as this cannot offer encyclopedic coverage of a very complicated subject. Because of space limitations, it must necessarily be highly selective. For this reason, it has not been possible to set every case or law cited here in its full historical context: to do so would require a multivolume study of the entire medieval period. As a result, some of the most significant political, economic, military, religious and social events of the thousand years of the Middle Ages will be mentioned only in passing or not at all.

The reader who wishes to refresh his or her knowledge about these developments will find some excellent sources in the bibliography. Four broadly based works listed there are good starting points: *The Oxford Illustrated History of Medieval Europe*, edited by George Holmes (2001); *The Early Middle Ages*, edited by Rosamond McKitterick (2001); the *Dictionnaire raisonné de l'Occident médiéval*, edited by Jacques Le Goff and Jean-Claude Schmit (1999); and *Medieval Europe, 400–1500*, by H.G. Koenigsberger (1998).

Some historical subjects lend themselves readily to a seamless chronological treatment. Medieval justice, alas, is not one of them. Too many things were going on at the same time — in England, France, Germany and in other European countries which are

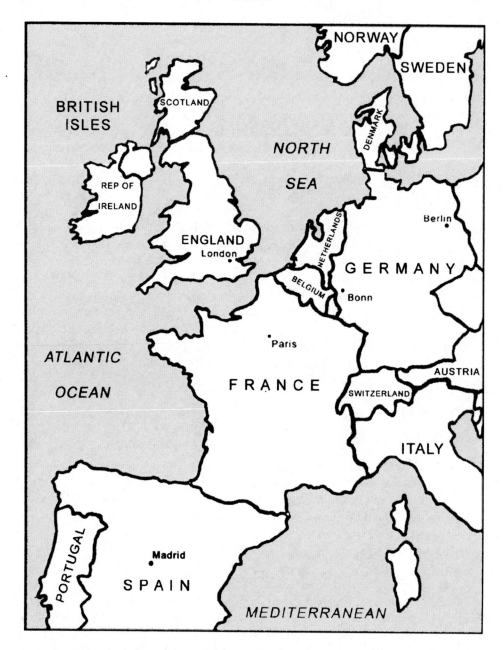

Map of England, France and Germany today. (Courtesy of Sue Barber.)

beyond the scope of this book. Moreover, medieval justice is characterized by multiple, overlapping, coexisting, changing, and conflicting laws and customs.

So although this book covers the thousand years of the Middle Ages, it does not do so in strict chronological order. Chapters are subject driven, not date driven. Chapter IV, for example, deals with "Feudalism and Justice in Medieval France." It is a long chapter and covers the ninth through the fourteenth centuries—a time span covered in some other chapters as well. In this book there are thus considerable overlaps in chronology. Within each chapter, however, events are presented in sequential order and are dated to help keep the chronological record straight. A selected chronology is included for this same purpose.

Chapters will begin with a short summary and will end with a section focusing on some of the most interesting cases and laws. Subheadings have been used generously for ease of reference and to break up, visually, what would otherwise be a dense text. The seven appendices shed light on points which are relevant but too detailed to explore in the text itself.

Geographic borders in Europe changed radically over the thousand years discussed here. To avoid digressions on the changing shapes of France or the Holy Roman Empire (a varying complex of lands in Western and Central Europe which endured for more than ten centuries), in many instances the names of modern states, e.g., Germany, will be used here, even though they might not have existed at that time. In the interests of simplicity, the only map used here is a modern one which shows England, France, Germany and neighboring states as they are today.

THE RELEVANCE OF THE PAST

What significance, if any, does medieval justice have for us today? The answer: a surprising amount. Numerous legacies of medieval justice can readily be identified. These will be discussed in the last chapter of this book, which also offers a brief summary of medieval justice.

1

Why This Book?

A common misunderstanding today is that there was no such thing as "medieval justice." The Middle Ages seem so far away from us now and medieval culture seems so radically different from our own that it is not easy to grasp the premises on which it was based. It is much easier to imagine that medieval life must have been based simply on religious or military coercion. Such an assumption, however, would be quite mistaken. Coercion did exist, as it does in every society, but medieval life was not based on force but on a complicated skein of unwritten customs and of written secular and ecclesiastical laws. Not all of them may be to our liking, but they were widely accepted at the time and their potency cannot be denied.

We must remember that patterns of life in the Middle Ages were not freely chosen. Even before they were born, virtually all medieval men and women were caught up in multiple relationships, dependencies and obligations — most of them permanent, many of them onerous and none of them of their own choosing.[1] People were tied to the land and were living in a densely woven social fabric. Manlio Bellomo, an Italian legal historian, reminds us that these same men and women also had "unshakeable certitudes to guide them, aid their understanding, and provide a notion of unity and order."[2] Their belief in justice — both divine and human justice — was one of these certitudes. As a result, law was one of the mainsprings of medieval society and directly touched the lives of most medieval men and women.

Indeed, the Middle Ages were remarkably litigious times. This can be seen from the fact that most of the records which have come down to us from this era are legal documents.[3] They show that a great deal of legal activity was going on. During the thirteenth century, for example, large numbers of students studied law, first at urban schools and then at the universities. This era alone has bequeathed to us about 7,000 manuscripts on Roman law (modified to suit the Middle Ages) and 8,000 manuscripts on canon law.[4] These are now held by European and American libraries.

Such works introduce us to the lively minds and technical skills of their authors, as well as to the careful attention they paid to the ever-changing political, economic and social currents of their day.[5] In fourteenth-century England, no fewer than 13,031 cases were brought in the Court of Common Pleas, the busiest branch of the king's court, in the two-year period 1327–1328. Each year, more than 15,000 different men and women were involved as litigants in this court alone.[6] On a personal as well as a community level, legal work was extremely important, too. For skilled practitioners it

This set of four illuminations on vellum, dating from about 1460, is the earliest known depiction of English courts and courtroom dress. Shown are the four courts at Westminster Hall. Left to right, from the top: the Court of Common Pleas (2), the Court of Exchequer (3), the Court of Chancery (4), and the Court of King's Bench (5). (Masters of the Bench of the Inner Temple).

offered lucrative, intellectually stimulating careers. Indeed, in the twelfth century, Nigellus Wireker, a satirical poet, complained that "Jurists are everywhere there is money and power, at the king's court and in the dwelling of the pope, in civil society and in the monasteries."[7] He added that in spite of "his dull mind and strong neck," even a donkey could understand that law was a good road to the summits of power.[8]

A legal career was one of the few ways in which an intelligent, ambitious young man could move up through the ranks of the relatively static society of the Middle Ages. Not surprisingly, legal work consistently attracted some of the finest medieval minds.

WHY A SURVEY MAY BE USEFUL

If we want to come to grips with medieval life as a whole, we must learn something about medieval justice. This, however, is easier said than done. Medieval society was colorful, diverse and complicated. Not surprisingly, medieval justice was equally so. As James Brundage, a specialist in medieval canon law, has pointed out,

> Medieval laws came in abundant variety. Multiple legal systems coexisted and overlapped within the same town or region, each with its own complex rules and conventions as well as its own system of courts that applied them. Manorial law, feudal law, municipal law, royal law, maritime law, merchant law, and canon law all nestled cheek by jowl with each other in medieval communities. Each claimed its special areas of competence, to be sure, but jurisdictional claims frequently competed with one another and disputes over jurisdictional questions erupted with lamentable regularity.[9]

But this is not all. As early as c. 1188, when *Glanvill*— the first treatise on English common law — was finished, its unknown author complained: "To put in writing, in their entirety, the laws and customs of the realm would be utterly impossible today … such a confused mass they are."[10] And when the classic French medievalist Marc Bloch (1886–1944) surveyed the European scene at mid-point in the Middle Ages, he found that three features were dominating the legal process: the tremendous fragmentation of judicial powers, their tangled interconnections and their relative ineffectiveness.[11]

Before the fourteenth century, anyone who traveled a long distance in Western Europe and who went from one country to another might find that his legal status changed radically during the course of one day. In country A in the morning, he might be of age; in country B in the evening, he might be a minor.[12] Medieval justice therefore turns out to be a surprisingly complicated subject. Moreover, just as legal status was subject to different interpretations, social relationships were, too. Medieval society was more of an *unequal* society than a strictly hierarchical one. Kings could have conflicting obligations to other kings, and lords to other lords.

Because of all these complexities, most legal historians today shy away from broadbrush general surveys of the field. They prefer instead to concentrate on tightly focused studies which can be examined in greater depth and which can, if necessary, be defended more easily. From the point of view of the general reader, however, such a conservative scholarly approach can result in works which may be brilliant but which can be appreciated only by other academicians. In fact, Jacques Chiffoleau, a French scholar, tells us that

> The painstaking study of [medieval] rules and judicial practices requires a technical competence so specialized that it often seems, both to general historians and to the public at large, to be a discipline which is slightly mysterious, isolated, and remote. [It] has therefore remained in the hands of legal scholars themselves [because] it does not sufficiently hold the attention of general historians, even when it does not scare them off by its extreme complexity.[13]

This survey is written by a "general historian" and tries to steer a middle course between academic complexity and a simple-minded approach. It is manifestly impossible in such a book to cover all of the multiple, overlapping and sometimes conflicting medieval legal systems. Two more modest goals, however, may be achievable. The first of these is to highlight some of the key elements of these intricate legal systems. The second goal is to give the reader the flavor of medieval times by discussing approximately 100 contemporary cases and laws.

CASES AND LAWS

So that they do not obstruct the flow of the text, many of these cases and laws have been put into separate sections at the end of each chapter. *It is important to understand that this has been done for illustrative purposes only, not to make a particular point or prove a particular thesis.* If there is any ulterior purpose in this unusual format, it is simply to whet the reader's interest in learning more about medieval justice on his or her own, once this book is finished.

Case law was certainly important in its own right. It played a key role in the development of legal systems in England and France, where it was the responsibility of the courts to apply the sometimes academic principles of the law to work a day disputes. Although legal texts and ordinances themselves can be deadly dull, most of the cases cited here are of considerable human interest. Some of them have been cited in considerable detail, using the exact (if translated) words that medieval people themselves used to record them. It would have been easy enough to paraphrase them but in their original form they give an "I-was-there" immediacy which would otherwise be lost.

We shall see, for example, well-meaning but angry and often frightened medieval men and women struggling to come to grips with a wide range of issues. These include blood feuds, werewolves, perjury, pig stealing, sorcerers and witches, ordeals (by fire, water, or battle), murder, a "perfect" rape, satanic dreams of women, a marriage made under duress, responsibility for the loss of a castle, blasphemy, the trial of one of the greatest nobles of France, a male transvestite prostitute, land disputes, the fictional outlaw Robin Hood and his real-life counterparts, Joan of Arc (relapsed heretic or saint?), punishment for adulterers, and rebellious barons.

In addition to their legal and human interest, these cases are worth studying for another reason as well. There was often a sizeable gap between the general principles and idealizations of the written law, on the one hand, and the practical applications of customary law, on the other. These applications could be decisively swayed by such under-the-table factors as political patronage or outright bribery. Studying the written law alone can therefore be misleading: it is the cases themselves which give us a real insight into the legal opportunities and pitfalls of daily life in the Middle Ages.

It is hoped that these cases will help the general reader to come to grips with medieval justice. As Janet Nelson, a modern scholar, says, "Actual cases, despite all their problems, are as close as we can get to how things happened — certainly far closer than the idealizations of written law."[14]

POSSIBILITIES FOR ERROR

The book tries to fill a scholarly gap. As far as is known, no other survey of this kind has been written, at least in English or in French. No such work is now listed in the holdings of the British Library in London or the Bodleian Library in Oxford. When Paul Brand, a British legal historian, was asked why this is the case, he replied candidly:

> I find it difficult to give a clear answer. I guess those of us who do know something about the subject typically know about particular kinds of law and particular places and times and are leery of straying too far off our own territory. It needs someone like you to see the whole picture and not be too afraid of getting some things not quite right.[15]

For a nonspecialist, writing on this subject can be daunting because scholars themselves frequently disagree. Conclusions are never set in concrete but differ from one expert to another. One reputable writer (John Morall) asserts that "France was the classic country of feudalism."[16] Another equally reputable scholar (Paul Brand) thinks otherwise. "England," he says, "was much more comprehensively 'feudalized' as a result of the Norman Conquest than France ever was."[17]

This lack of agreement is the result of a more fundamental problem. As Michael Swanton, a translator of the *Anglo-Saxon Chronicle*, has remarked, "Any work of scholarship is necessarily provisional."[18] A noted medievalist (H.G. Koenigsberger) concurs: "Few, if any, questions are finally answered. That has usually been one of the most prominent features in the study of European history."[19] Thus *Medieval Justice* runs the risk of getting a few things "not quite right," either as a result of simple mistakes made when working with 1,000 years of medieval history or by citing scholars whose judgments may not be universally accepted now.

Nevertheless, because it has not been attempted before, trying to describe medieval justice *as a whole*, rather than only one small part of it, seems to be a worthwhile challenge. The end result is, hopefully, a book of greater interest to the general reader than a traditional, narrowly focused academic analysis. If *Medieval Justice* does succeed in outlining some parts of the medieval legal system and giving the reader some of the flavor of daily life in the Middle Ages, it will have served a useful purpose. With this background in mind, and perhaps stimulated by some of the cases discussed here, the interested reader can then move on to the more specialized works listed in the bibliography.

2

Justice in the Early Middle Ages

By the beginning of the Early Middle Ages (about 500), Roman rule had ended nearly everywhere west of the Adriatic Sea. This era, formerly known as the Dark Ages, was marked by frequent warfare and a virtual disappearance of urban life. Apart from the Carolingian court established by the emperor Charlemagne, there was no large kingdom capable of providing political or military stability. Instead, the Christian church provided the main basis for social unity. Two different legal systems — barbarian law and Roman law — coexisted uneasily.

THE COMING OF THE BARBARIANS

The influx of German tribesmen into Western Europe used to be known as the barbarian invasions. (The Romans used the term "barbarian" to mean someone who did not speak Latin.) This process is now seen as a series of Germanic *migrations*, probably given impetus by the expansion of the Huns from their own homelands north of the Black Sea. The barbarians turned out to be a mixed blessing for the Romans. Rome often hired them as "federates" (auxiliary troops) to help preserve the integrity of the empire, but at other times, the Romans had to fight them.

In these latter campaigns, Roman soldiers managed to win some considerable victories. But the Roman Empire itself was rotten to the core and in the long run it could not hold out against the barbarians. Thus it was that in 476, the barbarian Odoacer, who had risen to be the Roman army's *magister militum* ("master of the soldiers," i.e., the senior officer of the imperial guard), deposed the 16-year-old Romulus Augustulus, the last Roman emperor, and had himself proclaimed king.

BARBARIAN LAW: THE ROLE OF CUSTOM

As they came to power the barbarians set up kingdoms of their own. The Visigoths controlled Gaul as far north as the Loire River. They ruled in Spain as well. Further north, the Alemanni and the Salian Franks held power. North Africa was in the hands of the Vandals. But barbarian rulers and their followers constituted only a small minority in the new kingdoms and retained their own tribal laws. The first compilation of these laws were the *Leges Barbarorum* (*Barbarian Laws*), which were written in

Latin and used some of the technical terms of Roman law. They date from the fifth to the ninth centuries.

Barbarian law was based on very different legal premises from those used today. Among them were the veneration accorded to tribal customs; the reliance on "personal" law, which resulted in conflicting legal jurisdictions (described below); *wergeld* (monetary payments to redress wrongs); and certain unique ways of proving the guilt or innocence of an accused person. These methods of proof, which will also be discussed below, included compurgation (oath swearing); ordeals (by hot water, by hot iron, or by cold water); and trial by battle.

Barbarian law was usually not handed down from the king but arose from the customs of a given tribe. The *Leges Barbarorum*, for example, drew heavily on local customs. In about 630 this was underscored by Isidore of Seville, whose *Etymologies* became one of the most-studied works of the Middle Ages. "The legal system," he wrote, "is based on law and on custom. The difference between them is that the law is written. Custom, on the contrary, is legitimized by its antiquity. *It is an unwritten law.*"[1] The importance of the oral transmission of the law in the early Middle Ages can hardly be overemphasized. To use an apt phrase coined by modern French scholars, the written word was then only "an islet lost in a sea of orality."[2]

THE SURVIVAL OF ROMAN LAW

Even after the disappearance of Roman political authority in the west, however, there was no decline and fall of Roman law itself. Instead, there was a gradual process of integration and adaptation of this law throughout the Middle Ages.[3] Thus Roman law never vanished entirely. The *Codex Theodosianus (Theodosian Code)*, for example, had been compiled in Latin in 438. Abridgements were made of it in the early Middle Ages, e.g., the *Lex Romana Visigothorum (Roman Law of the Visigoths)* of 506 and the *Brevarium (Breviary)* of Visigothic King Alaric II of 507. Through these versions, Roman law remained in use in Western Europe until the eleventh century.[4]

PERSONAL LAW AND CONFLICTING LEGAL JURISDICTIONS

The barbarians permitted their subjects to continue to live under Roman law. So, even though these two groups might live cheek by jowl in the same region, they were subject to different laws. The barbarians had tribal law; their subjects had Roman law. This unusual situation came about because customary barbarian law was *personal law*, that is, it was conceived of as residing in the individual, not in the territory where he or she happened to live. The Germanic conquerors themselves could therefore "profess" Gothic, Frankish, Lombard or some other kind of barbarian law, according to their tribal affiliations. Their subjects and the clergy, on the other hand, could profess Roman law, albeit in a "vulgar" (simplified) form.[5]

This fact gave rise to the problem of conflicting legal jurisdictions — an issue so vexing that the famous French medievalist Marc Bloch thought that it constituted "the most singular medley that ever confronted a professor of law in his nightmares."[6] In about 816, for example, archbishop Agobard of Lyon reported that in Frankish Gaul "One frequently sees conversing together five persons, no two of whom are governed by the same law."[7] An example of this would have been a conversation between a Roman, a Salian Frank, a Ripuarian Frank, a Visigoth, and a Burgundian.[8]

WERGELD

Under barbarian law, criminal offenses were seen as wrongs against individuals and their families, not as wrongs against society as a whole. As a result, amends could be made in cash or in goods. Each man or woman had his or her own monetary value, known as *wergeld* ("man-price" in Old English). Payments reflected the magnitude of a crime. Minor offenses could be rectified by a small payment. If a man were murdered, however, the murderer and his kin had to pay a high price to the family of the victim — 200 *solidi* in the case of a free Anglo-Saxon or a free Frank.[9]

Such payments, however, may have been intended merely as starting points in negotiations, rather than as the amounts which actually had to be paid. There were other fines as well. The *bot* was compensation for damages done to, and allowances for the repair of, a house or tools. The *wite* was a fine paid to the king by a criminal, to atone for his act.

The kin-group was responsible for bringing to justice anyone who had wronged a member of the kin. In extreme cases this could result in a "blood feud," i.e., a continuing state of conflict marked by killings and counterkillings. During such a feud, the kin-group could legally kill anyone who murdered one of its members. Though rare, this practice was accepted by Anglo-Saxon society because without such a lethal threat there was no other way to force a guilty person to submit to the legal process.[10]

Social rank, gender and whether a person was free or not free were extremely important in determining *wergeld*. A lord's *wergeld* was much higher than that of a common man. Clergy had their own rate of *wergeld*, which was a function of the social class into which they had been born. Royal directives governing *wergeld* were firm and very specific.

THE ORDEALS: PROVING INNOCENCE OR GUILT

The Roman form of legal proceedings, known as the *cognitio extraordinaria* ("extraordinary jurisdiction"), had relied on both oral and written testimony. It required stringent rules of evidence and proof. It gave significant investigative or "inquisitorial" powers to the judge. Under Roman law, the burden of proof was usually on the accuser. As the emperor Justinian's legal code put it in 533, "the burden of proof is upon the party affirming, not on the party denying."[11] It was thus up to the accuser to find credible witnesses who would support his allegations.

With the eclipse of Roman power in the West, the *cognitio extraordinaria* was abandoned. The Germanic tribes preferred their own traditional methods of proof. Under barbarian law, the accuser had to provide some kind of initial proof of the validity of his charges but, ultimately, the burden of proof could fall heavily on the defendant, who might have to submit to an ordeal to establish his innocence or his guilt.

Ordeals are now referred to as "irrational proofs" because their verdicts were believed to reflect the will of God, not rational compliance with man-made norms.[12] The ordeal was based entirely on theology. According to the thinking of the times, men did not judge other men by means of the ordeal: they simply relied on the will of God as revealed through it.[13] By invoking divine blessings on the ordeal before it began, priests played a critically important role. When, therefore, in 1215 the Fourth Lateran Council, which will be discussed later, banned priests from participating in the ordeal, this removed its religious foundations and legally brought it to an end.

By the ninth century, much of Western Europe was divided into *pagi* (the *pagus* was a small administrative unit about the size of an English county), each governed by a count. As the king's representative, the count presided over the local court, which adjudicated disputes between freemen. It was the men who "owed suit" or "performed suit" — that is, the men who had a duty of regular attendance at the court — who determined which procedure the court should follow and what kind of proof it should demand.

In this they appear to have had considerable latitude. Barbarian methods of proof will be discussed below.

COMPURGATION

This was the most common method of proof in the early Middle Ages. The parties involved had to swear on oath — several times — and deny that the charges which had been brought had any validity. The defendants swore: "By the Lord, I am guiltless both of deed and instigation of the crime with which [the plaintiff] charges me." In addition, they or the court itself would enlist a number of compurgators (oath helpers) who would take oaths, too, to demonstrate that they believed these denials. Their oath was: "By the Lord, the oath is pure and not false that [the defendant] swore."[14]

ORDEALS AS A LAST RESORT

As a general rule, the ordeals themselves were used only when there seemed to be no other way of determining a person's innocence or guilt. Thought to originally have been a custom of the Franks, they were widely used by other continental Germanic peoples after the year 500. They were invariably a means of last resort and were never called upon lightly or at random. A legal maxim in twelfth-century England held that "the ordeal of hot iron is not to be permitted except where the naked truth cannot otherwise be explored."[15] A similar principle existed in thirteenth-century Germany: "It is not right to use the ordeal in any case, unless the truth may be known in no other way."[16]

ORDEAL BY HOT WATER

This proof was endorsed by, among other notables, archbishop Hincmar of Reims (806–882), one of the great canon lawyers, theologians and political experts of Carolingian times. He was a political consultant to both the Frankish kings Louis I the Pious and Charles the Bald. For Hincmar, the ordeal by hot water had two important qualities. Water represented the great flood of the Old Testament, which spared only the virtuous. The flames used to heat the water brought to his mind the Last Judgment, when the wicked would be condemned to the fires of hell.

An early example of this ordeal was the state trial of Queen Teutberga of Lotharingia in 858, which involved both sex and politics in equal measure.[17] The queen was barren. Her husband, King Lothar, wanted to get rid of her, marry his mistress, and legitimize the children he had by her. He therefore accused his wife of sexual misbehavior. She retaliated by ordering one of her retainers to undergo the ordeal by hot water on her behalf. This courageous, loyal individual passed the order successfully; the queen was declared innocent. As a result, Lothar's children remained illegitimate and could not inherit the throne upon his death.

This is how the ordeal by hot water was conducted. On the day of the ordeal, a mass was celebrated. At the communion, the priest prayed that "this body and blood of Our Lord Jesus Christ to be to thee [the accused] this day a manifestation of guilt or innocence." Then a fire was kindled, and water — it was holy water now, because it had been blessed by the priest — was heated in a cauldron.

For minor offenses, the "single" ordeal would suffice. This required the accused to thrust his hand into the water up to his wrist. He was then free to jerk it out again. Alternatively, he might be made to retrieve a ring or a stone from the bottom of the cauldron, an enterprise which took more time. Serious offenses called for the "triple" ordeal, which required the whole forearm to be plunged into the water up to the elbow.

The hand and, if necessary, the forearm, too, would then be bandaged and sealed. If an inspection three days later showed that the injuries were healing well, the accused was pronounced innocent. If they were not, he was held to be guilty. Here is what the Anglo-Saxon king Athelstan (924–939) had to say about the ordeal by hot water:

> And concerning the ordeal we enjoin by command of God, and of the archbishop and of all the bishops: ... let [the water] be heated till it low to boiling. And be the kettle of iron or brass, of lead or of clay. And if it be a single accusation, let the hand dive after the stone [to retrieve it] up to the wrist; and if it be threefold, up to the elbow....[18]

ORDEAL BY HOT IRON

This proof involved the same preparations and the same procedures as the ordeal by hot water: prayer and fasting, a mass, blessings, bandaging the injuries and, finally, inspecting them three days later. To quote Athelstan again:

This final page from a ninth-century French law book is thought to depict the ordeal by hot iron. Symbolic flames are emerging from the head of the central figure, who may be clutching a hot iron bar in his right hand. (MS. lat. 4628.f.66v. Bibliothèque nationale de France, Paris.)

> Let the iron lie upon the hot embers till [the end of the Mass]; after that let it be laid upon the *stapela* [stake].... And let him [the accused] go thereto; and let his hand be enveloped, and be [opening it] postponed till after the third day, whether it be foul or clean within the envelope....[19]

In other ordeals by hot iron, sometimes the accused was blindfolded and forced to walk over a path studded with six, nine or twelve red-hot plowshares. At other times, without a blindfold, a man or a woman (when her chastity was at issue) had to hold a red-hot iron, or carry it for a given distance, usually nine feet. In Anglo-Saxon England the "simple" ordeal by fire called for a one-pound chunk of iron. However, "three-fold" (serious) charges, such as plotting against the king's life, counterfeiting, murder, robbery, arson or felonies, were judged by use of a three-pound piece.[20]

ORDEAL BY COLD WATER

The theology behind this ordeal was that water was a pure element which, when blessed and therefore made holy, would *refuse to accept a guilty person.* In one version of this mode of proof, the accused was bound hand and foot and was then thrown into a body of water — often contained in a large pit dug expressly for this purpose — which had been duly blessed by a priest. If the water accepted the accused, i.e., if he sank, he was innocent. If the water rejected him, that is, if he floated, he was of course guilty.

In another version of this ordeal, the accused, having been bound and foot, was slowly lowered into the water by means of a rope tied around the middle of his body. There was a knot in the rope, either tied close to his body ("a long hair's breadth" away) or some distance from it (about half a yard away).[21] If he sank and pulled the knot down with him until it broke the surface of the water, he was innocent. If both he and the knot floated, however, this proved his guilt.

SHORT-CIRCUITING THE ORDEALS

Despite the severity of these ordeals, they were conducted in such a structured, methodical manner that there was plenty of time for second thoughts and out-of-court settlements. Many people in the *pagus* were related; all of them had friends or relatives who were interested in a given case. Some of these men and women must have put themselves forward as peacemakers. Clerics were involved, too: witness the exploits of St. Gregory, discussed at some length below.

The ordeal came at the end of a legal process. Immediately before the ordeal itself, the accused had to spend three days in prayer and fasting, presumably getting in the process no end of well-meaning advice from other members of the *pagus*. Subjective factors played a large role. Even after the ordeal itself was over, there was still room for human intervention in what was in theory a direct, infallible appeal to the will of God.

Take the ordeal by hot water, for example. As soon as the accused yanked his scalded hand or forearm out of the hot water, his injuries were bandaged with a cloth, which was then sealed with a judge's signet. Three days later, the cloth was removed. If the wound was found to be "clean," that is, healing well, the man was proclaimed innocent. If it was "unclean," i.e., discolored or suppurating, he was pronounced guilty.

There were, however, no objective medical standards for what constituted healing or infection. A typical directive from the Middle Ages simply states that "if festering blood be found in the track of the iron, he shall be found guilty. But if, however, he shall go forth uninjured, praise shall be rendered to God."[22] Another contemporary source claims that a blister "as large as half a walnut" was a fatal sign.[23] It is thus a reasonable guess that the verdict of guilt or innocence was in large part subjective. Extraneous factors, such as politics or compassion, almost certainly played a role in the final judgment.

A king, for example, could assure for political reasons that the outcome of an ordeal would be to his liking. In the thirteenth-century *Saga of Saint Olaf*, for example, a ship captain, Sigurth Thorlakson, is falsely accused by the king of a murder. The king orders Sigurth to undergo the ordeal of hot iron. Just before the trial, however, Sigurth tells his men, "This king is crafty and deceitful.... It will be very easy for him to falsify this ordeal. I would consider it dangerous to risk that with him."[24] Deciding that prudence was the better part of valor, Sigurth and his men took advantage of a fair wind and set sail for the open sea.

There may have been compassionate outcomes, too, although they have not been recorded because the purpose of the ordeal was to obtain God's judgment, not man's sympathy. It is easy to imagine, though, that if a sympathetic judge thought the accused was an honorable man who had already suffered enough during the ordeal, he might be set free. On the other hand, a man who already had a reputation in the *pagus* as a bad character might fare less well. As the eminent English jurist and legal historian Frederic William Maitland put it,

> How these tests worked in practice we do not know. We seldom get stories about them save when, as now and again will happen, the local saint interferes and performs a miracle. We cannot but guess that it was well to be good friends with the priest when one went to the ordeal.[25]

TRIAL BY BATTLE

Also known as the judicial duel, this appeal to the will of God was a familiar custom to the continental Germanic peoples from about the year 500. Because physical strength, training and good luck played decisive roles here, this method of proof could not be short-circuited.

A judicial battle could be fought between men on horseback or on foot, armed with either lethal or non-lethal weapons. Not everyone was permitted to engage in trial by combat. In 1140, Pope Innocent II ordered that ecclesiastics should not take part in such a duel. Serfs could not challenge freemen. The sick, e.g., lepers, could not challenge the healthy. Bastards could not challenge those who were legitimately born. Children were not allowed to fight. Women were normally excluded from trial by combat. Very rarely, however, a wife might be allowed to fight her husband, with rigorous conditions being imposed to make the duel a fair one.

In 1228, a woman fought a man at Berne, Switzerland, and soundly defeated him.[26] German law provided that in such a case the man should be armed with three wooden clubs. He was to put be up to his waist in a three-foot-wide hole dug in the ground, with one hand tied behind his back. The woman was to be armed with three rocks, each weighing between one and five pounds, and each one wrapped in cloth. The man could not leave his hole but the woman was free to run around the edge of the pit.

If the man touched the edge of the pit with either his hand or his arm, he had to surrender one of his clubs to the judges. If the woman hit him with a rock while he was doing so, she forfeited one of her stones. Bizarre as it may seem to us today, this marital duel was very far from play-acting. For both parties, the penalty for defeat was death. If the woman won, the man was executed; if the man won, the woman was buried alive.[27]

Trial by battle was occasionally used even by monasteries to settle their differences. In 1287 the monks of Bury St. Edmund in England were embroiled in a dispute over the ownership of two manors in Suffolk. The monks came to the conclusion that they had such a weak case that trial by combat would be better than a jury trial. "After discussion of the case," they wrote, "since we were doubtful about the countryside, as friendly with and akin to our enemies, we decided that our right was to be defended by the duel."[28] The outcome of this duel, if it ever took place, has not been recorded.

CHAMPIONS

What happened when a person was challenged to trial by combat but was formally barred from accepting the challenge? In this case, a champion could be hired to do the fighting.

In England, parties in non-criminal cases were not allowed to fight in person and were required to use champions. The plaintiff's champion was, ideally, a witness to the possession of the property under dispute, on which the plaintiff based his claim. For this reason, he could not be the plaintiff himself. The defendant's champion was by definition someone who believed that the plaintiff's accusations constituted perjury.[29]

Champions were often family members or freeman retainers, but gradually a class of professional "hired guns" came into being. These freelance champions sold their skills to the highest bidder. In 1017, for example, when the Holy Roman emperor Henry II wanted to find out which of two robbers who were awaiting trial in different German cities was guilty, he hired champions to fight judicial duels with them.[30]

If a champion was defeated in a trial by combat, he might be punished by the amputation of a hand or a foot, or even by hanging. Needless to say, this line of work did not attract the best and the brightest. Champions were not held in high esteem. In thirteenth-century France, they were ranked with prostitutes and petty criminals. Germany lumped them together with actors, jugglers and bastards as undesirables who were "unlaw-worthy" and who were not permitted to give evidence or inherit property. Italy suspected them of being ex-convicts or men of unsavory reputations.[31]

England even had a special category of champions known as "approvers." These were career criminals who had turned crown witness (state's evidence) in the hope of lessening their sentences. Seeking a full pardon, they had also agreed to challenge, for a relatively brief period of time, other felons to trial by battle. A contemporary case records that one Robert, son of Patrick, "was captured at Kidderminster fleeing in company with thieves ... he confessed that he is a thief ... and he turns an approver to fight five battles."[32] This procedure may have been an easy way to get rid of convicted criminals: Robert himself might have been killed in combat or he might have managed to kill some or all of the other felons.

FAILURES TO END THE JUDICIAL DUEL

Despite its apparent advantages, doubts persisted about the legitimacy of trial by battle. Liudprand, king of the Lombards from 713–744, wrote: "We are unsure about the judgment of God and have heard of many men who have lost their cause unjustly through trial by combat."[33] Clerics were even more outspoken. Archbishop Agobard of Lyon was quoted earlier. He had something to say on this subject, too, being convinced that

the duel was opposed to Christian charity, to reason and to experience, which teaches us that the outcome of duels is often unjust and wrong, and which is confirmed by many examples from Holy Scripture showing that even the just man

Trial by battle c. 1249 between the "approver" Walter Bloweberme and the accused robber Hamo le Stare. Bloweberme, an accomplice who had turned crown witness, charged le Stare with complicity in a robbery and challenged him to trial by battle, shown on the right side of the illustration. Le Stare was defeated. Having thus been proved guilty, he was hanged from a nearby gallows, shown on the left side of the illustration. (Computer enhancement by Sue Barber of a copy of an illustration in the author's collection.)

can be defeated in battle; finally, the duel was opposed to the nature of judgment, which consists in wise investigations, not brutal power.[34]

These early misgivings, however, failed to end the judicial duel. It continued to be used frequently throughout the thirteenth century to settle disputes. Medieval law books in England, France and Germany accepted it as a normal part of the legal process. It was used in Italy, Spain and Eastern Europe as well. During the fourteenth and fifteenth centuries, though, it fell out of favor. In 1455, Philip the Good, duke of Burgundy, went to watch a trial by battle in Valenciennes, attracted to the spectacle only because "such things do not happen often."[35] The last judicial duel held in England occurred in 1492, at the end of the Middle Ages. Remarkably, trial by battle was not formally abolished in England until more than 300 years later — in 1819.

Illustrative Cases and Laws

A WEREWOLF CLAUSE (C. 500)

In European folklore, a werewolf was a man who turned into a wolf at night and ate animals, people or corpses, resuming his human form just before dawn. (Even in the sixteenth century, there were still executions in rural France of men convicted as being *loups-garous*, i.e., werewolves.) In the early sixth century, "werewolf" was used in the following legal decision on what should be done in the case of a raider who had seized a slave illegally and taken him abroad:

> If any foreign slave has been seized and taken overseas, and if he is found there by his master and names, in the *mallus publicus* [the official meeting-place of the free men of a local community in the Frankish world], the man by whom he was seized in his own country, he ought to gather three witnesses there. Again when the slave has been brought back from across the sea he ought to repeat his statement in another *mallus*, and should again gather three suitable witnesses.
>
> He ought to do the same at a third *mallus*, so that nine witnesses swear that they heard the slave make the same statement against his kidnapper in three *malli*, after which he who seized him should be denounced in court as a *werewolf* [that is, one who figuratively consumes another man's livelihood by depriving him of his slave]....[36]

A Barbarian King Condemns Perjurers (502)

Gundobad, greatest of the Burgundian kings, formulated two law codes. The first was for his own people — the *Lex Gundobada* or *Lex Burgundionum* of 484. Later, in about 500 he promulgated a broader code (now known as the *loi Gombette*) which applied to his Roman subjects and to cases which involved both Romans and Burgundians. In 502, he also issued an edict at Lyon condemning perjury by Burgundian oath-takers:

> We know that many of our people have become depraved through the failure of litigation and through an instinct of cupidity, to the extent that they do not hesitate to offer oaths in uncertain matters and to perjure themselves over known facts....
>
> If the party to whom the oath has been offered does not wish to accept it, but says that the force of truth can only be brought to his adversary by dint of arms, and if the other party does not then withdraw the suit, license to fight will not be denied.
>
> Then one of the witnesses who has come to give his oath shall undertake the challenge with God as judge; since it is right that if anyone says that he knows the truth of the matter without doubt and offers to take the oath, he should not refuse to fight.[37]

The Salic Law (c. 507–510)

One of the most important of the barbarian laws was the *Pactus Legis Salicae* (*Law of the Salian Franks*, or Salic Law). This was a penal and procedural code finally committed to parchment, in Latin, only after a long period of oral transmission. It is attributed to Clovis I (466–511), king of the Franks and ruler of much of Gaul.

The Salic Law combined elements of customary law, Roman written law, Christian ideals and royal edicts. It listed a long string of fines for different offenses. Here are some excerpts:

> If anyone steals a suckling pig, and it be proved against him, he shall be sentenced to 120 *denarii* — that is, three *solidi*.

If a slave steals, outside of the house, something worth two *denarii*, he shall, beside paying the worth of the object and the fines for delay, be stretched out and receive 120 blows. But if he steals something worth 40 *denarii*, he shall either be castrated or pay 6 *solidi*. But the lord of the slave who committed the theft shall restore to the plaintiff the worth of the object and the fines for delay.

If anyone kills a free Frank, or a barbarian living under the Salic Law, and it is proved against him, he shall be sentenced to 8,000 *denarii*. But if he shall have thrown him into a well, or into the water, or shall have covered him with branches or anything else to conceal him, he shall be sentenced to 24,000 *denarii*, which make 600 *solidi*.[38]

RESTITUTION AFTER A FRANKISH RAID (MID-520S)

The Clermont formulary (a collection of legal forms) records the case of a French family in the Auvergne whose home was occupied as a result of a raid by the Franks. Following the elaborate procedures of late Roman law, which were still in use, the head of the family filed a formal claim in the municipal archives:

> Therefore, your Excellency and you honourable men, who assiduously act in the common good, [I ask that] in this meeting of the council [you] approve on my behalf this appeal or plea, upheld for three days in the public places, with your signatures and marks affixed below, so that I may regain possession of my dwelling, as is necessary, either in the presence of the lords or of the judges of my opponents....[39]

JUSTINIAN CODIFIES ROMAN LAW (527–533)

At the death of the emperor Theodosius in 395, the Roman Empire had been divided into the Eastern (Byzantine) Empire and the Western (Latin) Empire. When Justinian I came to power in 527 in the eastern half, he found that the Roman laws there were disorganized, contradictory and inconsistent. A thorough revision was therefore necessary before they could be of any use. Accordingly, Justinian appointed a special commission for this purpose.

First, his commissioners revised the imperial constitutions by producing the *Codex Constitutionum* (*Constitutional Code*). This document has not survived but a revised edition of 534 exists as part of the broader *Corpus Juris Civilis* (*Code of Civil Law*). A second commission of legal experts then tackled the writings of Roman jurists. This led to the publication in 533 of the 50 books which comprised the *Digesta* (*Digest*, also known as the *Pandects*), which became the new law of Justinian's lands.

In the prologue to the *Digest*, Justinian explained to Tribonianus, one of his senior magistrates, the problems he had faced in undertaking this great codification:

> We have found the entire arrangement of the law which has come down to us from the City of Rome and the times of Romulus, to be so confused that it is extended to an infinite length and is not within the grasp of human capacity.... We have hastened to attempt the most complete and most thorough amendment of the entire

law, to collect the whole body of Roman jurisprudence, and to assemble in one book the scattered treatises of so many authors which no one else has herebefore ventured to hope for or to expect and it has indeed been considered by Ourselves a most difficult undertaking, nay, one that was almost impossible....[40]

Justinian also caused an outline of Roman law to be published at about the same time. This was the *Institutiones* (*Institutes*), which were to be used as a textbook in law schools. He also issued a large number of new ordinances — the *Novellae Constitutiones*, now referred to simply as the *Novels*— and pulled existing legislation together into the *Codex Iustianus*. Justinian's legal works comprised the chief laws of the Byzantine Empire but their importance did not end there. The *Corpus Juris Civilis* would later serve as a model for canon law and would have a major impact on medieval law schools, courts and monarchies.

St. Gregory of Tours: Oath Taking and Peacekeeping (late sixth century)

Bishop Gregory was a prolific writer whose *Histories* is one of our best sources on the complicated twists and turns of justice in the Merovingian kingdom of the sixth century. Gregory himself was usually at or near the center of these events and has left us a vivid if partisan record of them.

Queen Fredegund, for example, had an affair with the bishop of Bordeaux, which resulted in the birth of a boy. Gregory was charged with having spread rumors about this affair. In 580, using compurgation to defend himself, he first celebrated mass on three different altars and then took oaths on each of them. This compurgation ceremony persuaded the Council of Berny that he was indeed innocent of spreading the rumors.

Fredegund, for her part, prevailed in a related legal dispute involving the legitimacy of her young son. She rounded up 300 noblemen and got them to support her oath asserting that the real father of the boy was her dead husband.[41]

On other fronts, Gregory did his best to keep the peace in these fractious times. One of the key figures in a blood feud was a man named Chramnesind, whose father, brother and uncle had been killed by one Sichar. Chramnesind refused to accept Gregory's mediation. He and his supporters overran Sichar's estate, stole everything they could, killed some of his slaves, burned down not only Sichar's house but also those of his neighbors, and carried off all the cattle and valuable objects.

This breach of the peace so aroused the local citizens that the miscreants were summoned to appear before a judge in Tours to plead their cases. The judgment of the court apparently brought the feud to an end. Indeed, after the settlement Sichar and Chramnesind became good friends and often had dinner together. One night, however, Sichar drank too much and became very insulting. Chramnesind feared that unless he retaliated, Sichar would brag to Chramnesind's kinfolk about these unavenged insults.

Gregory tells us that

> When he heard Sichar's remarks, Chramnesind was sick at heart. 'If I don't avenge my relatives,' he said to himself, 'they will say that I am as weak as a woman, for I

no longer have the right to be called a man!' Thereupon he blew the lights out and hacked Sichar's skull in two. Sichar uttered a low moan as life left his body, and then fell to the floor.... Chramnesind stripped Sichar's corpse of its clothes and hung it from a post in his garden fence.[42]

Chramnesind then hurried off on horseback to find King Childebert. He threw himself at the king's feet and begged for his life. The meeting did not go well. Queen Brunhild, enraged because Sichar had been one of her favorites, ordered that Chramnesind's goods be confiscated. To escape her hostility, he fled to the neighboring territory of King Guthrum. Later, he petitioned Childebert again and this time managed to win a pardon by persuading the king that he had killed Sichar only to avenge an insult.

ABBOT ERMENOALD LOSES HIS CASE (C. 692)

A *placitum* (plural *placita*) was a medieval document recording the outcome of a lawsuit, e.g., a mutual agreement or a royal decision. Here is a lightly edited summary of one such document:[43]

Chaino was abbot of the monastery of St. Denis, located north of Paris. In about 692 he sent his *agentes* (representatives) to the royal palace at Nogent-sur-Marne to bring suit against Ermenoald, another Frankish abbot. Chaino's *agentes* claimed that Ermenoald had pledged to Chaino 1,500 pounds of oil and 100 barrels of good wine on behalf of Bishop Sigofred, probably as security for a loan. Ermenoald, they argued, had promised to make good this pledge but had not in fact done so.

The case was initially heard by bishop Sigofred. He ruled that Ermenoald, accompanied by three reputable friends of his who were qualified to be oath helpers, would have to attend a hearing and would have to swear before the bishop that he had never made the pledge or promised to pay it. If Ermenoald failed to do this, decreed the bishop, he would have to pay ten pounds of silver on the spot. Moreover, he would then have to come before the royal court and make his oath again, this time before the king himself.

The day of the bishop's hearing came but neither Ermenoald nor his *agentes* appeared in court. Chaino's *agentes*, however, were there in full voice. They defended their case over three days, as required by law, and charged Ermenoald with failure to appear, with failure to send anyone in his place, and with failure to provide a valid excuse for not complying with the bishop's summons.

Later, when the king and his magnates studied the warrants of suit, they judged that there was a valid case to be heard. Warno, count of the royal palace, formally explained to them that Chaino's *agentes* had defended their suit according to the law but that Ermenoald had failed to defend his own suit. Complying with local law, the king and magnates then ruled that Ermenoald either had to make a satisfactory payment to Chaino's *agentes* or be "subject to their distraint." (Distraint was the seizure of property in cases where a penalty had been imposed by the court but had not been paid.)

FOR THE REPOSE OF WALTOF'S SOUL (806)

Many *placita* dealt with land because in the Middle Ages land was the main source of wealth. An interesting *placitum* reflects the power of customary law in a land dispute in Germany.[44]

Three men — Binin, Rudwig, and Willibert — claimed that, while he was still alive, their friend Waltolf had begged them to give his land at Eimsheim to the monastery of Fulda (located northeast of Frankfurt) in alms, i.e., for the repose of his soul. Waltolf had initially given the land in question to these three men on a temporary basis, with the expectation they would pass it to the monastery as soon as he died. After his death, however, while Binin and Rudwig agreed to give the land to Fulda, Willibert refused to do so.

A case was accordingly brought against Willibert. Although there was no document recording Waltolf's wishes, Willibert was eventually forced to make a *traditio*, that is, a ritual transfer to Fulda of rights over the land. The ruling against him rested on a well-established custom: land given for alms-giving must be used for alms-giving, as the original owner had wished. Since life was lived in public in the Middle Ages, other members of the community doubtless remembered Waltolf's wishes and supported Benin and Rudwig. These two men prevailed by invoking norms about the obligations created by gifts of land — norms which were enforceable at law even without a document to back them up.

AN OPEN-AND-SHUT CASE? (828)

In a third *placitum*, a royal judgment given by Pippin I settled a dispute over monastic rent in Aquitaine.[45] Suit was brought by some of the hereditary peasant tenants who were working land at Antoigné, an estate belonging to the monastery of Cormery (located near Tours). They claimed that abbot Jacob and his advocate Angenus had unjustly raised their rent for this land.

Angenus and Magenar, provost (administrator) of the monastery, both appeared before Pippin and denied that they had raised the rent. To support their position, they submitted an estate survey which showed that the rent had not been raised over the last 30 years. Pippin then asked the tenants

> if the survey had been good and true, or did they wish to say anything against it or object to it, or not? They said and acknowledged that the survey was good and true, and they were quite unable to deny that they had paid that [rent] for a period of years.[46]

This was Pippin's ruling:

> Therefore we, together with our faithful men, have seen fit to judge that since these tenants themselves gave the acknowledgement as stated above that the survey was as they had declared it, and as it was written down in the document there before them, and that they had paid the said [rent] for a period of years, so also must they pay

and hand over the same each and every year to the representatives to that house of God.[47]

On the surface, this appears to have been such an open-and-shut case that we may ask why the tenants brought suit at all. They must have had a good reason but we will never know for sure what it was. One possible explanation involves the "30-year rule." This meant that, according to local custom, uncontested possession of land over a long period of time (30 years) became proof of ownership.

In the case cited here, Paul Fouracre, a modern scholar, has speculated that the survey was accurate but that it in fact reflected rent increases which had been imposed by an earlier abbot (Alcuin), who died in 804. If so, it is conceivable that the tenants were trying to revert to a previous lower level of rent and to do so before the monastery could invoke the 30-year rule and claim that the present higher level was the correct one.[48]

DEALING WITH SORCERERS AND WITCHES (NINTH CENTURY)

The ordeal was of special use in cases which were so threatening to the social order that only the most dramatic rituals could resolve them — it hardly mattered which way.[49] A Carolingian capitulary (royal ordinance) offers a case in point:

> Since we have heard that sorcerers and witches are rising up in many parts of our kingdom, whose magic has killed and injured many men, and since, as the holy men of God have written, it is the king's duty to rid the land of the impious and not to permit witches and sorcerers to live, we command that the counts should take great pains in their counties to search out and seize such people.... [I]f the suspects cannot be proved guilty by trustworthy witnesses, let them be tried by the ordeal, and thus through that ordeal either freed or condemned.[50]

3

Canon (Ecclesiastical) Law and Its Variants

Unlike customary law, which varied from one place to another, canon law was in principle universal — that is, with only a few exceptions, it applied everywhere in Western Christendom.[1] Its importance can hardly be overestimated. "Among the institutions peculiar to feudalism," the medievalist Marc Bloch tells us, "both the judicial system of the Church and its law were thus a sort of empire within an empire."[2] Indeed, canon law was so powerful a tool that as early as c. 850, French clerics forged what are now known as the Pseudo-Isidorian Decretals. (Decretals were the decrees of popes and ecclesiastical councils.) These documents, discussed below, were highly influential but almost entirely spurious.

There were, of course, many legitimate advances in canon law. A German bishop, Burchard of Worms, produced a masterful encyclopedia of canon law in about 1015. William the Conqueror set up new ecclesiastical courts in England in 1072. A self-educated jurist known as Irnerius is traditionally credited with establishing Bologna as an international center for the study of canon law in about 1084. Gratian's *Decretum* (c. 1140) remained an important source of canon law as late as 1917. The fusion of Roman law and canon law (c. 1165), known as the *ordo iudiciarius* or as the Romano-canonical procedure, had a decisive impact on continental Western European law.

THE IMPORTANCE OF CANON LAW

The word "canon" comes from the Greek *kanon*, "a rule or practical direction." Because the church played such a major role in most aspects of life in the European Middle Ages, canon law became a critically important part of medieval culture. All Christians, that is to say, all men and women — young and old, nobles and serfs, ecclesiastics and lay people alike — were subject to it. The canonists themselves were highly intelligent and well-trained men who have been figuratively described as medieval "ferrymen." That is, they were skilled at conveying their clients safely across the legal river between theology and Roman law.[3]

No medieval man or woman could afford to ignore canon law, not only because of the pervasive influence of the church but also because the boundaries between canon

26

law and secular law were very porous. Because ecclesiastical courts were generally well run, they attracted many cases that might otherwise have been heard by the secular courts. Ecclesiastical courts exercised jurisdiction over an enormous range of activities, few of which are now considered in the West to be the exclusive purview of any religious authority. Examples include a marriage made under duress, divorce (or, more accurately, annulment of marriage), adultery, wills, testaments, personal property, loans, bankruptcy, taxes, succession and even responsibility for the loss of a castle.

Canon law had a major impact in other fields as well. International law today owes its very existence to canon lawyers. The modern concept of the "state" comes from ideas worked out by medieval canonists who were studying how the church could best be organized. Moreover, the legal principles sorting out the relationships between *sacerdotium* (the authority of the church) and *imperium* (the authority of the state) were based on canon law. Few, if any, states accepted what the church thought was the proper relationship, so struggles between church and state became key factors in European history.

A cardinal presiding over a busy ecclesiastical court. (MS. 331. F1R. The Fitzwilliam Museum, University of Cambridge.)

Despite its modest beginnings, canon law gradually became a highly technical subject which was quite difficult to master. Contemporaries found that to do so required long years of concentration and study. As Frederic William Maitland, the eminent English legal historian mentioned earlier, said, "[Law] schools make tough law."[4] Canon law is still tough law and is probably best left to experts. Nevertheless, it is essential to say something about it here. We will try to avoid its reefs and shoals by steering well clear of technical shallows.

THE BEGINNINGS OF CANON LAW

Christianity was at first only a small, persecuted sect with no need for a complicated body of law. Initially, there was clearly some uncertainty what role law should play in religious life. Jesus himself had criticized the intricacies of the existing Mosaic (Jewish) law. He condemned as hypocrites the scribes and Pharisees who only went through the motions of following the law, neglecting "the weightier matters of the law: justice, mercy and faith."[5] He told his followers that without him the law could not be fulfilled: "I have come not to abolish the law but to fulfill it."[6]

Nevertheless, despite their initial ambivalence, the early Christians soon came to recognize the practical need for a law of their own. By the beginning of the second century, the first written compilation of canon law, known as the *Didache* or the *Doctrine of the Twelve Apostles*, was in use. Canon law was influenced chiefly by Roman law and contained very few Germanic elements. After they came to power, the barbarians, for their part, regarded canon law simply as another kind of personal law and took pains to have Christian clerics among their retainers.

These clerics were not only skilled at ministering to the Christian majorities in the barbarian kingdoms but were among the few literate men of the time. It was they who, beginning in the fifth century, first committed the Germanic laws to writing, in Latin (on the continent) and in Anglo-Saxon (in England). In so doing, they also made sure that these laws would protect Christian clergy, churches and church property.[7]

Canon law grew rapidly from these modest beginnings. Indeed, by the ninth century, the problem was not that there was not *enough* canon law but that there was already *too much of it*.[8] This body of lore included the canonical books of the Bible; the writings of the Church Fathers; conciliar canons and synodal decrees, which were the conclusions reached by Christian assemblies known as councils or synods; decisions made by the popes; and one pious forgery now referred to as the False (or Pseudo-Isidorian) Decretals.

THE PSEUDO-ISIDORIAN DECRETALS (C. 850)

Decretals gathered the decrees of popes and councils. Incorrectly attributed to Isidore of Seville, the Pseudo-Isidorian Decretals were probably written in the mid-ninth century by reformers working in the archdiocese of Reims.[9] These men wanted to prove that the hierarchical structure of the church, especially the pivotal role played by bishops and popes, was quite old. To establish this point, they shamelessly fabricated a set of ancient texts. Their reasoning was that if in the past the bishops and popes had wielded great power in the church, then they should do so in the present, too. The reformers were convinced, for example, that conciliar and synodal canons should not be valid without an explicit papal endorsement.

The Pseudo-Isidorian Decretals included 50 apostolic canons and 60 decretals of the popes. Of these 60 decretals, two were semi-forgeries and 58 were entirely spurious.[10] There was also a spurious gift, allegedly made by the emperor Constantine, of the western part of the Roman Empire, to Pope Sylvester. This infamous "Donation of Constantine" was claimed to be a present from Constantine to Sylvester for miraculously curing his leprosy and converting him to Christianity. Although doubts sometimes arose over the validity of this document, the Donation was used by canonists and popes from 1054 on to support papal claims to power. It was not shown to be a forgery until 1440.

The Pseudo-Isidorian Decretals became the most frequently copied canonical collection of the time.[11] They opened up many employment opportunities for legal experts because they mandated new requirements for evidence and procedure. This made canon law even more complicated than it had been before. The decretals were frequently cited by later reformers who wanted to centralize the church's authority in Rome. They were not unmasked as forgeries until long after the end of the Middle Ages: it was only in 1628 that the Calvinist pastor David Blondel proved them to be fakes.[12]

BISHOP BURCHARD'S DECRETUM (C. 1015)

Burchard was bishop of Worms, Germany, from 1000 to 1025. It then was a remote, dangerous area. Writing shortly after Burchard's death in 1025, his biographer tells us that when the bishop first came to Worms,

> He found [it] in ruins and almost deserted. Indeed, it was most suited not to man's use but to the lairs of beasts and especially wolves.... Robbers also boasted that this was the most fitting place to carry out the iniquity of their will.... If one of the citizens said something against their wishes, they went after him in nocturnal raids and, seizing everything he had, they took it with them, leaving the man either dead or half-dead.[13]

After overseeing the restoration of the city and successfully undertaking a number of other projects, Burchard arranged for a quiet monastic cell to be built for himself on a hilltop in a forest. "To this cell he withdrew," says his biographer,

> after royal councils and conversations with the king, synodal cares, and the diverse rumblings of the world.... Indeed, it was at this time that he labored not a little in this cell on his collection of canons. For he gathered together the canons into a single corpus [the *Decretum*] with the help of Bishop Walter of Speyer and at the suggestion and encouragement of Brunicho the provost; but he did this not out of arrogance but because, as he himself said, the rights of the canons and the judgments of penances had been utterly neglected and destroyed in his bishopric. He divided up this corpus or collection and distributed the canons over twenty books.[14]

Written in about 1015, the *Decretum* was an outstanding canonical and theological encyclopedia which tried to cover the whole span of canon law. Consisting of 1,785 canons organized into 20 books, it quickly became one of the most influential canonical collections of the eleventh and early twelfth centuries. Although not well-organized by today's standards, it was nevertheless a very useful guidebook for the clergy.

This is evident from the wide range of topics it covered. These included the powers of prelates and synods; the sacraments; penalties for different kinds of homicide; consanguinity and incest; monastic life; legal problems of single women; magic and sorcery; punishments for ecclesiastical crimes; feasts and fasts; civil rulers and the laity; church courts; sexual offenses; last rites for mortally ill Christians; questions to be posed by confessors; and theological issues.[15]

WILLIAM THE CONQUEROR ESTABLISHES CHURCH COURTS IN ENGLAND (1072)

Before the Norman Conquest of England in 1066, it was the customary Anglo-Saxon courts which had jurisdiction over ecclesiastical matters, with the local bishop as joint presiding officer. William the Conqueror changed this in an ordinance of 1072, which set up new ecclesiastical courts under the exclusive authority of the church. In its capacity as a major landlord of the realm, however, the church was already responsible for meting out justice to the peasants who were working church lands. Monastic houses and other religious establishments therefore continued to maintain the local courts previously established for this purpose.

Although it may have taken time for this new legislation to go into effect, the ecclesiastical courts eventually exposed the average citizen to the norms and doctrines of canon law. In England, these courts — sometimes called Courts Christian — tried to use this law to settle local disputes. It was so complicated, however, that it was not easy to apply correctly. A few prelates, such as Hubert Walter, archbishop of Canterbury from 1193 to 1205, could afford to keep resident canonical experts in their own households. Other, less fortunate bishops were forced to become legal experts themselves out of sheer necessity.[16]

IRNERIUS: "THE LAMP OF THE LAW" (C. 1084)

Despite Burchard's *Decretum*, much of canon law was still such a dense thicket that it was hard to cut a way through it. Considerable headway was made, however, by two scholars of near-mythic proportions in the field of medieval justice. The first was a self-educated jurist traditionally known as Irnerius, although he wrote his name as "Wernerius" and notaries called him "Guarnerius" or some variant thereof.

Modern scholarship shows that much of what has been said about him is the product of later legend (it is not even certain now that he ever taught in a law school), but he was reportedly such an inspiring, original instructor that he was known as *lucerna iuris*—"the lamp of the law."[17] He believed that the *libri legales* (the "legal books" containing Justinian's codification of Roman law) offered legal and peaceful solutions to problems which until then often had to be resolved by force.

Irnerius is reported to have drawn crowds of students to the law school of Bologna, even from the lands across the Alps. As the demand for trained judges and administrators increased in the late eleventh century, this school became the center of legal scholarship in Europe. Its prestige was so great that, from the thirteenth century on, law professors at Bologna demanded that they be addressed as *domini* (lords) and claimed knightly status. In their own eyes at least, the subjects they taught made them, according to a contemporary chronicler, "the fathers and brothers of princes."[18]

Irnerius was the first to treat law as a separate and autonomous subject, distinct from the traditional academic disciplines of ethics and logic.[19] On a more practical note, his introduction of marginal glosses (commentaries written on the margins of the text, rather than between the lines, as had been the usual practice) was a great help to students studying Justinian's *Corpus Iuris Civilis.* Since the law taught in medieval universities was a highly academic "learned law" — it was virtually "a professor's law"[20] — students had good reason to thank Irnerius.

A marginal gloss from a fifteenth century French treatise on legal procedure. The main body of the text is in French and gives the circumstances in which torture may be used. The marginal notes on the left are in Latin and cite the legal authority for each of the positions taken in the text. (Fr. 4367, fol. 54v, R 50887. Bibliothèque nationale de France, Paris.)

RESOLVING CONTRADICTIONS: GRATIAN'S DECRETUM (C. 1140)

The second near-mythic figure of medieval law was Gratian, who is known as the father of the systematic study of canon law. His work marks the beginning of the "classical" period of canon law (1141375), that is, the era in which it attained its definitive shape and lasting characteristics.[21] Gratian was a bold, innovative thinker who tried to bring order out of the legal chaos of his day. He succeeded so well that for centuries his *Decretum* was the text most widely used wherever canon law was taught. It still remained an important resource when canon law was officially codified in 1917.

His achievements were conceptual as well as practical. The great Italian poet Dante, for one, felt sure that Gratian had earned a place for himself in paradise by drawing a clear distinction between a person's *consciousness*, on the one hand, and the *acts* that he performed, on the other.[22] Gratian argued that a judge should focus only on the acts — not on the consciousness (the hidden thoughts or feelings) — of the accused. This was an important conceptual step because it gave canon law a legitimacy which was now independent of theology.

Few hard facts about Gratian's life have survived. He may have been a monk, a judge, a bishop or an abbot. His contemporaries at the law school of Bologna referred to him simply as *magister* (master or teacher), which suggests that he taught canon law there.[23] In about 1140, legend has it that he produced a massive collection of more than 3,900 texts of canon law, which he labeled *Concordia discordantium canonum* (*A harmony of conflicting canons*).

Modern scholarship now suggests that Gratian's *Decretum* was not a single book: there were in fact two recensions (scholarly revisions) of it.[24] Gratian himself was the author of the first, smaller version; his successors wrote the second, larger recension. Taken together, however, these works were and still are referred to simply as Gratian's *Decretum*.

Gratian set himself the ambitious goal of trying to resolve the many contradictions which had crept into the vast body of canon law. Although the structure of his book is complicated, his goal was quite clear. The first thing he wanted to do was to highlight the contradictions in the law. He then wanted to reconcile them. Since the classroom was the natural home for this kind of analysis, Gratian's *Decretum* soon became the basic text of canon law as taught in medieval universities.

Like any good teacher, Gratian tried to use vivid examples which students would remember. Here is an edited version of one of the 36 fictitious cases used in the second recension of the *Decretum*:

> A bachelor [let us call him Honorius] wanted a wife and children, so he married a prostitute. She was the daughter of a serf and the granddaughter of a freeman. Although her father wanted her to marry another man, the grandfather gave her to Honorius instead, only in order to control her sexual appetites. She was infertile. When Honorius discovered this, he slept with his own maid in hopes of having children. Later, after he had been convicted of adultery and had been punished, he asked another man to rape his wife so that he could divorce her. After the rape and the divorce, Honorius married an infidel woman, but only on the condition that she convert to the Christian religion.[25]

Gratian then poses eight questions for his students. No answers to them are given: Gratian's purpose in raising them was to stimulate thought and discussion among legal students. The questions are:

> Is it lawful for a man to marry a prostitute? If she is married only to control her sexual desires, does she deserve to be called a wife? Whose judgment should she follow — that of her free grandfather or her servile father? Was Honorius allowed to conceive children with a maid while his wife was still alive? What happens if, due to being raped, Honorius' wife lost her reputation? Can an adulterous man divorce his adulterous wife? May a man marry again while his divorced wife is still alive? Can a Christian man marry a non-Christian woman under the condition cited above?[26]

THE ORDO IUDICIARIUS: A FUSION OF ROMAN LAW AND CANON LAW (C. 1165)

By the end of the twelfth century, confidence in the ordeal had waned. It was falling out of favor because educated people no longer believed in its infallibility. Instead, they turned increasingly toward two more reliable methods of proof: judicial inquiry and written evidence. As noted earlier, the ordeal itself was officially banned by the pope at the Fourth Lateran Council in 1215. Even before then, however, it was gradually being replaced by the newly minted *ordo iudiciarius*, also known as the "Romano-canonical" procedure.

This was a fusion of Roman law, i.e., Justinian's *Corpus*, and traditional canon law. The *ordo iudiciarius* mandated new judicial procedures. It was first defined in about 1165 by the French jurist Stephen of Tournai, who summarily excluded the ordeal from any trial. Under the new *ordo*, said Stephen,

> The defendant shall be summoned before his own judge and be legitimately called by three edicts or one peremptory edict. He must be permitted to have legitimate delays. The accusation must be formally presented in writing. Legitimate witnesses must be produced. A decision must be rendered only after someone has been convicted or confessed. The decision must be in writing.[27]

One consequence of the growing reliance on the *ordo iudiciarius* was that it significantly increased the role of the secular authority. In the past, the secular leader of a given area, e.g., the count, had been present at but had not been the central player in a trial. He might chair the proceedings of the court but could himself play only an advisory role. In theory, it was the court alone which "declared" or "found" the law: "The court passes judgment, not the lord," an English text tells us.[28] In fact, however, it was the men who "owed" or "performed suit" who dictated the course of the trial and who decided its outcome.

Under the new *ordo*, the count (or his superior) became in effect both judge and jury. Thus during the twelfth and thirteenth centuries the power of the judicial institutions of kings, lords and city-states expanded considerably. Ironically, however, not long thereafter this trend was offset to some extent by a new development. In the later part of the thirteenth century, legal scholars began to argue that fundamental procedural norms were really part of *natural law*.

"Natural law" was law said to be derived from nature itself. Gratian equated natural law with divine law, that is, the revealed laws of the Bible, especially the Golden Rule. Since natural law was God-given, rulers could not meddle with it. It therefore followed that if procedural norms did in fact reflect natural law, they lay beyond the control of the ruler.[29] "Positive law," on the other hand, was the opposite of natural law. Being man-made, positive law could appropriately be changed by men.

CANON LAW AND JURISPRUDENCE

Canonists of the late twelfth and the thirteenth centuries showed a keen interest in jurisprudence. (In this connection, "jurisprudence" means the philosophy of law.)

They studiously explored the relationships between such convoluted issues as law, justice, custom, equity (fairness), free will, and the "constant man."[30]

Gratian himself declared that equity was the mother of justice. Equity was thus the wellspring of every valid law: a law that was patently unfair did not have to be obeyed. On the vexing question of what role *custom* should play in law, Gratian sided with Roman jurists and Christian theologians by arguing that custom could indeed be treated as law, but only under certain circumstances. By this he meant that to be a law, a custom must not contradict truth, reason, Christianity or natural law. Moreover, it must have been followed by a community for a considerable period of time.

Medieval canonists also drew from Roman law a fundamental legal maxim that we still live by today: ignorance of the law is no excuse. In principle, it is certainly unfair to punish someone for breaking a law that he or she does not know exists. In practice, however, for the legal system to work at all it is essential to posit a knowledge of the law. Otherwise, virtually all lawbreakers could use ignorance of the law as a valid excuse for their actions.

THE DOCTRINE OF THE "CONSTANT MAN"

Canonical jurisprudence addressed a wide range of hypothetical issues, some of which might easily occur in real life. A forced consent to marriage was one of them. Gratian and others (see Oldradus da Ponte's *Concilium No. 35,* below) believed that a woman could not be given to anyone against her will because free will was an essential component of any valid marriage. This premise seems clear enough on the surface, but in some situations it was not at all obvious what "free will" meant. Let us take some cases which came before the medieval popes.

In one case, a young man and a young woman were in bed together. The girl's father burst into the room and surprised the couple in the act of intercourse. He demanded that the young man immediately agree to marry his daughter. The young man apparently agreed. Was this in fact a valid betrothal? Pope Alexander III (1159–1181) said that it was — but not, however, if the man had acted out of a fear so great that it "would move a constant man."

Here it must be explained that

> The 'constant man' was a mythical creature invented by classical Roman jurists as a benchmark against which to measure degrees of coercion. They described this fictitious figure as 'constant' in the sense that he was courageous, resolute, and steadfast in character; one who was not easily frightened and who was fully capable of standing up against idle threats or bullying tactics.[31]

Alexander III also ruled that a boy whose parents had used violence to get him to agree to a betrothal did not have to marry the girl in question because he had not agreed out of free will. Other popes took a similar line. Urban III (1185–1187) held that threats from her parents nullified a nine- or ten-year-old girl's agreement to marry a youth of her parents' choosing. Pope Gregory IX (1227–1241) concluded that the threat of a grave penalty for failure to consent would invalidate the consent. On the other side of the coin, Clement III (1187–1191) ruled that a woman who had lived with a man for 18 months could not expect a judge to believe she had not been doing this of her own free will.

Canonical judges, then, had to rely on both their legal texts and on their common sense to determine what it would take to strike fear into the stalwart heart of a "constant man." Physical violence would of course invalidate consent — if, for example, the men in a wedding party actually beat a young woman with wooden poles to get her to marry the prospective groom. But the mere fact that in this particular case the men came to the wedding armed with long poles (ostensibly to help them vault the drainage ditches) was not considered enough to frighten a "constant man," so the marriage was declared to be valid.

MOVING TOWARD A UNIFORM CODE OF CANON LAW (THIRTEENTH AND FOURTEENTH CENTURIES)

During this period, the church also worked hard to create a uniform body of canon law and to give it a coherent structure. Jurists and legal scholars were looking for the "sure haven" of an agreed text to serve as a fixed reference point in their juridical debates.[32] A step in this direction was pope Gregory IX's massive collection of laws, known as the *Liber Extra* (*Outside Book*) because it lay outside of Gratian's work.

This important book, drawn from decretals and from papal decisions in individual cases, was the most important source of new canon law. Published in 1234, the *Liber Extra* affirmed two important technical concepts of canon law.[33] The first is referred to as *exclusivity*. It held that laws which were not included in the *Liber Extra* or in Gratian did not automatically have to be applied in a given case. The second concept was *textuality*. This stated that the laws which were in the *Liber Extra* were especially important in the contexts of the passages in which they appeared; their format and exact wording were especially important, too.

A MODERN CODE OF CANON LAW (1983)

From its earliest beginnings, canon law has never been static. It has always been a work in progress and this is why it survives today. Important codifications on the path to what after the end of the Middle Ages would become the official body of canon law — the *Corpus iuris canonici* (1582) — included the *Liber Sextus* (*Sixth Book*) issued by Boniface VIII in 1298 and the *Decretales Clementinae* (*The Decretals of Clement V*) promulgated in 1314. These and related works are the foundations of canon law today.

The *Corpus iuris canonici* itself proved to be so durable that it did not have to be revised extensively for 335 years: the first major revision was not published until 1917. A second revision, promulgated in 1983, remains the current *Codex juris canonici* (*Code of Canon Law*) for the Roman Catholic Church. It consists of 1,752 canons arranged in seven books.

Illustrative Cases and Laws

BISHOP BURCHARD LAYS DOWN THE LAW (1014)

Burchard also drafted the *Lex Familie Wormatiensis* (*Law of the Retainers of the Bishop of Worms*). Worms was still a rough place even after 25 years of Burchard's stewardship. In the opening paragraph of his law, he explains why the law had to be set down and enforced:

> I Burchard, bishop of the church of Worms, on account of the strenuous lamentations of the wretched, and the frequent schemes of those many people who tear like dogs at the *familia* of St. Peter [the dependents of the bishopric of Worms], imposing various laws on them and oppressing the weaker among them by their judgments; ... I have ordered that these laws be written down, so that no advocate or agent or official or any other person among them may impose on them anything new; rather, let it be known before everyone that there is one and the same law, common to rich and poor alike.[34]

Burchard's law consists of 31 articles. Among other things, they deal with dowry and inheritance, restitution for injustices, *wergeld*, marriage, oath taking, judicial duels, penalties for abducting a young woman, debts, and the ordeal by hot water. What is most striking, however, is the very high level of violence which existed within Burchard's household itself. Indeed, the good bishop found it necessary to order that

> On account of the murders which arise daily in the *familia* of St. Peter as though among beasts, because often for nothing, or on account of drunkenness or pride, one person rages against another as though insane, so that in the course of one year thirty-five of the servants of St. Peter [i.e., serfs] have been killed for no reason out of the servants of the church, and their murderers rejoice and are covered with more glory than repentance, on account of this great injury to our church, with the counsel of our faithful people we have decreed this correction:
> That if anyone of the *familia* wishes to kill his fellow needlessly, that is, without any of the following reasons, namely that the other might wish to kill him, or is a brigand, of if the killer is defending his goods and family, we establish that he shall lose his hair and skin and be branded on either side of his jaw, and shall pay the *wergeld* and make peace with the kinsmen of the dead man in the accustomed way, and the kinsmen shall be constrained to accept this peace.[35]

BURCHARD'S CORRECTOR (C. 1015)

Book XIX of Burchard's *Decretum* contains a detailed list of questions which priests were instructed to put to women who were making their confessions. These questions reflect some of the Germanic beliefs which had survived long into the Christian era. They undoubtedly reflected priestly fantasies and subconscious fears as well. Because this book recommended penances for various sins, it was known as the *Corrector*. Two examples will suffice to show its contents.

The priest was instructed to ask the woman in the confessional:

Have you shared the belief of many women in Satan's retinue? That during the silence of the night, after lying down on your bed and while your husband rests on your breast, you have the power to leave through the closed door, though you are a bodily being, and to traverse through space with other women like you? That you have the power to kill with invisible weapons baptized Christians redeemed by the blood of Christ; to eat their flesh after cooking it and to replace their heart with straw, or a piece of wood, or some other thing? That after eating your victims you have to revive them, or to give them a respite for living? If yes, [the penance is] 40 days fasting and a penance for seven years.[36]

Have you done as women do: they take a living fish, and push it into their vagina, keeping it there until it has suffocated and after boiling or grilling it, they give it to their husband to eat so that he will become more passionate towards them? If yes, two years of fasting.[37]

GRATIAN ON MARRIAGE (C. 1140)

The *Decretum* makes difficult reading for beginners — a fact which has prompted James Brundage, a modern scholar, to joke that "this merely confirms the tradition that Gratian was a law teacher."[38] A shortened, edited citation from Gratian's "On Marriage" may show its convoluted line of reasoning:

The first institution of marriage was effected in Paradise in such a way that there would have been "an unstained bed and honourable marriage" resulting in conception without ardor and birth without pain. The second, to eliminate unlawful movement, was effected outside Paradise in such a way that the infirmity that is prone to foul ruin might be rescued by the uprightness of marriage ... it is clear that [a married couple] are not commanded to join together solely for the procreation of children ... for what is done outside of the intention of generation is not an evil of marriage but is forgivable on account of the good of marriage, which is threefold: Fidelity, Offspring, and Sacrament.[39]

CLERICS ARE FORBIDDEN TO TAKE PART IN THE ORDEAL (1215)

The Fourth Lateran Council officially ended the ordeal in 1215. It took some time for this papal decision to become public knowledge, so the ordeal did not end immediately. It lingered on in Germany and in southeastern Europe until fading out there by 1300.[40]

The Council's statement had been unequivocal:

Canon 18: No cleric may pronounce a sentence of death, or execute such a sentence, or be present at its execution.... Nor may any cleric write or dictate letters designed for the execution of such a sentence.... Neither may any cleric act as judge in the case of ... archers, or other men of this kind devoted to shedding blood.... *Neither shall anyone in judicial tests or ordeals by hot or cold water or hot iron bestow any blessing;* the earlier prohibitions in regard to dueling remain in force.[41]

Once clerics were barred from participating in the ordeals, the "holy" aspect of these proceedings vanished entirely. Thus they could no longer be relied upon to reflect the will of God. As a result, new ways had to be invented to find out whether a person was innocent or guilty. As will be discussed below in the chapter on medieval crime, the ultimate solution — which is still with us today — was trial by jury.

"The Most Illustrious Jurist of His Time": Oldradus Da Ponte (c. 1350)

Oldradus da Ponte was an Italian who studied law at Bologna and then went on to become a judge, a law teacher and a senior member of cardinal Peter Colonna's ecclesiastical court in Avignon. The Italian poet Petrarch, said to be the greatest scholar of the fourteenth century, knew Oldradus well and described him as the most illustrious jurist of his time.[42]

Oldradus was the first medieval jurist to produce large numbers of *concilia*, which were detailed analyses of the law relevant to specific cases, and *questiones* (questions) in the same vein. Many *concilia* and *questiones* were based on actual cases. Sometimes, however, they were adapted for use in law schools or as models for jurists to follow. The examples used below have been shortened and edited for purposes of clarity.

A Marriage Made Under Duress (c. 1350)[43]

Oldradus' *Consilium* No. 35 stages this scene and raises an obvious question:

> A certain layman named Johannes, aspiring to marry a certain Margaret, even though he knew from her friends that she did not want to marry him, seized her violently and, though she was unwilling and inwardly resistant, through force and the threat of death he was able to carry her off and rape her repeatedly. Later, in the presence of certain other persons, he compelled her to utter the words of the marriage ceremony. Afterwards he held her imprisoned, unwilling and resistant, raping her again. For twelve days or thereabouts he kept her shut up in the house. She fled as soon as the opportunity arose and immediately protested publicly that she had never consented to this marriage. It is asked: is there a contract of marriage between them?

Oldradus' answer is as follows:

> And briefly it must be said that given the facts above, no marriage was celebrated between these two people. The reason is that marriage is contracted through the legitimate consent of a man and a woman.... [A]lthough these events took the form of a marriage contract, i.e., the words of marriage and the carnal joining, the substance of a marriage contract, namely Margaret's consent, was absent. The aforesaid words and carnal joining cannot complete a marriage contract by themselves.... Margaret fled when she was able.... [I]n a marriage contract, consent ought to be free.... Here, however, it was not free, and only through force and threats could Johannes have intercourse with her. And therefore there was no marriage between them.

Man in the stocks. (MS. Dounce 195, fol. 107r. The Bodleian Library, University of Oxford.)

RESPONSIBILITY FOR THE LOSS OF A CASTLE (C. 1350)[44]

In his *Questio* No. 92, Oldradus addresses the hypothetical guilt or innocence of a knight who lost a castle:

> A king was holding a castle and when he had a war with his enemies, he made an agreement with a certain knight that, in return for a payment, the knight would guard it. That knight gave custody of the castle to a certain person. Through that person's fault, the enemies came and occupied the castle. Now it is asked whether the knight would be held liable.

Oldradus looked at this case from several different angles and explored it at some length. His basic conclusion was that

> According to the law of the nobles of our land: if the knight gave custody to another noble, he is not held liable; if to a non-noble, he is held liable.[45]

Such a finding was, he said, consistent with the *ius commune*. This was the combination of Roman law, canon law and feudalized justice which was taught in medieval universities between the eleventh and the sixteen centuries and which formed the common law of continental Western Europe — but not that of England, which had a common law all of its own.

A ROYAL ORDINANCE
AGAINST BLASPHEMERS (1397)

We have seen that the boundaries between canon law and secular law were very porous. These two systems of law could and did overlap. Here, for example, are some of the penalties decreed by the French king Charles VI (1368–1422) for blasphemy against the Virgin Mary and the saints:

Passers-by jeer at a man in the stocks. (*Coutumes de Toulouse*, MS Latin 9187, fol. 30. Bibliothèque nationale de France, Paris.)

For the first offense: Confinement in the pillory [the stocks] between the hours of *prime* [early morning] to *none* [mid-afternoon].... Passers-by may throw mud or other refuse at the eyes of the guilty person, but not stones or other objects which might wound him. Afterwards he shall spend a whole month in prison, living only on bread and water.

For the second offense: The guilty person is to be put in the pillory on a market day or a holy day [when there would be a great crowd in the market square]. His upper lip will be split open by a hot iron, so that the upper teeth can be seen.

For the third offense: The lower lip will be split open.

For the fourth offense: Both lips will be severed.

For the fifth offense: If by bad luck the person blasphemes a fifth time, his tongue shall be cut out entirely, so that subsequently he will not be able to say anything more.[46]

4

Feudalism and Justice in Medieval France

The physical insecurity of life in ninth-century France gave rise to feudalism, a pattern of culture with several unique institutions which will be discussed below. Within certain limits, feudal lords had the right of *justitia* (justice) in the lands they ruled. Royal judicial sessions, known as *curia regis in parlemento* (literally, "the king's court in a session for discussion"), gradually evolved during the thirteenth century into an omni-competent supreme court of France — the Parlement.

THE HEYDAY OF THE SOLDIER

In ninth-century France, the decline of the Carolingian monarchy and the fero-cious attacks of foreign raiders, especially the Vikings, led to a state of near-anarchy. The Northmen, as they were called, assaulted French cities, towns, landed estates and monasteries. Contemporary historians chronicled how they struck:

> The Northmen with a hundred ships entered the Seine on the twentieth of March [845] and, after ravaging first one bank and then the other, came without meeting any resistance to Paris.... The Northmen returned down the Seine and coming to the ocean pillaged, destroyed, and burned all the regions along the coast.[1]

In addition to attacking Paris several times, the Vikings also pillaged Bordeaux, Toulouse, Orléans, Angers, Amiens, Cambrai, Reims, Soissons and the rich valley of the Seine. Reflecting on these woes in the mid-ninth century, an Italian cleric predicted that henceforth "each man will put his trust only in the sword."[2] He was certainly right.

To protect their lives and property, knights and commoners alike forged recipro-cal ties with the nearest lord who had enough forces at his disposal to be able to guar-antee their common defense. This era has aptly been called "the heyday of the soldier."[3] The reason is clear enough: unless a castle, a village, a city, a monastic house or a church was protected by armed men, it ran the risk of being assaulted, captured, looted and possibly destroyed.

41

THE EMERGENCE OF FEUDALISM

We can define feudalism as a fragmented system of reciprocal rights and duties which arose from a pervasive breakdown of law and order.[4] In theory, the king stood at the apex of a hierarchy of power but in practice his power was limited by custom, by powerful nobles and by the church. There was no real consensus about where the lords and the clergy ranked in relationship to each other: both claimed to be the most important. Both agreed, however, that the peasants were beneath them.

Western European feudalism was born in France. The Normans brought Norman feudalism with them when they conquered England in 1066. It flourished there, too. Indeed, later on, England was in some respects much more comprehensively "feudal-ized" than France ever was.[5] France was, nevertheless, not only the center of European intellectual life but also the land of feudalized justice in its purest form.[6]

Feudalized justice intermixed elements of Roman law and barbarian law with the personal interests of the feudal lords themselves. It is a more useful term than "feudal law," which implies that every feudal *seigneurie* (lordship) followed the same law. This was not in fact the case: the laws of different lordships were rarely identical. Feudal-ism existed in other countries as well but generally mirrored the characteristics which first appeared in France. These included the three social groups; homage; fealty; vas-salage; and the fief.

THE THREE SOCIAL GROUPS

Feudal society was divided into three distinct groups, although there was always some ebb and flow between them. The ambitious commoner on his way up the social ladder might pass the impoverished petty noble on his way down. Each of these groups had existed prior to the emergence of feudalism but, under it, the power of the mili-tary element in society was greatly enhanced.

In a sermon of 995, Ælfric, an Anglo-Saxon monk, described the social makeup of feudalism:

> The *laboratores* [peasants] are those who, by their labor, provide us with the means of subsistence; the *oratores* [ecclesiastics] are those who intercede with God for us; and the *bellatores* [lords and knights] are those who protect our cities and defend our land against invading armies.[7]

Peasants formed the vast majority of the population. Many of them — perhaps two-thirds of the English population in the twelfth century — were villeins (serfs) hold-ing land in villenage.[8] That is to say, they were neither slaves nor free men, but were bound to the lord's land and could be brought back to it by force if they ran away.[9] They did all the back-breaking work: at one point, their life-expectancy was only about 35 years. Manorial courts, by which the lord of the manor exercised jurisdiction over his tenants, governed their lives.

The ecclesiastics exerted a pervasive influence on society, not only spiritually but also economically. Monks were the best farmers of medieval times and did much to bring marginal areas under cultivation and to improve crop yields. Moreover, the abbots and bishops were often lords in their own right and governed large agricultural domains worked by peasants or lay-brothers.

Lords and knights formed a distinct military, political and social elite. Scholars believe that one of the hallmarks of feudalism was that, under its sway, public authority (including some kinds of justice) passed decisively into the domain of private right. This privatization and control of justice was especially pronounced in France. The *bellatores*, for example, could exercise for their own benefit many of the legal and police powers which in later eras would be wielded by a local or national government only for the public benefit.

These aristocrats did not face many onerous social restrictions, either. One of them, however, was that as the Parlement of Paris made clear, a knight who had acquired a tenement in villenage could not do any manual work himself if he wanted to retain his elevated status. A provincial French saying explains why: "To plough, to dig, to carry a load of wood or manure" were actions which would automatically lead to a loss of knightly privileges.[10]

HOMAGE, FEALTY, VASSALAGE, AND THE FIEF

Under feudalism, complex ties of obedience and protection bound man to man. These ties were legal contractual obligations formed voluntarily between two free men — a prospective vassal (a knight) and his superior (a lord). This relationship was sealed by the ceremony of homage, which was a simple but moving event. In it, the vassal-to-be knelt before the lord, put his hands between the lord's hands, and uttered four short but binding words: "I am your man."[11] By an oath of fealty, the vassal promised to give the lord his loyalty and support.

By paying homage and by swearing this oath, the vassal committed himself to fight to the death to defend his lord's interests if called upon to do so. He also had to be present at the lord's court for trials, administrative deliberations and ceremonial events. When the use of money became more common toward the end of the eleventh century, vassals were also responsible for paying feudal taxes known as "aids." These were levied when the lord was captured and held to ransom; for knighting the lord's eldest son; for marrying the lord's eldest daughter; and to assist the lord's heir in "redeeming" his father's land by paying a succession duty known as "relief."[12] If the lord decided to go on a crusade, his vassals might have to contribute to this adventure, too.

In return for all this, the lord committed himself to protect the vassal, his family and his retainers, militarily and legally — that is to say, both on the field of battle and in the lord's court. The lord also had to support his vassal financially. The lord usually did the latter by granting the vassal a portion of land called a fief. Legally, a fief can be defined as an estate in land held from a lord on condition of homage or service.

The fief was a key institution in the Middle Ages. Fiefs varied greatly in size, ranging from enormous estates or whole provinces to plots of just a few acres. The latter, of course, hardly fit the classic picture of vassalage. The income generated by fiefs varied enormously as well. With the exception of allodial land (land which was held freely, without any obligation of service to a lord), a knight did not own outright the fief which provided his livelihood.[13]

In the mid-ranges of the income scale, it is estimated that to support himself and his household at an acceptable but not princely level of comfort, a knight needed to have somewhere between 15 and 30 peasant families working his fief.[14]

Each fief developed its own laws and customs, which limited the power of the lord. The wise lord heeded these restrictions on his own freedom of action because he needed the advice of his vassals and their financial and military support. If his own fief was big and rich enough, a vassal could set himself up as a lord simply by subdividing and sub-letting the fief to his tenants. The practice, known as subinfeudation, inevitably led to a further fragmentation of local authority, spreading wealth and power more broadly. Homage to more than one lord became common in France.

The count of Champagne, for example, owed homage to 10 different lords for various parts of his county. Alternatively, a knight who was little more than a well-armed thug could, like a Mafia chief of later times, offer free peasants "protection" — both from himself and from others like him — if they would simply acknowledge him as their lord. This practice also exerted a centrifugal effect on medieval society.

A lord was master of his own castle but visitors to medieval castles today may agree that the lord and his household lived in cold, damp, dark, spartan surroundings. As the medievalist Sidney Painter put it,

The life of the feudal class was simple and crude and its members enjoyed little more luxury than the peasants who tilled their fields.... The knight's castle was extremely simple and must have been most uncomfortable.... [I]f one of us were offered the choice between spending a winter night with the lord or [with] his serf, he would choose the comparatively tight mud hut with the nice warm pigs on the floor.[15]

Nobles and their ladies shown here embarked on a hunting (hawking) expedition. In the background, peasants till the nobles' fields and then cool off from the August heat by a quick dip in the river. Behind them looms the lord's castle. ("le Mois d'août," from *Les Très Riches Heures du duc de Berry*. Chantilly, musée Condé. Réunion des Musées Nationaux Agence photographque.)

Top left: Bonaguil Castle (late fifteenth century): remains of one of its defensive towers. *Top right:* Bonaguil Castle: stairwell in a defensive tower. *Bottom left:* Bonaguil Castle. *Bottom right:* moat with drawbridge.

The Spread and Decline of Feudalism

From France, feudalism gradually spread in different forms to Italy, Spain, Germany, the Slavic territories, England, Scotland, Ireland, Wales, and (via the crusades) even to the Middle East. It reached its widest extent between 1000 and 1200. The last example of medieval fortification in France was the by-then-anachronistic Bonaguil Castle, built by the baron Bérenger de Roquefeuil between 1480 and 1520 in southwestern France.

Feudalized justice itself began to fade away as soon as kings were able to extend their judicial grip over their entire realm. This they did by putting in place a network of itinerant justices or permanent representatives. The affirmation of royal authority first occurred in England under the Norman and Angevin kings. It came about later and more slowly in France under the Capetians.[16] The itinerant justices of Normandy, Flanders, and England became models for the earliest French *bailli* (bailiff) of the twelfth century. From the thirteenth to the fifteenth century, these French officials were the principal agents of the kings' efforts to build up an effective central administration to take the place of feudalism.

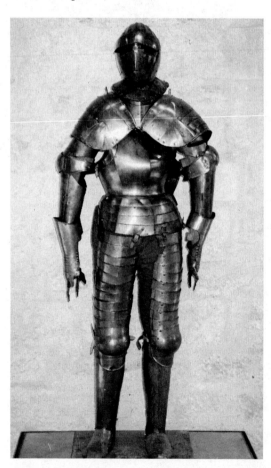

Occupying an important position in the bureaucratic hierarchy, these officials exercised a wide range of duties: maintaining law and order, promulgating the king's edicts, calling men up for military service, paying salaries to local officials and sending tax revenues to the king's treasury. Their legal role was equally important. The *bailli* presided over the local court which determined the appropriate customary law to be applied to each case. These men also exercised jurisdiction over cases affecting the royal domain and the rights of the king. A *grand bailli* (senior bailiff) was the equivalent of an English sheriff, who acted on behalf of the king and whose considerable powers will be discussed later.

The limits of Justitia (justice)

Justitia covered a much broader spectrum of activities than the term "justice" implies today. *Justitia* included

Bonaguil Castle: suit of plate armor, c. 1500.

not only the police power of arrest and punishment but also the financial power to authorize markets, tax transactions taking place in them, and levy tolls on the use of public highways.[17] Although a noble in France could exercise great power within his own fief, the grant of a fief did not automatically carry with it the formal right of "high justice," i.e., the power to impose the death penalty or to settle disputes involving the personal status of nobles or their landed properties.

France presents a mixed picture here. *Justitia,* including high justice, was by the year 1000 a right of some of the lords who were allodists (men who owned their lands) and castellans (masters of castles). The great lords of Flanders, Normandy and Béarn, for example, could exercise the death penalty.[18] In other cases, vassals — no matter how powerful — could not exercise high justice on their own authority. Sometimes it was neither the lord or the vassal who had this right, but only the prince or another third party.

Due to unusual local circumstances, however, there were a few atypical cases where a fief did carry with it the right to exercise justice. In the thirteenth century, Beauvaisis (near Clermont in south-central France) was one of them. This anomaly gave rise to a local maxim: "Fief and justice are the same thing."[19] More commonly, however, as Antoine Loisel, a seventeenth-century legal scholar who wanted to unravel the diverse provincial customs which made up the customary laws of France, put it: "Fief, jurisdiction and 'justice' have nothing in common."[20]

DIFFERENT LEGAL SYSTEMS IN FRANCE

France also presents a mixed picture on the role of residual Roman law. By the mid-thirteenth century, northern France was the *pays de droit coutumier* (land of customary law).[21] In this region, Roman law was not positive (mandatory) law. As a result, a judge did not have to rely on it. He could invoke it only if he wished, especially in a difficult case where the customary law might be obscure. The south of France, on the other hand, was the *pays de droit écrit* (land of written law). Here, Roman law was positive law: it could not be ignored and had to be applied.

The legal system was still in flux. The major cities of France retained and applied their own laws. Outside the cities, feudal lords exercised great power and could set up their own legal systems if they so wished. This was done by lay and ecclesiastical nobles alike. Examples include the dukes of Burgundy and of Brittany; the abbots of famous abbeys such as Sainte-Geneviève and Saint-Germain-des-Prés; and the bishop of Metz, whose legal provisions were known as *atours* (literally, "finery").[22] It was the interplay between the *ius proprium* (the customary law of each city or province) and the *ius commune* (continental common law) which made French law a constant work-in-progress.[23]

"FEUDAL JURISDICTION" AND THE SCOPE OF ROYAL POWER

"Feudal jurisdiction" was a powerful weapon when wielded by a great lord or a king. It meant legal jurisdiction over the disputes stemming from the contract of vassalage or affecting the fief *per se*.[24] At first, although the lord himself retained ultimate responsibility for feudal jurisdiction, he did not personally sit in judgment on his vassals. This state of affairs changed over time, however, and by the end of the tenth century each great lord in France and his subordinates, the counts, presided over their own *curia* (court), staffed with judges and legal experts.

These nobles were all vassals of the king of France, but the most powerful of them governed territories far larger than the royal domain itself, which was limited to the area around and to the south of Paris.[25] In their own lands — in Flanders, Vermandois, Champagne, Burgundy, Normandy, Brittany, Maine, Anjou, Blois, Toulouse, Gascony and Aquitaine — the great lords did not, as a practical matter, recognize the sovereignty of the king.[26] Thus until late in the twelfth century, the king of France could influence his vassals only by whatever feudal jurisdiction he could wield, not by his direct commands.

Properly deployed, however, the contract of vassalage was a truly formidable weapon. When French kings had a strong case, and as their own power increased during the twelfth century, they could demand that their vassals comply with this contract. In 1202, for example, Philip II Augustus, the French king, confiscated all the French fiefs of the English king, John, because John was his vassal but had failed to answer a summons to Philip's court.

One of the reasons Philip was successful in this ploy was that John had only a weak claim to these lands. John's French subjects knew this. A contemporary French account, however, confines itself to a more legalistic explanation of why John lost his fiefs:

> Then when the court of the king of France had met, it judged that the king of England should be deprived of all the land which up to then he and all his ancestors had held of the kings of France, because for a long time they had refused to furnish nearly all the services due for these lands and they were not willing to obey their lord in anything.[27]

As they slowly built up a centralized financial and administrative apparatus, later French kings restructured their feudal relationships to solidify their own power. Louis IX played a highly personal and sometimes informal role in dispensing justice. According to the king's biographer (Jean, sire de Joinville), who probably began writing his famous *History of Saint Louis* in the 1270s,

> In summer, after hearing mass, the king often went to the wood of Vincennes [near Paris], where he would sit down with his back against an oak, and make us [Joinville and others] all sit around him. Those who had any suit to present could come to speak to him without hindrance from an usher or any other person. The king would address them directly and ask: "Is there anyone here who has a case to be settled?" Those who had one would stand up. Then he would say: "Keep silent all of you, and you shall be heard in turn, one after the other." Then he would call Pierre de Fontaines and Geoffroi de Villette, and say to one or the other of them: "Settle his case for me." If he saw anything needing correction in what was said by those who spoke on his behalf or on behalf of any other person, he would himself intervene to make the necessary adjustment.[28]

Louis IX also relied on French friars as his legal agents. These *enquêteurs* ("inquisitors") were charged with scrutinizing local government and correcting any abuses.

LEGAL PRIVILEGES FOR BASTIDES
(THIRTEENTH AND FOURTEENTH CENTURIES)

Bastides were semi-fortified "new towns" first built by the count of Toulouse, Alphonse de Poitiers (1249–1271), brother of King Louis IX. Later, lords acting under the orders of the French kings Philip the Bold and Philip the Fair and the English king Edward I (the latter in his capacity as Duke of Aquitaine) built them, too. More than 300 *bastides* were constructed in southwestern France. Many of these sun-washed villages are still lovely, vibrant communities today. Monflanquin, Pujols and Montjoi, for example, are each formally designed by the French government as *un des plus beaux villages de France* (one of the most beautiful villages of France). Castelsagrat, founded in 1269 under an *acte de peréage* (a shared sovereignty agreement) between Alphonse de Poitiers and a local lord, is lovely, too.

Usually laid out on a checkerboard square or on a rectangular plan, the *bastides* were originally created to bring together a populace which had been scattered and diminished by years of warfare. *Bastides* not only put people under the direct protection of the count and the church but were also organized around a central marketplace (rather than around a church), so that goods and services could readily be exchanged. To encourage people to settle in these new towns, they were offered certain legal privileges.

Typically, these included a guarantee of military security, protection against a lord's arbitrary use of power, exemption from military service, the right to inherit, exemption from onerous taxes, and the right to have a say (through an assembly of 12 sworn men known as the *jurade*) in the day-to-day running of the *bastide*. Carefully drafted charters in Latin spelled out the rights and responsibilities of all the parties concerned.

The *Charte des coutumes de Monflanquin* (*Charter of the customary laws of the* bastide *of Monflanquin*), granted by Alphonse de Poitiers in June 1256 and reconfirmed by him in 1269, is a good case in point. The first of its 37 clauses clearly states its purpose:

> From Alphonse to you who read these words, greetings. Know that, to the inhabitants of our *bastide* Monflanquin in the diocese of Agen, we grant the freedoms and customary laws listed below.[29]

Some of the subsequent clauses provided that:

- Taxes would not be imposed without the consent of the inhabitants.
- The inhabitants would have the right to buy and sell goods and to marry whom they chose.
- Neither the seneschal (the chief administrative officer of a noble's household) nor the bailiff could arrest anyone or seize their goods unless a serious crime had been committed.
- No matter what the provocation, no inhabitant was permitted to engage in a duel or in trial by combat. If a man were challenged and refused to fight, he would not be considered guilty but could seek legal remedies, such as calling witnesses.
- Before taking up their duties, the seneschal and the bailiff had to swear before

the village assembly that they would behave honorably, would render justice impartially to everyone and would observe the customary and written laws of Monflanquin.

• Adulterers, both men and women, would have to choose one of two punishments: either paying a fine of 100 *solidi* each or running through the village entirely naked.

THE PARLEMENT

Courts in France suffered from two shortcomings endemic to medieval justice. The first was that litigants did not give up easily: indeed, they proved to be remarkably tenacious. The second shortcoming was that since there was usually no way to

Top left: Pujols: narrow lane overlooking the Séoune valley. *Top right:* Pujols: roof angles. *Opposite top left:* The *bastide* of Monflanquin was granted a contract of *paréage* (shared sovereignty) in 1252 and the right to a customary law in 1255. An open town to begin with, Monflanquin was fortified by the English at the end of the thirteenth century. The church of Saint-André was completed in 1290 as part of these defenses. Its monumental doorway is now a registered historical monument in France. The stone steps have been worn smooth by countless feet over more than 700 years. *Opposite top right:* Circular window, church of Ste. Foy, in the twelfth century *bastide* of Pujois. *Opposite bottom left:* Pujols: Details of a half-timbered medieval house. *Opposite bottom right:* Pujols: remains of a thirteenth century pillory. Also known as the stocks, a pillory was used to punish offenders. It consisted of a wooden frame with holes in which the head, heads or feet could be locked. Pujols had a gallows, too, which is no longer standing.

Top: The twelfth century *bastide* of Pujols. *Bottom:* Pujols: Church of St. Nicholas. The bell tower was formerly the *donjon* (main defensive tower) of the town but was partially destroyed c. 1228. The bell was installed when the church itself was built in 1457. *Opposite top left:* Pujols: Angel holding a coat of arms. *Opposite top right:* Pujols: Le Bastidou, a fifteenth century house, now a gift shop. *Opposite bottom left:* Pujols: Archway of *donjon* (main defensive tower) overlooking the valley. *Opposite bottom right:* Pujols: The thirteenth century Hotel de Bailli (bailiff's office), now a private residence.

Church and shops in the *bastide* of Castelsagrat in southwest France, founded in 1269.

enforce judgments of the courts, these judgments either had to be compromises or otherwise acceptable to all parties in a dispute.

The French solution to these intractable problems was to have a final court of appeals: the Parlement of Paris. The Parlement grew out of the *curia regis* (king's court) with its professional legal advisors. This court had been held from time to time by early French kings to get advice from their principal vassals and prelates on feudal and political issues. It also dealt with legal cases submitted to the king as the sovereign judge.

By the mid-thirteenth century, these judicial sessions were being described as *curia regis in parlemento* and were being handled separately from its other business. Because the Parlement became the ultimate court of appeals, it attracted an ever-growing share of litigation from lower courts, especially from the *Grands Jours* (literally, "Great Days), which were assizes (provincial sittings of a court of justice) attended by magnates from the Parlement of Paris.

By the middle of the reign of Louis IX (1229–1270), a special *Chambre aux Plaids* (pleading chamber) was set up in Paris on the site where the modern Palais de Justice now stands. The *Chambre aux Plaids* came to be known as the *Grand Chambre* (Great Chamber). It was there that final decisions were announced. Other chambers appeared, too. The *Chambre des Enquêtes* (inquiry chamber) conducted judicial investigations which gave rise to these final judgments, and the *Chambre des Requêtes* (petitions chamber) were both instituted in the fourteenth century. The *Chambre de la Tournelle* (the "tower chamber," so-called because it was located in a turret of the palace) handled criminal matters.

The town square in Montjoi, a *bastide* dating from 1256. Built along the ridge of a narrow hill-top in southwest France, Montjoi is lined with half-timbered wattle and daub homes. Wattle and daub is an ancient method of building walls by weaving vertical wooden stakes (wattles) with horizontal twigs and then plastering them with mud or clay (daub).

Although vacant seats in the Parlement were supposed to be filled only by election or appointment, from the fourteenth century on, members of the Parlement who wanted to retire often gave their seats to their sons or simply sold them to the highest bidder. With about 50 lawyers in the Parlement, its legal procedures quickly became so complex that a handbook for practitioners was needed and was available by the 1320s.

Writing in 1323, this is how Jean de Jandun, a French scholar, described the Parlement:

> Nearly every day, the members are seated on elevated seats lining two sides of the chamber. These men are named after their professions: some are attorneys at law, others are notaries public. All of them, pursuant to their rank and royal orders, work for the public good. They present petitions which have been weighed in the scales of the most scrupulous fairness. In the Great Chamber, complex problems are being dealt with, requiring the greatest calm and seclusion. Seated in their tribunal are these always alert and able men, the masters of the Parlement. Their infallible knowledge of law and custom enables them to discuss the issues in all depth and latitude, and to render definitive final verdicts.[30]

Despite this array of highly skilled legal talent, judicial procedures in the Parlement could be painfully slow. In fact, one dispute between a monastery and a bishop ground on in the Parlement and in lesser French courts for more than a century.[31]

In *The Prince*, written in 1513, the Italian diplomat and author Niccolò Machiavelli had good things to say about the Parlement:

> Among kingdoms which are well organized and governed, in our own time, is that of France: it possesses countless valuable institutions, on which the king's freedom of action and security depend. The first of these is the parliament and its authority.... There could be no better or more sensible institution, nor one more effective in securing the security of the king and the kingdom.[32]

Modern historians, however, think of the Parlement as both a servant of and as a counterbalance to royal power. On the one hand, the *arrêts* (final decisions) of the Parlement were the authoritative statements of the king's law. On the other, the Parlement was also responsible for formally registering the king's edicts and letters patent.[33]

If the royal edicts and letters patent did not conform to established principles of justice and law and did not reflect the common interest, the Parlement could withhold registration and could argue against such ill-advised measures. After the end of the Middle Ages, successive Parlements would systematically oppose royal reform measures and would become the agents of privilege and reaction. This reactionary opposition ended only when the Parlement itself was abolished in the early years of the French Revolution and several of its members were sent to the guillotine.

Illustrative Cases and Laws

BECOMING A VASSAL (820s–830s)

The contract of vassalage was a key feature of feudalism. It involved two interlocking ceremonies. The first was *commendation* (homage), which occurred when a man formally gave himself to a superior by putting his hands between those of the other man. The second ceremony was the *oath of fealty*, in which a man pledged fidelity to his lord. Many detailed references to these legal ceremonies can be found in documents from medieval France. Here are some examples:

• A contemporary account tells us how King Harald of Denmark commended himself to Louis the Pious in 826: "Soon [Harald] delivered himself, with joined hands, to the king ..., and the emperor himself took his hands between his own glorious ones."[34]

• In 837, the emperor Louis gave to his young son Charles the Bald the titular command of all the land between Frisia (that part of the Netherlands and Germany fronting the North Sea) and the Seine. The magnates of the area had to become his vassals. Therefore, according to the Annals of St. Bertin, "the bishops, abbots, counts and royal vassals who had benefices in the aforesaid regions commended themselves to Charles and confirmed their fealty with an oath."[35]

• In a charter of homage and fealty of 1110, Bernard Atton, viscount of Carcassonne, acknowledged to Leo, abbot of the monastery of St. Mary of Grasse, his fealty and homage for the castles, manors, and places which the patrons, my ancestors, held from his and his predecessors and from the said monastery as a fief.... [I]f I or my sons or their successors do not observe to thee or to thy successors [the duties specified in the charter], we wish that all the aforesaid fiefs should by that very fact be handed over to thee and to the said monastery of St. Mary of Grasse and to thy successors.[36]

French abbots prevent a battle between their monks (1064)

The most comprehensive range of legal documents on judicial combat is found in France. In Angers in 1064, for instance, monks of the monastery of Saint-Serge were ready to come to blows with the monks of Saint-Aubin. The issue was land to be used for building a weir at the water mill of Varennes. The cartulary of Saint-Serge (a book holding copies of charters and title deeds of the monastery) reveals that this dispute

> grew so great that the members of the household of each monastery were preparing to contend with staves and shields against each other concerning this matter. Such a turn of events disturbed abbot Daibert of Saint-Serge beyond measure, especially since it might cause monks to want to fight against other monks. He, employing the greatest supplication, sent word to abbot Otbrannus of Saint-Aubin lest such an unheard-of evil as this occur and lest monks, who ought to show the example of concord and peace to others, become the cause of perdition. He [Otbrannus], complying with Daibert's healthy suggestions, did not delay in coming to meet Daibert.[37]

Thanks to the intercession of the two abbots, a compromise about the weir was reached in Angers on 27 April 1064. "On the next day," we are told, "it was reaffirmed and authorized in the chapter house of Saint-Aubin, with all the monks, and others who had gathered here for that reason, listening."[38]

Giving a man fair warning (1091)

Before the thirteenth century, only feudal customs had any weight in France: public law hardly existed, especially as far as nobles were concerned. So long as a French noble did not injure or insult his lord, the family of the lord, another vassal of the lord or that vassal's family, he could treat lesser people more or less as he pleased. This lack of legal restraint gave him relatively free rein to use sword, lance, war horse and armor to defend his "honor" or simply to express his aggression.

Even efforts by kings to establish some law and order were often ineffective. For seven years (1089–1096), William II Rufus ("Rufus" means "red" and referred to the king's ruddy complexion) waged war on Normandy to recover it from his elder brother, Robert. Normandy was a lawless, dangerous place at that time. The best that the king and Robert could do to make travel for noncombatants safer was to issue a joint decree in 1091. If a man wanted to kill an enemy in Normandy, they ordered, he must first give him fair warning — by blowing a horn before attacking.[39]

Monks' Champions Fight a Judicial Duel Over a Marsh (1098)

The monks of St. Martin of Tours complained to count William of Poitou that the monks of Holy Cross of Talmont, a neighboring monastery, had fraudulently taken possession of a marsh at Angles. The count ordered the abbot of Holy Cross to appear before him to answer this charge. Odo de Roches, a local judge, listened to the claims of both sides and decided that the issue should be decided by judicial combat.

Accordingly, two champions were chosen, armed and led to the church to take oaths. St. Martin's champion swore that the marsh had been given to his sponsors. His opponent countered this was a lie and accused the other champion of perjury. Once the fighting began, however, it did not take long to reach a clear-cut decision:

> And when the champions came together to do combat the injustice did not remain in doubt for very long, but was quickly revealed by the Lord. In fact, the champion of the monks of Holy Cross and their allies was shamefully defeated and laid low without delay, and he thus acquired nothing else for the monks of Holy Cross save the highest shame and greatest harm.
>
> Weighed down with shame and sadness on account of this defeat, [the monks of Holy Cross], weeping and overcome with sadness, departed along with those others who had wanted to seize the marsh belonging to Saint Martin. The monks of [Saint Martin] and their champion, on the other hand, offering immense thanks to the most just judge, God, and their patron saint, Saint Martin, returned quickly and joyfully to their house in order to take possession of their rights.[40]

A Judicial Battle Over Mills Along the Seine (c. 1100)

According to the cartulary of the monastery of Saint-Serge, when the Seine was in spate it enlarged a certain river landing near Angers. As a result, where there had formerly been room on the riverbank for only two mills, there was now room for five. Three new mills were duly built there.

A man named Engelardus claimed to be the rightful inheritor of the river landing and of all five mills. The monks of Saint-Serge, however, denied this, asserting that they had only rented out the site and thus still retained ownership of it and the mills. This quarrel went on for so long that the bishop of Angers, Geoffrey of Mayenne, found it necessary to intervene personally and went to the site to inspect it.

He was unable to resolve the matter, however, and decided that a judicial battle should be fought between Engelardus and the monks. The spot chosen for the combat was a villa known as Vi. Two champions were selected and were led to the church for the mandatory oath taking. Then, armed with shields and wooden staves, they fought for nearly a whole day.

Ultimately, there was no doubt about the outcome: "And just as it is written that God opposes the prideful, so he weakened the champion of Engelardus, so that [his sponsors] were utterly terrified."[41] All parties then agreed to a compromise which favored the victor but gave something to the loser, too. This settled the dispute, at least temporarily. Subsequent entries in the cartulary, however, indicate that the dispute was revived later on.

NAVIGATION AT THE PORT OF ARLES (1150)

Arles was and still is the last major city on the Rhone river. In Roman times, it was situated on a rocky outcrop from which navigation on the river could be watched and controlled. By the twelfth century, Arles had a flourishing trade with ships sailing down the river or entering it from the Golfe du Lion in the Mediterranean. The city drew up a navigation code to facilitate this fluvial and maritime traffic. Here are two of its provisions:

> *Concerning fishermen near the river:* Also we decree that any fisherman who lives near the river for the sake of fishing shall be expected to swear once a year in the court at Arles, that he will help any vessel belonging to a man of Arles which shall go out or come into the river if it be exposed to danger. And if it should happen that the vessel or vessels suffer shipwreck, which God forbid, he shall likewise be expected to save the vessel and its cargo, and for every pound they save they shall have twelve *denerii* and they shall take only two *solidi* for the labor from foreigners.
> *Concerning vessels:* Also we decree that, if any vessel be in the river and be moored to a post or stay at Le Gras on account of a contrary wind, the mates of those vessels shall be expected to send their small boats with mariners to help any vessel which may wish to enter the river.[42]

A GREAT NOBLEMAN OF FRANCE
IS TRIED FOR MURDER (1259)

The Coucy dynasty held one of the four most important baronies of medieval France. The power of this family was matched only by its pride and arrogance. "*Coucy à la merveille!*" ("Coucy, what a wonder!") was its battle cry. The motto of Enguerrand IV de Coucy, the senior member of the family, was

> *Roi ne suis,*
> *Ne prince ne duc ne comte aussi;*
> *Je suis le sire de Coucy.*
>
> (Not king, nor prince,
> Duke nor count am I;
> I am the lord of Coucy.)[43]

Enguerrand IV de Coucy was described by a contemporary as "the most experienced and skillful of all the knights of France."[44] Nevertheless, he made a nearly fatal mistake. His foresters arrested three young noblemen who had been caught hunting in the Coucy forest. Although these squires were carrying bows and arrows, they did not have hunting dogs with them or any of the other equipment needed to take valuable big game, such as stags or wild boars. Nevertheless, Enguerrand IV had them all hanged immediately like common thieves, without benefit of a trial of any sort.

These unfortunate young men had been retainers of the abbot of St. Nicholas-aux-Bois in nearby Laon. The abbot and the women who were cousins of the squires appealed to king Louis IX for justice. The king decided that Coucy's rank afforded him no immunity and that, as a result, he should be tried and punished much like a common criminal. Here are some lightly edited excerpts from the record of the trial:

> The blessed king, having made sufficient and due inquiry as to the said deed, had Enguerrand cited [brought] before him. He then had him arrested by his knights and sergeants, taken to the Louvre, put into prison and held there unchained. [A common criminal would have been chained.]

The barons of France came to Enguerrand's defense. Eager to protect the status of the high nobility, they warned the king that Enguerrand

> neither should nor would submit himself to an inquest in such a case, since it would touch his person, his honour and his inheritance. He was, however, ready to defend himself by battle and he denied that he had ever hanged the aforesaid youths or ordered them to be hanged.

The hanging eight thieves who tried to rob the shrine of St. Edmund, c. 1130. (The Pierpont Morgan Library, New York, MS M.736, f.19v.)

The king, however, refused to allow trial by combat, on the grounds that

> one would not easily find anyone willing to fight for this kind of person against the barons of the realm.... Therefore the blessed king did not accept the [barons'] request, but had my lord Enguerrand taken on the spot from there back to the Louvre by his sergeants and kept and guarded there.

Although the king initially wanted to sentence Enguerrand IV to death, he was persuaded to forgo it on the advice of the peers. Nevertheless,

> he condemned my lord Enguerrand to pay twelve thousand Paris pounds, which sum he had sent to Acre [a Christian fortress in Palestine] to be spent in the aid of the Holy Land. And this did not stop him from condemning [Enguerrand] to lose the wood where the youths had been hanged.... Also he

condemned him to make and endow three perpetual charities for the souls of those hanged. And he stripped him of all *haute justice* ["high justice," i.e., the right to impose the death penalty] over hunting and fishing, so from that time he could neither imprison nor put to death anyone for any offence committed there.[45]

The historian Barbara Tuchman, who in 1978 chronicled the exploits of the Coucy dynasty, tells us that in this case, "Legal history was made and later cited as a factor in the canonization of the King."[46]

WHEN AN AGREEMENT SHOULD NOT BE HONORED (1283)

Philippe de Beaumanoir was a bailiff of Clermont in south-central France. He occupies a special position in French legal history because his *Coutumes de Beauvaisis* (*Customary Laws of Beauvaisis*), written in 1283, is one of the best early customaries (collections of local legal customs) and was the first one to include actual cases.

Customary law held that certain kinds of agreements were not to be honored. An example is the case of Pierre, who sold firewood:

> Pierre had wood to sell, and he appointed an agent to sell it. The agent sold the wood to several people, with payment to be made on the following All Saints Day; and when All Saints Day had passed, the debtors came to the agent who had sold and delivered the wood to them, and asked for an extension of the payment they owed for the sale of the wood, and he gave them a year's extension.
>
> And when Pierre, who was the owner, discovered this, he dismissed the agent and sued the debtors and asked them to pay, and they answered that they had an extension from the person who had sold them the wood. And Pierre did not want to ratify this extension, for his agent did not have the authority or the power to extend the date just because he had sold the wood and set the original payment day. And on this issue they requested a judgment.

This is the ruling handed down in the case:

> It was judged that the extension would not be enforced, and by this judgment you can see that the agent has no power to act except as concerns what he was appointed and given to do by his master's authority. And it would be a bad thing, when an agent had created debts owing to his master on a day certain, for him to be able to give an extension later on.[47]

WEAPONS FOR TRIAL BY COMBAT (1306)

France is the best source of legal documents on judicial combat between well-armed nobles. Because such fights were common in southern France, in 1303 king Philip the Fair's issued an ordinance in Toulouse to regulate them. Updated in Paris three years later, this document became the definitive statement on how trial by combat should be conducted by the gentry. It directed that

> Since it is the custom that the plaintiff and the defendant come into the camp bearing with them all of their weapons and armor, which they intend to use against each

other, or to defend themselves, leaving from their camps on horse, they [should] tether up the horses and cover them in blankets bearing their blazon [coat of arms], wearing lowered visors, gorgets [armor protecting the throat], glaives [broadswords] in their hands, scabbarded swords and daggers, and in all states and manners in which they intend to attach each other, be it on foot or on horse....[48]

Suits Against an Abbess (1357)

Not all the problems the Parlement addressed were of earthshaking proportions. This entry in the court records of Paris reflects a minor dispute, though it must have been important enough to the men and women directly concerned.

The Parlement was the king's court so all its proceedings were conducted in the king's name, as in the following case:

> To the bailiff of Senlis, greetings. A number of inhabitants of the village of Chacrisse have explained to our Court that they have certain suits which they are moving or hoping to move in our Parlement and elsewhere against the religious abbess and convent of Notre-Dame of Soissons....
>
> [These suits concern] certain taxes on wine that the nuns are seeking and trying to collect from the said inhabitants and also concerning a certain number of men at arms, which the said nuns assert they are to have from the said inhabitants, or a certain sum of money to pay for them, which men at arms the said nuns are held to provide to us whenever we personally go to war ourselves.
>
> To prosecute these suits, [the villagers] must pay certain expenses and therefore must apportion and collect a tallage [contribution of money] among themselves; they must draw up letters of procuration and name proctors; and they must come together to consider the defense and prosecution of these suits. These things they do not dare to unless they first be granted license to do so. Since some of them are men subject to us, and others are men subject to several other lords, so they say, they entreat us that our Court provide for them.[49]

The case ended with an order to the bailiff "to do everything necessary" for the prosecution and defense of these suits. He was further directed to send one of his sergeants to the village make sure all was done properly.

A Parlementary Suit Over a Castle (1368–1380)

Guillaume du Merle was lord of the castle of Messei on the Varenne River in Normandy. The castle had been occupied by the English during one phase of the Hundred Years War (which will be discussed in the section on Joan of Arc) but they had withdrawn from it under the terms of the Treaty of Bretigny. They left the castle in very poor condition.

Two villages were located near the castle. The inhabitants of these villages alleged that Guillaume had not only forced them to refortify the castle at their own expense but later, realizing that it could still not be defended adequately, he had then forced them to tear it down. They claimed, moreover, that afterwards he "forced them again to repair, fortify and restore the said place's walls, towers, and moats, and to do guard duty there both day and night."[50]

The details of this case are somewhat murky but what is clear is that Guillaume had some of the plaintiffs imprisoned at Caen for 14 weeks or even longer. Their goods were seized and they were fined as well. The Parlement, however, was moved to come to their rescue, stating that

> they are paupers and miserable persons without the means to live or to prosecute their rights…. [They are] led to such beggary that they may die of hunger and help-lessness in the said prison unless we provide needed relief."[51]

Accordingly, Parlement ordered the viscount of Falaise, the senior local official, to

> proceed to the prison and free the prisoners, taking sureties from them, and sum-mon [Guillaume du Merle and his supporters] to the present Parlement … to answer our proctor and the said plaintiffs concerning the aforesaid and to proceed as justice requires. We order you not to allow anything further to be done in prejudice of the plaintiffs, and that you restore to them their goods…. You shall certify to us the inquest you have made on this matter and whatever else you have done, and forcefully compel those whom you adjourn to be present.[52]

The villagers were released from prison but it took the Parlement fully six years to reach a provisional decision about their case. In this decision, the Parlement found that the villagers were in fact required to stand guard duty in the castle. Later, in a compromise which finally settled the matter in 1380, the villagers agreed to help pay for the rebuilding and upkeep of the castle, except for its walls and towers, which were the most expensive components. In return for this concession, the villagers were required to guard the castle only during times of imminent danger, and then only at night.[53]

5

Anglo-Norman Justice in England Before the Common Law

Medieval justice followed a much different course in England than it did in France or other European countries. Anglo-Saxon law (a form of Germanic law) flourished in England from the sixth century until the Norman conquest of 1066. The Normans introduced feudalism and strong, centralized government to England — but not Roman law. Instead, a new body of Anglo-Norman law gradually evolved, based both on long-established Anglo-Saxon customs and on Norman feudalism. The Romanized canon law, however, was adopted by the English church in 1072.

THE ANGLO-SAXONS AND THEIR LAWS

The Anglo-Saxons were a mixture of Germanic newcomers with Celts already living in England and with Danish and Viking invaders. After the last Roman troops were pulled out of England in 407, the Anglo-Saxons took over Roman lands and replaced Roman law with their own laws. Most matters were regulated by the customs of the ethnic groups involved. Laws were written in Old English, not Latin. They were relatively independent of Roman law, being derived from several indigenous English sources. These included folkright, i.e., unwritten tribal rules; laws issued by the king; written statements of custom; and private compilations of legal rules.

The tension between "folkright" and "privileges" was a fundamental characteristic of Anglo-Saxon law. Each tribal kingdom had its own folkright, which governed a wide range of issues, including property, succession and contracts. Folkright could be overcome, however, by royal enactments or grants known as privileges. These gradually became more important than folkright itself and helped to strengthen the power of tribal kings.[1]

Before the tenth century, Anglo-Saxon law focused chiefly on monetary remedies for criminal offenses, i.e., stating how much money should be paid to an injured party or his kin. The king consulted his *witan* (wise men) in difficult cases. He also received some of the fines imposed for crimes. Later on, the law was broadened to include new penalties, such as declaring a criminal to be an outlaw, confiscating his goods or inflicting punishment, up to and including death. Law began to address policing and administrative issues as well.

The first Anglo-Saxon laws, known as "dooms," are attributed to Æthelbert of Kent and were drafted around 605.[2] Written in English, they constitute the earliest body of law expressed in any Germanic language.[3] The influential British legal scholar William Stubbs found that these laws tended to address narrowly defined matters of greatest concern to particular individuals. There was much less attention to weightier political and legal issues of concern to society as a whole. "The great bulk of the laws," he wrote,

> concern chiefly such questions as the practice of compurgation, ordeal, wergild, sanctity of holy places, persons, or things; the immunity of estates belonging to churches; and the tables of penalties for crimes, in their several aspects as offenses against the peace, the family, and the individual.[4]

Early Anglo-Saxon communities were small and relatively poor. Villages were scattered over a wide, unruly area. Warriors had to fend off invaders and were fond of fighting each other. Literacy was uncommon. Nevertheless, even in these inauspicious circumstances a broad range of contemporary documents, i.e., charters, *Notitiae* [Notices], the Domesday Book, cartularies, chronicles, *gesta* ["deeds"] and *miracula* ["miracles"], all attest to the fact that a good deal of interesting legal activity was going on. Examples include:[5]

• The forfeiture (loss of property or money because of a breach of a legal obligation) in 1043 of queen Emma and bishop Stigand of Elmham for encouraging king Magnus of Norway to invade England.

• A mid-eleventh-century dispute over the port of Sandwich and its revenues, which pitted king Harold Harefoot against archbishop Eadsige; the officials of Christ Church, Canterbury; and abbot Ælfstan of St Augustine's church, Canterbury.

• The execution of three men, and the branding of a cleric, for robbing the Abbey Church of Waltham Holy Cross in the mid-eleventh century.

• A quarrel between the infamous earl Sweyn (d. 1055) and his mother over the identity of his father. Sweyn later seduced Eadgyfu (or Edviga), abbess of Leominster, and then murdered his cousin, earl Beorn, while under a flag of truce. For the latter outrage, a military assembly headed by the king formally declared Sweyn to be a *nithing* (a man without honor.) This judgment made him an outcast in any part of the northern world and temporarily forced him to take refuge in Flanders.[6]

• The trial of a man named Thorkel and his wife for the murder of their son (pre-1066).

ALFRED THE GREAT

Alfred was king of Wessex, a Saxon kingdom in southwestern England, from 871 to 899. He repulsed Danish invaders, revived learning in England itself, and issued a code of laws which laid the foundations for the English common law. Asser, a Welsh scholar who was Alfred's friend, wrote a biography of the king in 893 which reveals Alfred's personal involvement in Anglo-Saxon justice.[7]

An ealdorman was the chief royal official of an Anglo-Saxon shire (county). He presided over the shire court, took one-third of its profits, and recruited the shire's soldiers. A reeve was the general overseer of an estate. Alfred looked into almost all the judgments made by his ealdormen and reeves. If he thought a given ruling was unfair, he would require the judge to explain how he reached it. If the judge did not know what the law was on this particular issue, he was forced to study the law, even if he was illiterate. Thus it came about, Asser tells us, that

> Nearly all the ealdormen and reeves and thegns [nobles], who were illiterate from childhood, applied themselves to learn this unfamiliar discipline [reading], no matter how laboriously, than to relinquish their powers of office; and if anyone of them was slow on the uptake, the king insisted that he should find someone else to help him — by reading out books in English day and night, or whenever he had the opportunity.[8]

THE NORMAN CONQUEST

The military conquest of England by William, duke of Normandy, in 1066 marks a decisive turning point in English history in both foreign and domestic policy. His victory over Harold, who had claimed the title of king of England, brought England into much closer contact with continental Europe. Domestically, William brought strong, centralized government and Norman feudalism into England.

As rebellious Anglo-Saxons forfeited their rights, their lands passed to the Normans on feudal terms. William handed out much of the country to about 180 of his most powerful supporters and their retainers. Every estate in England was thus a feudal tenement held directly or indirectly from the crown. There was no more allodial land. A new Norman aristocracy largely replaced the old Anglo-Saxon nobility.

An entry in the *Anglo-Saxon Chronicle* for the year 1086 gives us a balanced description of William's simultaneous dedication to law and order and to his own interests. On the plus side, we learn that

> The good order that William established is not to be forgotten. It was such that any man ... might travel over the kingdom with a bosom full of gold unmolested; and no man durst kill another, however great the injury he might have received from him. He reigned over England, and being sharp-sighted to his own interest, he surveyed the kingdom so thoroughly [by means of the Domesday Book — see below] that there was not a single hide of land [a hide was the standard unit of assessment for taxation] throughout the whole of which he knew not the possessor, and how much it was worth, and this he afterward entered in his register.[9]

But there was another side of the coin, too:

> Truly there was much trouble in these times, and very great distress. [William] caused castles to be built and oppressed the poor. The king was also of great sternness, and he took from his subjects many marks of gold, and many hundred pounds of silver, and this, either with or without right, and with little need. He was given to avarice and greedily loved gain.... The rich complained and the poor murmured, but he was so sturdy that he took no notice of them; they must will all that the king willed, if they would live, or keep their lands,... or be maintained in their rights. Alas, that any man should so exalt himself....[10]

THE DOMESDAY BOOK (1086)

Twenty years after they conquered England, the Normans made a vast, highly detailed survey of their new lands and possessions. Writing in 1086, bishop Robert of Hereford said that the survey

> covered all the lands of every shire, and the property of every magnate in fields, manors, and men — whether slaves or free man, cottagers or farmers — and in plough-teams, horses, and other stock, and in services and in rents....[11]

William's inspectors overlooked nothing. An entry in the *Anglo-Saxon Chronicle* complains that William had England investigated

> so very narrowly that there was not one single hide, not one yard of land, not even (it is shameful to tell — but it seemed no shame to him to do it) one ox, not one cow, not one pig was left out, that was not set down in this record. And all the records were brought to him afterwards.[12]

This famous survey, originally known as "the description of England," was summarized for the king in two volumes. Since the mid-twelfth century, these two books have been known collectively as the Domesday Book, so-named after the last day at the end of time — "doomsday" — when people were believed to face a divine judgment of their lives from which there was no appeal. The Domesday Book is neither a collection of laws nor a treatise on law but rather a "geld-book," that is to say, a compilation of the facts necessary for assessing the crown's land tax (geld). Remarkably, the Domesday Book has survived and is now on display at the Public Record Office in Kew, outer London.

In terms of medieval justice, one key feature of the Domesday Book was how its findings were confirmed. According to the *Inquisitio comitatus Cantabrigiensis* (*The Inquisition of the County of Cambridge*), a document which formed part of an early draft of the Domesday survey, confirmation was done under oath by a county court in which a proto-jury system seems to have been in use. This was a local jury drawn from the middle classes of the rural population. It usually consisted of eight people: four Englishmen and four Normans.[13]

ANGLO-NORMAN LAW

The Normans retained much of the Anglo-Saxon legal system, including the ordeal and outlawry (putting a fugitive beyond the protection of the law). They also built up a bureaucracy for their central government and began to keep written financial and, later, legal records. Clerics or literate laymen administered the law.

The Normans accepted the late Anglo-Saxon legal doctrine that serious transgressions resulting in injury or death were crimes against society as a whole, not merely offenses against an individual and his kin. The conquerors introduced a few innovations: a new body of forest law to prevent poaching of the king's game, use of trial by combat in conjunction with the Saxon ordeals, greater reliance on sworn testimony, and bringing ecclesiastical cases under canon law. Nevertheless, the feudalized justice of Norman France did not entirely displace the traditional Anglo-Saxon courts, to which we shall now turn.

County Courts[14]

In the immediate post-Conquest era, county courts did not meet very frequently. It was probably not until the late twelfth century that they began to convene once a month. They did not require the attendance of all free men living in the shire, but only those of a certain wealth. By the late thirteenth century, only men owing "suit of court" (the duty to be present at the court) had to attend and to make judgments at the court. This duty was attached to particular holdings of land. A few exceptional counties also had a separate set of doomsmen, who were freeholders who owed suit of court on a permanent basis as a duty attached to their land. There was no separate duty on other landholders to attend the county court.

The county court was not only a judicial meeting but a coming together of many of the leading men of the shire to discuss any matters that needed to be resolved. In the thirteenth to fifteenth centuries, at least 150 men, and occasionally many more, might be present.[15] It sometimes met in the open air but could also be held inside — in a house, the hall of castle, or a monastery. A royal representative originally known as the shire-reeve presided over this court. His title was later shortened to our familiar word "sheriff."

Courts of the Hundred

This court ranked lower in the judicial hierarchy. The hundred itself ranged in size from no more than one or two villages in some counties (Kent and Sussex) to much bigger areas and multiple villages in other counties (the West Midlands). In the Danelaw — that part of the northern, central and eastern regions of England colonized by Danish invaders in the late ninth century — the term *wapentake* was used instead of hundred and "plowland" was used instead of "hide." During the 1270s there were 628 hundreds or *wapentakes* in England. The number of hundreds in each shire varied considerably. For instance, Devon had 35 and Oxfordshire 14 of them in the 1270s.[16]

The hundred court was usually presided over by a bailiff, but twice a year the sheriff himself visited each hundred in his jurisdiction.[17] In pre-conquest times, the hundred court was the main court for most cases. King Edgar (959–975) ordained that if a man "denies the doom of the hundred, and the same be afterwards be proved against him," he was to be fined ever-increasing amounts if he did this three times. But "for the fourth time," Edgar ordered, "let him forfeit all that he owns, and be an outlaw, unless the king allow him to remain in the country."[18] Disputes only went to the county court if the hundred court failed to give justice. Under the Normans, however, the hundred court seems to have declined in importance.

CHURCH COURTS

Before the Norman Conquest, ecclesiastical disputes had been handled by the Anglo-Saxon courts. As mentioned earlier, this changed in 1072 when William set up new courts within the exclusive authority of the church. There were two different kinds of court belonging to the church after 1066: those dealing with ecclesiastical matters under the 1072 edict, and manorial courts which dealt with the peasants who worked monastic and other ecclesiastical lands. These latter courts seem to have resembled the manorial courts held by laymen for their tenants.

MANORIAL COURTS

Introduced from France by the Normans, manorial courts soon became a key part of medieval English life. They usually addressed civil matters, such as land transactions and dealings between the lords and their peasants, but petty crimes could be dealt with, too. Unlike the courts of the shire and hundred, manorial courts could perhaps be considered as "personal courts" for the lord. Every lord had the right to hold his own court for the tenants of his fief and to exercise his feudal jurisdiction over them. He was also entitled to pocket the fines imposed on tenants for their offenses. The manorial court was thus a useful source of income for him.

A manorial court which was convoked on the lord's authority alone was known as a "court baron." One which was held under royal franchise and could punish minor offenses was a "court leet." There were many other kinds of specialized courts as well — the *curia regis*, franchise courts, and the courts of the Danelaw.

"PIEPOWDER" COURTS

There were also open-air courts for merchants and traders. These were known as "piepowder" courts (the word comes from the French *pied-poudreux*, i.e., "dusty-footed") because the men who used it still had dust on their feet. Their itinerant callings kept them moving from market to market and from fair to fair. For this reason, piepowder courts had to reach legal decisions relatively quickly.

The speed with which a piepowder court could decide matters can be seen in a suit brought at the court of Colchester in 1458. At 9 a.m., the plaintiff filed suit to recover a debt. The defendant failed to appear, despite repeated summonses. At noon, judgment was given in favor of the plaintiff. At 4 p.m., the defendant's goods, which had been seized by the court, were handed over to the plaintiff.

Illustrative Cases and Laws

FROM THE DOOMS OF ÆTHELBERT, KING OF KENT, 560–616[19]

Anglo-Saxon laws (dooms) left little to the imagination:

> For seizing a man by the hair, 50 *sceattas* shall be paid as compensation.
> If a bone is laid bare, 3 shillings shall be paid as compensation.
> If the outer covering of the skull is broken, 10 shillings shall be paid in compensation.
> If an eye is knocked out, 50 shillings shall be paid as compensation.
> If one man slays another, he shall pay the *wergeld* with his own money and property, which whatever its nature must be free from blemish.
> If a freeman lies with the wife of another freeman, he shall pay the husband her *wergeld*, and procure a second wife with his own money, and bring her to the other man's home.
> If anyone destroy another man's organ of generation, let him pay with three *leudgelds* [the amount owed for manslaughter]; if he pierce it through, let him make *bot* [compensation] with six shillings; if it be pierced within, let him make *bot* with six shillings.

ANGLO-SAXON LAW EVOLVES (AFTER 871)

Anglo-Saxon law became more complex and more sophisticated under king Alfred (r. 871–899) and his successors. It still contained lists of fines for different kinds of offenses but now embraced a broader range of subjects, such as conspiracy, sanctuary and feuds. Alfred ordained that:

> *Of plotting against a lord*: If anyone plot against the king's life, of himself, or by harboring exiles, or of his men; let he be liable with his life and in all that he has....
> *Of churchfryth* [sanctuary under the protection of the church]: We also ordain to every church which has been hallowed by a bishop, this *fryth* [right of sanctuary]: if a *fahman* [a "foeman" in a blood-feud] flee to or reach one, that for seven days no one can drag him out.... If he himself be willing to deliver up his weapons to his foes, let them keep him for 30 days, and then let them give notice of him to his kinsmen.
> *Of feuds*: We also command that if a man who knows his foe be homesitting fight not before he demand justice of him. If he have such power that he can beset his foe, and besiege him within, let him keep him within for seven days, and attack him not, if he will remain within. And, then, after seven days, if he will surrender, and deliver up his weapons, let him be kept safe for 30 days, and let notice of him be given to his kinsmen and friends.[20]

The dooms of kings Alfred, Guthrum and Edward the Elder also gave the exact words to be used for a wide variety of fealty and other oaths. "Thus shall a man swear fealty oaths," they decreed:

By the Lord, before whom this relic is holy, I will be to [the name of the lord] faithful and true, and love all that he loves, and shun all that he shuns, according to God's law, and according to the world's principles, and never, by will or force, by word nor by work, do ought of what is loathful to him; on condition that he keep me as I am willing to deserve, and all that fulfill that our agreement was, when I to him submitted and chose his will.[21]

A CLEVER THIEF (C. 897)

As mentioned earlier, one of the reasons for studying medieval cases is to narrow the gap between written law and local custom. Let us see how a clever thief escaped punishment.

The Anglo-Saxon thief Helmstan, who had previously gotten into serious trouble, was now charged with stealing the belt of a man named Æthelred.[22] Helmstan knew that if he lost the case and was convicted, he would no longer have any legal standing. This meant he could not defend his own property. Indeed, even before the case came to trial, his enemies were so sure he would lose that they were already beginning to claim his lands — even those to which he held written title.

He therefore decided to turn to an old friend, Ealdorman Ordlaf, who proved to be extremely helpful. First, Ordlaf told Helmstan that if he promised to stay out of further trouble he could have life tenure of the lands he farmed but did not own outright. More importantly, Ordlaf also got in touch with king Alfred on Helmstan's behalf and rigged the court procedure so it would favor Helmstan. With this kind of backing, it is not surprising that Helmstan won his case and was declared to be innocent.

DEALING WITH COUNTERFEITERS (978)

King Æthelred the Unrædy (978–1016) — "unrædy" means "unadvised" — made London coinage the standard for the whole realm and tried to suppress counterfeiters. He decreed that

> The coiners [i.e., counterfeiters] should lose their hand, and it should be placed above the money-smithy. And the coiners who work in the woods, or make similar things anywhere, are guilty of their lives, unless the king wishes to have mercy on them.
> And let the moneyers be fewer than they were before; in every important port three, and in every other port let there be one moneyer.... And they who guard the ports shall take care upon pain of my displeasure that each coin conform to the standard at which my money is received.... And let all guard the money, just as I have commanded and as we have chosen all to do.[23]

A RESOURCEFUL ABBOT (C. 990)

Custom played a major role in a case involving Ramsey Abbey in England. This abbey was founded by Ailwine, a Saxon noble, in 969. The institution's *Chronicon* (chronicle), attributed to the monk Florence of Worcester, is a valuable source on English life during late Anglo-Saxon days and immediately after the Norman Conquest. From it we learn that the abbot had become involved in a suit which he knew would be very expensive and in which he had a weak case. This is how he won the case:

> [the abbot knew that] a suit which demanded the outlay of much revenue would be dangerous to contest: using therefore a more effective plan, he deceived the efforts of the other side with a clever trick, obtained the attention of the king, and with modest petition skillfully intimated ... the wickedness of his opponents; he added twenty marks in gold wherewith to earn the king's favour; he acquired also the support of the queen at the price of five marks, that she might faithfully bring her holy prayers into the royal ears....[24]

KING CANUTE UPHOLDS THE LAWS (1020)

In 1018, the Danes and English had agreed at Oxford to follow the laws of king Edgar. In his charter of 1020, Canute ordered them to do so:

> If any be so bold, clerk [a member of the clergy] or lay, Dane or English, as to go against God's will and against my royal authority, or against secular law, and be unwilling to make amends, and to alter according to my bishops' teaching, then I pray Thurcyl my earl, and also command him, that he bend that unrighteous one to right if he can; if he cannot, then will I with the strength of us both that he destroy him in the land or drive him out of the land, be he better, be he worse....
>
> And I will that all people, clerk and lay, hold fast Edgar's law, which men have chosen and sworn at Oxford ... and eschew all unrighteousness; that is, slaying of kinsmen, and murder, and perjury, and witchcraft and enchantment, and adultery, and incest.... [N]o man [shall] be so bold as to marry a hallowed nun or *mynchen* [novice]; if any have done so, be he outlaw towards God, and excommunicated from all Christendom, and answerable to the king in all that he has, unless he quickly alter and deeply make amends to God....[25]

"WITH SAKE AND WITH SOKE" (C. 1066)

The legal formula for a baron's judicial power over his tenants was expressed in two English words which are now rendered as "sake and soke."[26] The first word referred to the cause of a dispute; the second, to the act of seeking a lord or a formal assembly for resolving this dispute. Sake and soke were used in an alliterative phrase first recorded during the reign of Edward the Confessor (1042–1066) but became in the Norman age the formal description of a baron's judicial rights. The full phrase was: "with sake and with soke, with toll and with team; and with infangenetheof." When Edward the Confessor gave the towns of Old Windsor and Staines to the abbey of Westminster, for example, he used this phrase.

To put it in modern terms, "with sake and with soke" meant that the monks were directed to set up a manorial court to make sure the estate ran smoothly. "Toll" meant that the abbey had the right to take a payment when others sold their cattle or goods.

"Team" was the right to hold a court where men accused of illegal possession of cattle or other items could be tried. The method of proof here was the testimony of witnesses who had seen "toll" when these goods actually changed hands. "Infangenetheof" was the right to punish a thief caught on the estate in possession of stolen property.

HENRY I ON THE ANGLO-NORMAN LAW COURTS (1108)

Henry I was William the Conqueror's youngest and most intelligent son. Nicknamed Henry Beauclerc ("good scholar") because he could read, he governed Normandy, made peace in England, and built up the crown's executive powers and its bureaucratic capabilities. He was also known as the "Lion of Justice" because justice was strengthened and expanded under his reign. Royal justices, for example, were sent out to tour the countryside.

Other legal milestones under Henry I included the first of the "pipe rolls" (records of the crown's income and expenses, so-named because of the pipestem-like form of these rolled sheepskin parchments) and the first appearance of the court of exchequer, which handled the king's revenue and had jurisdiction over cases involving it.

A writ was a written command from the king to the sheriff to see that justice was done. In a writ of 1108, Henry I put his personal, imperious stamp of approval on the four most important lay courts of his kingdom. These were the royal court, the shire or county court, the hundred court, and the lord's honour court. (An "honour" was a group of estates.) Henry I ordained as follows:

> Know that I grant and order that henceforth my shire courts and hundred courts shall meet in the same places and at the same terms [the four sittings of English courts] as they met in the time of King Edward, and not otherwise. And I do not wish that my sheriff should make them assemble in different fashion because of his own needs or interests. For myself, if ever I should wish it, will cause them to be summoned at my own pleasure if it be necessary for my royal interests.
>
> And if in the future there should arise a dispute concerning the allotment of land, or concerning its seizure, let this be tried in my own court if it be between two tenants in chief. But if the dispute be between the vassals of any baron of my honour, let it be held in the court of their common lord. But if the dispute be between the vassals of two different lords, let the plea be held in the shire court.... And I will and order that the men of the shire so attend the meetings of the shire courts and the hundred courts as they did in the time of King Edward.[27]

6

Henry II and the Rise of the English Common Law

Henry II (reigned 1154–1189) and his advisors created the institutional foundations for the English common law, so-named because, unlike feudalized justice, it was common to all men in all regions of the country. Three interrelated factors helped bring about the common law: the strong monarchy established and maintained by post-conquest kings; the growth of the jury system, which eventually displaced the ordeal as a method of proof; and a centralized royal court system, where cases would be decided by professional judges and clerks applying the same standards. One of the historic milestones in the rise of the common law was Magna Carta, the "Great Charter" of English liberty, conceded by King John to rebellious barons in 1215.

ONE LAW FOR ALL: THE COMMON LAW

Common law arose from the decisions of the new central courts, which used prior judgments and common sense, rather than formal written enactments of law, to resolve disputes. Judges in these courts applied what the eminent eighteenth-century legal commentator William Blackstone said was

> the first ground and chief cornerstone of the laws of England, which is, general immemorial custom, or common law, from time to time declared in the decisions of the courts of justice; which decisions are preserved among our public records, explained in our reports, and digested for general use in the authoritative writings of the venerable sages of the law."[1]

This way of "making law" turned out to be so successful that until late in the nineteenth century, English common law was still being made primarily by judges, not by legislators. Modern law in the United States and in the Commonwealth of Nations owes an enormous debt to the common law of England.

Common law had deep roots in Anglo-Norman justice. Henry II created a strong, centralized monarchy which made it possible for him and his advisers to take some bold steps on the legal front. These included:

• encouraging the development of the jury system;

• sending out justices to the counties of England "on eyre" (literally, "wanderings" but, in reality, on official visits);

• creating a centralized royal court to hear civil disputes;

• making sure there was enough continuity in judicial personnel so that a coherent, nationwide body of custom could emerge;

• requiring courts to keep detailed written records of their work;

• allowing courts to hear only those kinds of cases approved by the king;

• and, finally, integrating the local courts into a single legal structure which covered the whole country.[2]

Imposing royal justice in the provinces, Henry II made wrongdoers tremble, as the following story, drawn from a collection of miracle stories, shows:

> By royal command, men who had committed homicide, theft, and the like were traced in the various provinces, arrested and brought before judges and royal officers at St. Edmunds and put in jail, where, to avoid their liberation by some ruse, their names were entered on three lists by command of the judges.
>
> Amongst them was one Robert, nicknamed the putrid, a shoemaker from Banham, who was certain that he saw and heard himself put on the list. In the midst of his prayers, afflictions, tears and devotions he made a vow to God and St. Edmund that if he saved him from this peril he would give him the best of his four oxen.
>
> At daybreak, when they were taken out and their names checked against the written list, for them to be purged by the ordeal of water, the name of Robert was found in none. Pleased and full of joy, he returned home and, not forgetting his vow, took the ox and offered it to God and St. Edmund with great devotion....[3]

RELATIONS BETWEEN CHURCH AND STATE: THE CONSTITUTIONS OF CLARENDON (1164)

Clarendon was a royal hunting lodge which Henry II also used as a meeting place to discuss legal and political matters. In 1164 he presented to the bishops assembled there a number of rigorous "constitutions" (legal provisions), which effectively redefined the relations between church and state. These constitutions were drafted to limit the privileges of clerics and restrict the power of church courts, which, thanks to the rapid growth of canon law, had begun to encroach on secular, i.e., royal, justice.

The new constitutions tilted the balance of legal power decisively toward the king. Among their provisions — some old, some new — were the following:

• clerics could not make judicial appeals to Rome, nor even leave England, without the king's permission;

• the powers of the church to excommunicate lay people, place them under interdict, or try them on the basis of secret information were curtailed;

• confirmation of the custom that when bishoprics or monasteries were vacant (that is, they had no presiding bishop or abbot), the king could choose a successor and, in the meantime, he would receive the income from these institutions;

• certain types of cases involving patronage, debts and lands were put under the purview of the secular courts; and

• "criminous clerks" (priests charged with serious crimes) would be subject to secular punishment.

This last provision proved to be the most controversial. It provoked a long-running dispute between Henry II and Thomas Becket, archbishop of Canterbury, which ended with the assassination of Becket on the steps of Canterbury Cathedral in 1170. This famous murder will be discussed below.

A WORD WITH SEVERAL MEANINGS: ASSIZE

The word "assize" can be confusing today because it has numerous meanings. A word of explanation is therefore needed here.

"Assize" comes from the French *asseoir*, "to sit down." A general definition is "a sitting, or session, of a court of justice." At first, assize meant the procedures for the presentment (indictment) and trial of suspects. It was also applied to court sessions held in English counties. In medieval France, it meant the provincial sessions held by the Parlement of Paris. The twelve men testifying in a possessory assize were known as an assize, too. "Assize" was used for writs as well, and to mean legislation in general. Writs of assize, for example, included *mort d'ancestor* (death of an ancestor) and *novel disseisin* (recent dispossession), both of which are discussed below.

EARLY USE OF THE JURY SYSTEM: THE ASSIZE OF CLARENDON: (1166)

To restore law and order after a preceding period of anarchy, Henry II issued a number of ordinances in the Assize of Clarendon in 1166. These took power away from the local courts (and thus from the local lords) and returned it to the crown. In terms of legal history, the most important provision of this assize was the establishment of a jury of presentment (indictment). This institution would ultimately evolve into the jury system of the Crown Courts of Britain and the grand jury of the United States.

A jury of presentment formally stated the criminal charges against the accused. The Assize of Clarendon provided that

> King Henry has ordained on the advice of all his barons, for preserving peace and maintaining justice, that inquiry be made through the several counties and through the several hundreds *by twelve of the more lawful men of the hundred and by four of the more lawful men of each vill* [township], upon oath that they will tell the truth, whether in their hundred or in their vill there is any man who is accused or said to be a robber or a murderer or anyone who has been a harborer of robbers or murderers or thieves since the lord king was king. And the justices shall make this inquest by themselves, and the sheriffs by themselves.[4]

It must be noted that in England at this time there was no *trial* by jury. The grand

jury could testify against a lawbreaker but he still had to go through an ordeal to establish his guilt or innocence. The second article of the Assize of Clarendon makes this
clear:

> And he who shall be found by the oath of the [jury of presentment] cited or charged
> as having been a robber or murderer or thief or a harborer of them since the lord
> king was king, let him be arrested and go to the judgment of water [the ordeal], and
> let him swear that he was not a robber or murderer or thief or a harborer of them
> since the lord king was king, to the value of five shillings so far as he knows.[5]

Even if "the judgment of water" proved the accused to be innocent, his troubles
did not end there if previously he had behaved badly. In such a case, the assize demanded
that he be exiled; if he returned to England without royal permission, he was to be
declared an outlaw:

> Moreover, the lord king wills that those who shall be tried [by the ordeal] and shall
> be absolved by the law, if they have a very bad reputation and are publicly and scan-
> dalously denounced on the testimony of many lawful men, shall forswear the king's
> lands, so that within eight days they shall cross the sea unless the wind detain them;
> and with the first wind which they have thereafter they shall cross the sea, and they
> shall never return to England unless by the mercy of the lord king; and there let
> them be outlaws, and if they return let them be taken as outlaws.[6]

BRINGING JUSTICE TO THE COUNTIES: THE GENERAL EYRE (1175)

Under Henry I, justices had sometimes been sent into the countryside to hear
criminal pleas. Henry II had higher legal and political ambitions. A contemporary
chronicler, Richard Fitzneale (c. 1130–1198), was treasurer of England under both Henry
II and Richard I. In his *Dialogus de scaccario* (*Course of the Exchequer*) he tells us that

> the King [Henry II] once more essayed to renew the "golden days" of his grandfa-
> ther; and, making choice of prudent men, he divided the kingdom into six parts, so
> that the justices chosen, whom we call "Justices in Eyre," might go on circuit
> through them and restore the rights which had lapsed. They, giving audience in
> each county, and doing full justice to those who considered themselves wronged,
> saved the poor both money and labor.[7]

Thus England was divided into six judicial circuits which were visited regularly
by the king's itinerant justices. The general eyre consisted of visits by professional judges
sent out from Westminster to make sure justice was being done in the counties. Soon
it became such an established part of the legal regime that there should be an eyre visitation of the whole of England every other year.[8]

The first visitation, by two groups of two justices, took place in 1174–1175.[9] *Bracton*, the greatest legal treatise of the Middle Ages (see below), describes the arrival of
the justices and their assistants in about 1250:

> First let the writs be read which authorize and empower them to proceed on eyre, that their authority may be known. When these have been heard, and if the justices so wish, let one of the senior and more distinguished among them publicly declare in the presence of all the reason for their coming, the purpose of the eyre and the advantage to be gained from keeping the peace.... And [let him then declare] that the king orders all his lieges, in the faith whereby they are bound to him and as they wish to save their possessions, to lend effective and diligent counsel and aid for the preservation of his peace and justice and the suppression and extirpation of wrong-doing.[10]

Although the eyre's visits were not frequent, they were extremely unpopular. During each visit, the business of all other courts in that county ground to a halt. All the important men in the county had to attend the eyre and justify their activities. The county itself faced stiff amercements (punishments by fines set by the court), while individual lawbreakers faced heavy punishments as well.[11] So unpopular was the eyre that a contemporary chronicler tells us that in 1233 the men of Cornwall "fled to the woods"" when the justices approached.[12]

The justices left few stones unturned. They empanelled juries in each county and after 1194 they were expected to give each jury a copy of the "chapters" (articles of inquiry) of their eyre. There were more than 50 chapters, which cast such a wide judicial net that it is worth looking at one of them in some detail. It covered:

> Purprestures [illegal enclosures or encroachments upon the land or property of another] made against the king: whether on land or in the sea or in fresh water, whether within a liberty or without or elsewhere, no matter where. [A liberty was a right or immunity enjoyed by prescription or by grant.]
>
> Deceased Christian usurpers: who they were, and what chattels they had, and who has them; chattels of slain Jews and their pledges, debts and charters, and who has them; forgers and clippers of coins; burglars and malefactors and their harbourers in time of peace; fugitives: if any have returned after flight without permission of the lord king.
>
> Outlaws and their chattels: who has them, and whether outlaws have returned without warrant; those who have not pursued as they ought outlaws and burglars who crossed their lands; defaults, that is, of those who have been summoned to be here before the justices and are not present, and of those who did not come on the first day [of the eyre].
>
> The escape of thieves; poachers in parks and fishponds, who they are; the excesses of sheriffs and other bailiffs: whether they have fomented litigation for the purpose of acquiring lands or wardships or of obtaining money or other profits by which justice and truth are stifled or suffer delay; [and] sheriffs and other ambidextrous bailiffs who take bribes from both sides.[13]

Visitations of eyre were seen as sessions of the king's court. Judgments rendered at sessions of the general eyre were made in accordance with the customs of the king's court, not in accordance with the local customs of a given county. Pleas usually heard by the hundred and county were automatically transferred to the justices on eyre.[14] As a result, these judgments were applied nationally, not just locally.[15]

PROTECTING PRIVATE PROPERTY:
THE ASSIZE OF NORTHAMPTON (1176):

One of Henry II's early decisions was to give private property the protection of the courts. Previously, if a powerful man coveted his neighbor's land, he could simply seize it by force, expel the rightful owner and use the property for his own benefit. The owner would have to rely on sluggish and expensive legal maneuvers in hopes of ever getting it back.

To correct this abuse, Henry II ordered that if anyone ejected the occupant of land by force and without a court order, the injured party now had a recourse: he could complain to the king's chancellor. The chancellor would then order the sheriff to round up twelve men, known as an "assize," to testify under oath before the king's justices. If these men agreed that the owner had indeed been wrongfully ejected, he was reinstated on his property and the man who had seized it was heavily fined.

If, on the other hand, the twelve men found that the owner had not been so ejected and thus the defendant was innocent, the plaintiff was fined for making a false accusation. Known as possessory assizes, such cases not only meted out royal justice but also enriched the royal treasury: no matter which side won, the fine always went to the king.[16]

It was in the Assize of Northampton that Henry II divided England into six judicial circuits and ordered that they be visited by six groups of three judges each. The royal justices broadened the scope of their eyre by focusing on feudal matters as well. Men had to appear before them to swear oaths of fealty to the king. The justices also collected information about the custody of castles and inquired into "escheats, churches, lands and women, who are in the gift of the king."[17] ("Escheats" were reversions of lands to the lord of the fief when there were no heirs capable of inheriting under the original grant.)

In this process of expansion, the king's court ceased being a communal court where its justices were merely presiding officers: they now became judgment givers.[18] This assize made some modest changes in the provisions of the Assize of Clarendon and, among other things, set up a possessory action known as *mort d'ancestor* (death of an ancestor).

This action dealt with the situation where a close ancestor had died in possession of land but the lord — who was entitled to take possession until the heir came of age or until the lord had ascertained who the heir was and had been paid his relief (succession duty) — was refusing to admit the heir to possession of his ancestor's land. *Mort d'ancestor* made sure the heir got what was rightfully his.

The assize instructed judges to hear recent pleas of *novel disseisin*, an action by which "possession [of land] lost by wrongful force may be restored."[19] Judges were also given instructions on how to discharge their judicial, political, financial and other duties.

ROYAL COURTS AND LEGAL EDUCATION

Any court with royal justices was described as the *curia regis* (king's court). This included the eyre courts, the Exchequer court, and the traveling court that sometimes accompanied the king and did business as he moved around the country. In 1178, Henry II appointed two clerks and three lawyers from his household to hear and redress complaints from all over the country. At one point, it was thought that this marked the origin of the Court of the Common Bench, the most important royal court for civil litigation, but it now appears that the Common Bench slowly emerged from the Exchequer and became a separate institution only in the mid-1190s.[20]

THE INNS OF COURT

Legal education was available in the vicinity of Westminster, perhaps as early as the 1250s. By 1300, law in England had become an intricate profession, subject to special rules regulating professional conduct.[21] It was administered by intelligent, literate laymen who were specially trained in this discipline. The Inns of Court were set up in the 1340s at the boundary between the City of London and Westminster to provide a focal point for legal studies. Later, in the sixteenth century, the Inns were formally recognized as having the right to admit candidates to the bar, that is, giving them approval to practice law before a court as a barrister.

Like many other medieval legal institutions in Europe, the Inns of Court are still in business today. The famous eighteenth-century essayist and lexicographer Samuel Johnson once praised them as being "the noblest nurseries" of humanity and liberty in the Kingdom."[22] Located near the Royal Courts of Justice, they include the Inner Temple, the Middle Temple, Lincoln's Inn, and Gray's Inn. The Temple, now a large, gated compound which contains the two legal societies of the Inner and Middle Temple, is aesthetically the most impressive.

The name "Temple" refers to the fact that in 1185 Heraclius, patriarch of Jerusalem, consecrated a church in London for the use of the Knights Templar, an armed monastic order dedicated to protecting pilgrims in the Holy Land. The Temple Church became the English headquarters of this order because of the growing importance of London itself. This is how William fitz Stephen, a contemporary observer, described legal London in the late twelfth century:

> The city, like Rome, is divided into wards; it has annual sheriffs instead of consuls; it has its senatorial order and its lower magistracies; it has drains and aqueducts in the streets; it has its appointed places for the hearing of cases deliberative, demonstrative, and judicial; it has its several courts, and its separate assemblies on appointed days.[23]

When the Knights Templar were dissolved by the pope in 1312, their church was assigned to a rival order, the Knights Hospitallers. Lawyers studying and practicing the new common law, which was not taught in the universities, became tenants of the church. The English poet Geoffrey Chaucer, author of *The Canterbury Tales*, one of the greatest literary achievements of the Middle Ages, mentioned "the Temple" in 1381. Gradually, the offices of the lawyers there became known as the Inner Temple and the Middle Temple. By 1440 the Paston Letters (described later) refer to the Inner Temple as a separate society.

Joseph Nicholls' 1738 illustration, "The Fountain in the Middle Temple": one of the earliest surviving pictures of this famous legal institution. (By kind permission of the Masters of the Bench of the Honourable Society of the Middle Temple. Photographic Survey, Courtauld Institute of Art, ref. B58/1050.)

Legal education at the Inns of Court was originally a seven- or eight-year period of study. A senior barrister, known as the lector (reader) gave lectures and presided over oral arguments and discussions. In addition, moots (mock trials) were held in the evenings after dinner. Although medieval legal instruction was primarily oral, i.e., by discourse and disputation, the lectures were based on written material, namely, the statutes themselves. Another text, the register of writs, was also used in teaching. It seems likely, too, that law students used written reports of cases, as well as listening to the cases themselves.[24]

Here is a law school case, lightly edited, from the reign of Edward IV (1461–1470 and 1471–1483). It may have been used for instruction in the Inner Temple:

> *The question*: Suppose that as a result of knight-service to the king, a man holds land in two different English counties — in Norfolk and in Suffolk. He has two sons but dies while they are still minors. The laws of Norfolk provide that the elder son is the heir. The laws of Suffolk provide that the younger son is the heir. When the elder son comes of age, in what way can he claim ownership in the tenements in Suffolk?[25]

In the text of the case, there is at this point a long, convoluted legal exchange and commentary involving as many as 22 different students or lawyers. In the interest of brevity, only the first two replies will be given here, followed by a few words of explanation.

> *First answer:* The elder son, when he comes of age, may have the livery of the tenements in Norfolk; and when the younger son sues livery of the tenements in Suffolk, the elder may enter upon him.
> *Second answer:* That cannot be, for when two offices are returned to the Chancery, and one is contrary to the other, anyone who wishes to have livery must traverse the office which is against him. Thus when the elder son comes of age he must show in the Chancery that he is the elder son and the other the younger, and thereupon [they will be at issue] until it is found for him or admitted by the king's attorney, then he shall have livery in both counties.[26]

Some explanations are needed here.[27]

• All land in England had standard rules of inheritance under primogeniture which did not vary from one county to another. Ultimogeniture (inheritance by the youngest) was, however, characteristic of some unfree tenants and some tenants in towns. As a result, it was not local custom that led to the contradictory findings that in Norfolk the eldest son was the heir but that in Suffolk the younger son was the heir. A more likely explanation was that the jurors of the "inquisition post mortem" in Suffolk believed that the elder son was in fact illegitimate, most probably because he was born before the marriage of his parents.

• Knight-service was one of the standard forms of service by which tenants held their lands from lords. It involved a theoretical duty to either serve for a limited period in the king's army or to pay a fee in lieu of such service. Livery means legal possession. The Chancery was the office of the Lord Chancellor.

• The first answer means that the elder son should attempt to take possession of the land by direct forcible action. If so, he would either successfully get possession or would take some kind of nominal possession. In the latter case he could then sue his younger brother for dispossessing him.

• The second answer means that direct forcible action is not required because, when there are mutually inconsistent verdicts from the formal enquiries into who is entitled to inherit the lands, neither of the competing heirs will get possession until one of the contradictory verdicts has been overturned in the court of Chancery and a further verdict has been issued to clarify the matter. It is this verdict, then, which will establish a single rightful heir to all the lands.

THE LIMIT OF LEGAL MEMORY (1189)

In England today, title to certain rights and easements can still be established, at least in theory, by proving continuous and peaceful possession of such rights and easements since "time out of mind." This lovely phrase means "when legal memory begins." The first Statute of Westminster (1275) provided that no future litigant can base his claim to lands on the possession of those lands by an ancestor during any reign before that of Richard I, who was crowned on 3 September 1189. This date, then, marks the limit of legal memory.[28]

REGISTRAR OF WRITS (C. 1200)

The common law, carried throughout the counties of England by itinerant justices on eyre, involved the use of royal writs. Civil cases were based on these writs, which, as we have seen, were written orders issued in the king's name, directing the defendant to appear at the king's court or at some lesser court. The proper writ had to be used for a specific kind of complaint, e.g., trespass. Royal writs were needed for all legal actions involving land. There were so many royal writs that by about 1200 they had been compiled into a Register of Writs.

EDWARD I RESHAPES THE COMMON LAW (1275–1290)

Edward I has been called "the English Justinian" because the large number of statutes promulgated during his reign (1272–1307) reshaped the unwritten common law.[29] They are important because for many centuries they constituted the basic statute law of England. Four of these enactments deserve special mention:

• The first Statute of Westminster (1275) authorized measures against criminal defendants who refused to accept jury trial. It also modified land law.
• The Statute of Gloucester (1278) restricted the jurisdiction of local courts and expanded the number of actions in which damages could be awarded.
• The second Statute of Westminster (1285) dealt with a number of topics. These included helping to keep land in the family by confirming the "estate tail" in land, i.e., an estate which was limited only to certain heirs, excluding all others. It also provided that land should be considered an asset for "judgment debts," that is, debts which a court had judged to be valid. Improvements were also made in how assets were handled when death occurred.
• The 1290 enactment Quia Emptores ("Because Purchasers," the first two words of the statute) was an attempt to preserve existing seigniorial rights. It changed the mechanisms for granting land.

Illustrative Cases and Laws

MABEL DE FRANCHEVILLE (1158): FOUND TO BE ILLEGITIMATE, A LADY LOSES HER LANDS

William de Sackville, a rich nobleman, had extensive lands in Essex and in other neighboring counties.[30] When he died, his daughter, Mabel de Francheville, came into possession of them on the grounds that she was the rightful heiress. However, her cousin, Richard of Anstey, wanted to get William's property for himself. In 1158, Richard brought suit against Mabel in the king's court, asserting that she was illegitimate because the marriage of her parents had been annulled by the church. Richard further argued that as William's nephew (he was the eldest son of William's elder sister), the lands should go only to him as the rightful heir.

Since illegitimacy was a matter for the church courts, not the royal court, Mabel's status was discussed at length, first before the archbishop of Canterbury, then before papal judges, and finally before the papal court of audience in Rome. The final judgment was that Mabel was indeed illegitimate. The Anstey case was thereupon sent back to the king's court in England where, five years after the suit had begun, William's lands were awarded to Richard.

Richard kept detailed records of what the case cost him. He spent the considerable sum of £350. This included payments to three canon lawyers, as well as gifts of money and of horses to other men who went to court with him. These latter folk, however, were not lawyers, but simply friends and neighbors who wanted to demonstrate, by their presence in court, their support for Richard.

This case is a good example of the complexities and expenses of medieval justice under Henry II. It also suggests that in the 1150s, while professional (canon) lawyers were indeed available for litigation in the church courts, the same was not true in the lay courts. If lay lawyers had been available, Richard — obviously not a man to spare any expense when his social and financial future hung in the balance — would certainly have hired them and would carefully have recorded this expense. From this and other indications, modern scholars conclude that it was not until 1300 that professional lawyers became available in lay courts, too.

MURDER IN THE CATHEDRAL:
HENRY II AND THOMAS BECKET (1170)

The feud between Henry II and his archbishop of Canterbury, Thomas Becket, came to a head in 1164 with the Constitutions of Clarendon. It continued until Becket's assassination on the steps of Canterbury Cathedral six years later, which will be discussed below.

In the Constitutions of Clarendon, the king had proposed a complicated scheme for dealing with criminous clerks. These malefactors would be initially summoned to the king's court and would be tried there on matters within the jurisdiction of that court. They would then be tried in a church court (under lay supervision), with the church giving up its right to protect a clerk from secular punishment once he had confessed his guilt or was convicted.[31]

Henry II felt this was a necessary step because the most severe penalty the church could inflict on a cleric who did something illegal was simply to defrock him. As a result, a cleric who committed a murder could easily escape the death penalty likely to be meted out to a lay murderer.

Becket opposed the "criminous clerks" provision on the grounds that no one should be punished twice for the same offense: to defrock a priest and then to hang him was to punish him twice.[32] Still, under heavy pressure, Becket had grudgingly agreed to accept the Constitutions of Clarendon. He signed his consent but refused to set his seal to them, thus indicating his deep reservations. He also did penance for signing them by fasting and by not celebrating mass at the cathedral.

Henry II decided not to mount a frontal attack on his rebellious archbishop. Instead, he charged Becket with having failed in his feudal duty to produce £30,000 — a huge sum in those days — which was allegedly due to the king from Becket in his previous capacity as chancellor. Henry II planned to imprison Becket on this charge but the archbishop fled by night from a friendly abbey and took refuge in France, first in Flanders and then in the Burgundian monastery of Pontigny.

Years later, in 1170, to arrange a secure succession while he himself was still alive, Henry II had the archbishop of York crown his eldest son, Henry the Younger. Longstanding English custom decreed, however, that only the archbishop of Canterbury could crown a new king. Becket retaliated by excommunicating the archbishop of York and his supporters. Under the terms of a compromise which diplomatically made no mention of the Constitutions of Clarendon, Henry II and Becket subsequently agreed that Becket should return to England and recrown young Henry at a second ceremony.

Upon arriving in England, however, Becket took further punitive steps against the archbishop of York and his followers. When Henry II learned of this, he was holding his Christmas court in Normandy. Enraged, he is said to have blurted out a fateful question: "Will no one rid me of this troublesome priest?" Four of the king's knights decided to carry out what they assumed was the royal will. They at once sailed back to England to murder the traitor Becket.

One of Becket's supporters was the monk Gervase of Canterbury. Gervase was present at Becket's death. This is what he reports:

> There arrived [at the monastery of Canterbury Cathedral] four courtiers, who desired to speak with the archbishop, thinking by this to discover the weak points. These were Reginald Fitz-Urse, Hugh de Morville, William de Traci, and Richard Brito....
>
> Fitz-Urse hastened forward, and with his whole strength he planted a blow upon the extended head [of Becket]; and he cried out, as if in triumph over his conquered enemy, "Strike! Strike!" Goaded on by the author of confusion [the devil], these butchers, adding wound to wound, dashed out his brains.... They now returned through the cloister, crying out, "Knights of the king, let us go; he is dead!" And then they pillaged whatever they found in the archbishop's residence.
>
> See here a wonder. While he was yet alive, and could speak, and stand on his feet, men called him a traitor to the king; but when he was laid low, with his brains dashed out, he was called the holy Thomas, even before the breath had left his body.[33]

"HOLY THOMAS" AND TRIAL BY BATTLE (LATE TWELFTH CENTURY)

A nearly contemporary account reveals that the name of "holy Thomas" quickly became a force to be reckoned with:

Two men who been adjudged to a duel [trial by battle] came together, one being much bigger and stronger than the other. The stronger man catches the weaker one, lifts him high above his head, ready to throw him hard on the ground. The smaller man, hanging thus in the air, lifts up his mind to heaven and says a short prayer: "Help, holy Thomas martyr."

The danger was great and sudden and the time for prayer short. There are witnesses who were present: the stronger man, as if oppressed by the weight of the holy name, suddenly collapsed under the one he held and was vanquished.[34]

GLANVILL (C. 1188): THE FIRST DETAILED STUDY OF ENGLISH COMMON LAW

The *Tractatus de legibus et consuetudinibus regni Angliae* (*Treatise on the Laws and Customs of the Kingdom of England*)—commonly known as *Glanvill*—was the first treatise on English common law.[35] The opening rubric of this famous work sets the stage:

> Here begins the treatise on the laws and customs of the kingdom of England composed in the time of Henry the Second, when justice was under the direction of the illustrious Ranulph de Glanvill, the most learned of that time in the law and ancient customs of the kingdom; and it contains only those laws and customs which are followed in the king's court at the Exchequer and before the justices wherever they are.[36]

This work was traditionally ascribed to Ranulph de Glanvill, who was justiciar (chief minister) of England under Henry II. It seems likely, however, that a later justiciar (either Hubert Walter or Geoffrey Fitzpeter) may have been responsible for this treatise. Carefully organized and very detailed, *Glanvill* reflects the increasing centralization of the English court system. Because it greatly extended the scope of the common law at the expense of canon and feudal law, it is worth citing here at some length.

Much of *Glanvill* is devoted to procedure, especially to writs. The standardized writ was known as the *precipe* (command), which was the first word after the formal salutation. We learn from *Glanvill* that

> When anyone complains to the lord king or his justices concerning his [land], and the case is such as it ought to be, or the lord king is willing that it should be, tried in the king's court, then the complainant shall have the following writ of summons:
> The writ for making the first summons—"The king to the sheriff, greeting. Command [*Precipe*] N. to render to R. justly and without delay one hide of land in such-and-such a vill, which the said R. complains that the aforesaid N. is withholding from him. If he does not do so, summon him by good summoners to be before me or my justices on the day after the octaves of Easter, to show why he has not done so. And have there the summoners and this writ. Witness Ranulf [sic] Glanvill, at Clarendon."[37]

Because of its standardized format, this writ was easy for the Chancery to handle. All that had to be done was to fill in the writ so it identified the sheriff, the plaintiff, the defendant, the location and size of the plot of land involved, and the return date, i.e., the date on which the writ had to be in the hands of the king's court, with a report from the sheriff, written on the back, showing what he had done. This was called a returnable writ. Legal scholars see the existence of returnable, standardized writs as evidence of a central court which was trying to develop a way to stay in close touch with the sheriff.[38]

In this era, a case could be decided in one of two ways — either trial by combat or by a form of jury known as the Grand Assize. Concerning trial by combat, *Glanvill* tells us that

> If [the demandant] chooses to defend himself by battle, then he himself, or some other suitable person on his behalf [a champion], must deny the right of the demandant word for word as he has set it out. It should be noted that once [trial by battle has been chosen], the tenant must defend the land by battle, and cannot any longer put himself upon the [grand] assize.
>
> When the battle is fought, the vanquished champion is liable to a penalty of 60 shillings for crying craven ["I surrender"] and shall lose also his law. Moreover, if the tenant's champion is defeated, his principal shall restore the disputed land ... and shall never again be allowed to bring this same plea in court. For those matters which have been determined in the king's court as the result of battle are settled forever.[39]

Judgment by the Grand Assize was equally final. *Glanvill* emphasizes that

> Once the demandant has stated in court that he has put himself upon the assize, and has expressly said this to the justices sitting on the bench, he cannot afterwards retrace, but must stand or fall by the assize.... If nothing happens to prevent the assize from proceeding, then the case will be as conclusively settled by assize as by battle.[40]

Perhaps as a sign that times were changing, *Glanvill* clearly favors the Grand Assize over trial by battle:

> This assize is a royal benefit granted to the people by the goodness of the king acting on the advice of his magnates. It takes account so effectively of both human life and civil condition that all men may preserve the rights which they have in any free tenement, while avoiding the doubtful outcome of battle. In this way, too, they may avoid the greatest of all punishments, unexpected and untimely death, or at least the reproach of the perpetual disgrace which follows that distressed and shameful word [craven] which sounds so dishonourably from the mouth of the vanquished. This legal constitution is based above all on equity; and justice, which is seldom arrived at by battle after many and long delays, is more easily and quickly attained through its use.[41]

Glanvill points out two other advantages in the Grand Assize as well:

> Fewer *essoins* [excuses for non-appearance] are allowed in the assize than in battle ... and so people generally are saved trouble and the poor are saved money. Moreover, in proportion as the testimony of several witnesses in judicial proceedings outweighs that of one man, so this constitution relies more on equity than does battle; for whereas battle is fought on the testimony of one witness, this constitution requires the oaths of at least 12 men.[42]

Finally, in its discussion of "dower" (dowry), *Glanvill* also gives us an insight into the role of women in English law in the late twelfth century:

In common English law usage [dower] means that which a freeman gives to his wife at the church door at the time of his marriage. For every man is bound both by ecclesiastical and by secular law to endow his wife at the time of his marriage....

It should be known that a woman cannot alienate any of her dower during the life of her husband. For since legally a woman is completely in the power of her husband, it is not surprising that her dower and all her other property are clearly deemed to be at his disposal. Therefore any married man may give or sell or alienate in whatever way he pleases his wife's dower during his life, and his wife is bound to consent to this as to all other acts of his which do not offend against God.[43]

One of the distinctive characteristics of dower, however, was that although the husband could indeed grant away his wife's dower during his own lifetime, after his death she could claim it back.

ARTICLES OF THE BARONS (1215)

King John's unsuccessful attempts to defend the lands held in France by England led him to impose extortionate taxes at home. Those who could or would not pay were punished severely. John's administration of justice was heavy-handed, capricious and widely disliked. Moreover, he had gotten into a quarrel with the pope about who should be the archbishop of Canterbury. As a result, John himself was excommunicated and England was placed under interdict, which meant that all religious services there came to a halt.

The cumulative weight of these problems was so onerous that in January 1215 a group of barons, clad in armor *cap-à-pie* (literally, "head to foot," that is, fully armed for battle) appeared before the king and demanded that he grant them a charter of liberties as a safeguard against such autocratic procedures. To force the king to comply, the barons took up arms against him and captured London in May 1215.

The next month, representatives of both sides held negotiations at Runnymede, a field conveniently located between the royal castle at Windsor and the baronial camp at Staines. The Articles of the Barons, sealed in John's presence, marked his formal acceptance of its terms. The Articles made this explicitly clear, stating that "These are the articles the Barons seek and the Lord King concedes."

MAGNA CARTA (1215)

After the Articles of the Barons had been sealed, the king's chancery used them to draw up a royal grant. This grant became known as Magna Carta (the Great Charter of 1215), so-named to distinguish it from the Charter of the Forest (1217). Magna Carta was reissued with some revisions in 1216, 1217 and 1225 and then, without any further changes in the 1225 version, in 1264 and 1297. There are four copies of the original charter of 1215 — two in the British Library in London and one each in Lincoln Cathedral and Salisbury Cathedral. The one shown here is from the British Library and is formally described as "Letter patent of King John, single vellum sheet, in Latin, Runnymede, 15 June 1215." Tradition holds that it was discovered in a London tailor's shop in 1629.

Magna Carta has long been considered as the greatest charter of English liberties and has had an enormous impact on constitutional law (including the United States' Bill of Rights). It is important to recognize, however, that it was not written as a stirring defense of individual freedom but chiefly because ecclesiastical and lay magnates wanted to make sure that their customary feudal rights were officially acknowledged by the king. They also wanted to make sure that the collapse of central government and lawlessness which had prevailed in the recent past under King Stephen (reigned 1135–1154) did not resurface.

As a result, the preamble and the 63 clauses of Magna Carta focus on the broad range of feudal issues of most immediate concern to the barons.

Top: Edward I confirming Magna Carta (MS. Douce 35, fol. 25r. The Bodleian Library, University of Oxford). *Bottom:* Magna Carta. (Cotton Augustus II f. 106. By permission of the British Library).

These included freedom for the church; feudal laws regarding both the lands held directly from the crown and the subtenants working these lands; matters relating to merchants, trade, towns and cities; legal reforms; appropriate behavior for royal officials; royal forests; and guarantees that henceforth the king would adhere to the charter (if he did not, the barons would wage war against him.)

What makes Magna Carta so important from a legal point of view is that it established for the first time a constitutional principle of immense significance, namely, that *the power of the king could be curtailed by a written grant.* Magna Carta strongly affirms the doctrine that no man — not even the king himself— is above the law. Here are some of Magna Carta's key legal provisions:

> The city of London shall have all its ancient liberties and free customs, as well as by land as by water; furthermore, we decree and grant that all other cities, boroughs, towns, and ports shall have their liberties and free customs. (Clause 13)
>
> No bailiff for the future shall, upon his own unsupported complaint, put anyone to his "law," without credible witnesses brought for this purpose. (Clause 38)
>
> No freeman shall be taken or imprisoned or disseised [have his property seized] or exiled or in any way destroyed, nor will we go upon him nor send upon him, except by the lawful judgment of his peers or by the law of the land. (Clause 39). This is the precursor of the fifth amendment "due process" clause of the Constitution of the United States and of many similar provisions in American state laws. (Due process is the course of proceedings established by the legal system to protect individual rights.)
>
> To no one will we sell, to no one will we refuse or delay, right or justice. (Clause 40)
>
> We will appoint as justices, constables, sheriffs, or bailiffs only such as know the law of the realm and mean to observe it well. (Clause 45)
>
> If anyone has been dispossessed or removed by us, without the judgment of his peers, from his lands, castles, franchises, or from his right, we will immediately restore them to him.... (Clause 52)[44]

Magna Carta gradually became more a reference book of basic legal principles rather than a code of current law. In the fourteenth century, for example, Parliament would interpret the phrase "judgment by peers" to mean that all men have a right to trial by jury. In the United States, the national and state constitutions still echo Magna Carta. Indeed, it is the bedrock of the Anglo-American idea of personal freedom, namely, that the government cannot act against an individual without going through the proper legal procedures — the due process of law.

TO AVOID THE GREATEST OF CRIMES (C. 1215)

The importance of feudal rights and of *feudal duties* as well can be clearly seen in the case of William Marshal, earl of Pembroke, at the time of Magna Carta. One of the finest knights and greatest magnates of the Middle Ages, Marshal was King John's closest advisor and played a prominent role in the negotiations leading up to Magna Carta. Some of these meetings are said to have been held north of London at the shrine of St. Alban, the premier Benedictine abbey-church in medieval England.[45]

Even though King John treated Marshal very shamefully — accusing him of being a traitor, seizing his castles, taking hostage his two older sons, and even trying to force his own knights to challenge Marshal to trial by combat — the earl remained loyal to the king as his feudal lord.[46] He has no hesitation in taking John's side against the barons. Catherine Armstrong, a modern scholar, explains why:

> Of all the bonds of feudalism, the greatest and most important bond was the one of fealty, of loyalty to one's lord. To break this bond and oath was treason, and this was the greatest of crimes. William Marshal was the epitome of knighthood and chivalry. He did not simply espouse it. Marshal's entire life was governed by his oaths of fealty and by his own innate sense of honor. If Marshal had taken his lands, castles, and knights to the side of the rebellion, King John would have lost his crown and perhaps his life.[47]

Recognizing Marshal's great virtues and abilities, his peers chose him as regent for the nine-year-old Henry III after John died in 1216. Marshal himself died three years later and is buried in the Temple Church.

BRACTON (C.1220S-1250S)

This was the greatest legal treatise of the Middle Ages. Henry de Bracton was a thirteenth-century judge of the English court which traveled wherever the king went. This was known as the *coram rege* (literally, "before the monarch"). Bracton himself is traditionally, but probably incorrectly, thought to have been the author of the *Treatise de legibus et consuetudinibus angliae* (*On the Laws and Customs of England*). This has long been referred to simply as *Bracton*.

Whoever he was, the author explains clearly why he undertook such an arduous and lengthy work:

Carved wooden doorway at St. Alban's shrine, north of London.

Since [English] laws and customs are often misapplied by the unwise and unlearned who ascend the judgment seat before they have learned the laws and stand amid doubts and the confusion of opinions, and frequently subverted by the greater [judges] who decide cases according to their own will rather than by the authority of the laws, I, Henry de Bracton, to instruct the lesser judges, if no one else, have turned my mind to the ancient judgments of just men, examining diligently, not without working long into the night watches, their decisions … and have collected without I have found therein worthy of note into a *summa* [treatise], putting it in the form of titles and paragraphs, without prejudice to any better system, by the aid of writing to be preserved to posterity forever.[48]

The author of *Bracton* used as raw material for his book the plea rolls (court records) of England, which contained the writs, pleadings, verdicts and judgments of each civil action since the death of Henry II in 1189. By using continental common law (the *ius commune*), too, *Bracton* tried to make sense of the whole of English law as it then existed. The end result was so successful that *Bracton* was described by the famous legal historian Frederic William Maitland as "the crown and flower of English jurisprudence."[49]

Bracton was a very useful legal handbook because many of its examples were drawn from real life. How, for example, should homicide be judged? *Bracton* looks at several different kinds of cases:

By chance, as by misadventure, when one throws a stone at a bird or elsewhere and another passing by unexpectedly is struck and dies, or fells a tree and another is accidentally crushed beneath its fall and the like. But here we must distinguish whether he [the perpetrator] has been engaged in a proper or an improper act. Improper, as where one has thrown a stone toward a place were men are accustomed to pass, or while one is chasing a horse or ox someone is trampled by the horse or ox and the like, here liability is imputed to him.

But if he was engaged in a lawful act, as where a master has flogged a pupil as a disciplinary measure, or if [another is killed] when one was unloading hay from a cart or cutting down a tree and the like, and if he employed all the care he could, that is, by looking about him and shouting out, not too tardily or in too low a voice, but in good time and loudly, so that if there was anyone there, or approaching the place, he might flee and save himself, or in the case of the master by not exceeding mean and measure in the flogging of his pupil, liability will not be imputed to him. But if he was engaged in a lawful act and did not employ due care, liability will be attributed to him.[50]

7

Medieval Inquisitors

The medieval church claimed jurisdiction over almost every aspect of behavior and belief. Clerics were convinced that they had not only the right but also the duty to intervene vigorously to suppress heresy. They were certain that, left unchecked, "heretical leprosy" would spread and would jeopardize the salvation of many souls. Equally important, they feared that by infecting the rest of society, heresy would also destroy the Christian foundations of contemporary life. For both these reasons, medieval inquisitors used judicial processes to identify heretics. The inquisitors' goal, however, was not to punish them but to encourage them to repent and return to the fold of the church.[1]

INQUISITIO

The earliest meaning of the Latin word *inquisitio* was simply "the act of looking for something."[2] By the first century BCE, Cicero and others were using it in the narrower sense of inquiring into specific matters. Under Roman law, *inquisitio* and *inquirere* (the latter is the verb from which the first word sprang) came to mean a formal stage of legal procedure, i.e., searching for evidence to support an accusation. Gradually, *inquisitio* took on a new meaning under Roman law. It now referred to the duty of the magistrate in a criminal case to discover the truth about any issue coming before his court.

During the heyday of the medieval era, there was no single centralized authority which we can label as *the Inquisition*. Such authorities did appear, but only later: in Spain (1480), in Portugal (1536), in Rome (1542), and in Spain's New World colonies (Mexico and Peru, both in 1570). For this reason, it is more accurate to refer to medieval *inquisitors* in the Middle Ages rather than to a medieval *Inquisition*.

In fact, the concept of a highly centralized, all-seeing, all-knowing Inquisition is an image assembled from the facts and fears of later eras, notably the sixteenth-century Reformation, and from the role of Spain as the ardent defender of the established church.[3] An Orwellian "Big Brother is watching you" Inquisition never played a role in medieval life because it did not exist then. To medieval men and women, the inquisition was simply another judicial process, not a monolithic institution.

As we have seen in the chapter on Anglo-Norman justice, the *Inquisitio comitatus Cantabrigiensis* (*Inquiry of the County of Cambridge*) formed part of an early draft

Left: Details of the south *portail* (monumental entrance) of the abbey of St. Peter in Moissac. The top panel depicts the mortal sins of avarice and luxury. A rich man is seen on his deathbed: while his wife weeps, a demon carries off his soul to hell. *Right:* The south *portail* of the abbey of St. Peter in Moissac, southwest France. Built by Abbot Roger in 1135, this is one of the high points of medieval Christian art.

of the Domesday survey of 1086. William the Conqueror's officials were conducting an *inquisitio* into the rights of the king and others. In practice, the medieval inquisitorial procedure was — with three exceptions — not very far removed from contemporary procedures in canon and secular law courts. The exceptions were: the identity of witnesses was kept secret; there were restrictions on the role of the defense counsel; and the overall purpose of these proceedings was penitential, not exclusively punitive.[4]

Inquisitors were of two kinds. Some were local clerics charged by bishops to exercise judicial authority within a given diocese. Others had broader authority. They were usually members of one of the mendicant orders (Franciscans or Dominicans) and were appointed by a papal judge to suppress heresy in an entire region.[5] These carefully chosen, intelligent, well-trained men were known as *inquisitores heretice pravitatis* (inquirers into heretical depravity).

THE ROOTS OF HERESY

In the Western world today, heresy is not a burning issue. This was literally not the case, however, in the Middle Ages. Then it was an exceedingly grave crime which easily could result in burning at the stake; in other extremely savage forms of execution; or in beating, branding or the amputation of limbs.[6] Trials for heresy enjoyed widespread popular support and were endorsed by the church, the state and the universities. The University of Paris, the greatest authority in the West on such matters, fully concurred in the church's decision to turn over Joan of Arc to the secular authorities to be burned at the stake as a condemned heretic.

Heresy can be defined as adamant adherence to an opinion which runs contrary to church dogma on an important issue. It involves the denial, by a baptized and professed Christian, of a proposition which has been endorsed by the church as constituting a revealed

Top: Heretics embracing the faithful. (MS. Bodl.270B, fol. 123v detail. The Bodleian Library, University of Oxford.) *Bottom:* Detail of the tympanum (recessed sculptured face) of the abbey of St. Peter in Moissac. This shows Christ sitting in majesty, surrounded by symbols of the four Evangelists.

Punishment by branding and amputation. (*Costumes de Toulouse*, MS Latin 9187, fol. 29v. Bibliothèque nationale de France, Paris.)

truth. There were different degrees of heresy. A person could fall into "formal" heresy only when two conditions were both satisfied.

First, he or she had to decide of their own free will not to accept the church's teachings on an important doctrinal point. Second, he or she had to persist stubbornly in holding onto their erroneous opinion, despite the best efforts of ecclesiastics to explain their error and to bring the strayed lamb back into the fold. Formal heresy, in short, had to be both freely willed and pertinacious. A less serious failing was "material" or "objective" heresy. This occurred when a person simply did not understand that what he or she was denying was a revealed truth.

In the Middle Ages, heretical beliefs were held by a number of sects. Among the most important of these were the Waldenses, the Cathars (to modern eyes, the most interesting of the three groups), and the Beguins. A word about each of them is in order here. The date listed after the name of each sect represents some important point in its rise and fall.

THE WALDENSES (1184)

In 1170–1176, a merchant named Valdes (known as Valdo or Peter Waldo) preached in Lyon as a layman. He tried and failed to win ecclesiastical approval. Nevertheless, he and his followers (called the *Pauperes*, or the Poor of Lyon) still continued to preach. The result was that in 1184 pope Lucius III banned the sect.

Unrepentant, the Waldenses rejected the church's concept of purgatory and some of the sacraments. They called for a simple moral lifestyle, criticized the laxity and short-comings of the church itself, refused to take oaths, and wore a distinctive style of clothing. Their teachings became very popular, spreading into northern France, Spain, Flanders, Germany, southern Italy, Poland, and Hungary. When excommunication failed to suppress the Waldenses, the church resorted to capital punishment.

By the end of the thirteenth century, this threat had forced some members of the sect to return to the orthodox fold. Others were persecuted so vigorously that they had to abandon their distinctive dress. At the end of the fifteenth century, the remote Cottian Alps (between southeastern France and northwestern Italy) became the last refuge of the Waldenses. They managed to endure, however, and in 1848 they finally received full civil rights as a Swiss Protestant church.

THE CATHARS (1244)

The Cathars flourished as a heretical sect in Western Europe in the twelfth and thirteenth centuries. Their religion first arose in the Balkans in the tenth century. Although the word "Cathar" was once thought to come from a Greek word meaning "pure," another theory holds that it is a play on German words implying a cat worshiper. The Cathars were rumored to have performed an "obscene kiss" on the rear end of a cat.[7]

Philosophically, the Cathars were dualists, that is, they believed there were two cosmic forces at work in the universe. One was a force for good (God); the other was a force for evil (the devil). The material world itself was evil. Human nature was essentially good. The Cathars taught that men and women should free themselves from the snares of this world and should aim at communion with God. They thought of themselves as good Christians, but rejected the church's teachings on many fundamental issues.

For example, they considered Jesus to have only been an angel. They also strongly condemned the ostentatious wealth, corruption and moral laxity of the church itself. Indeed, such highly visible abuses of power were probably the reason why Catharism was famous in its own time as appealing to "the poorest of the poor."

Members of this sect were of two types: the elite *parfaits* (perfect ones) and the more numerous *croyants* (believers). The former were the leaders and devoted much of their time to contemplation and austerities. They were strict ascetics: for them, sexual intercourse and eating meat were both forbidden. The more numerous "believers," on the other hand, were held to much less rigorous standards and were permitted to raise families.

The Cathars were particularly strong in southern France; for this reason, they were often referred to as Albigensians, after the city of Albi in that region. At the end of the twelfth century, a community of Cathar women had been established in the little town of Montségur in the eastern Pyrenees. By the beginning of the thirteenth century, the number of Cathars there had grown appreciably. As a result, they asked Raymond de Péreille, the local lord, for permission to build a headquarters for their sect atop an isolated limestone outcropping, difficult of access and nearly 4,000 feet high, silhouetted against the blue skies of the Pyrenees.

This prominence was known as the *Pog*. The Cathars laboriously hacked a path in the steep slopes of the *Pog*. This track, still an arduous climb, remains the only practicable route to the top. About 500 Cathars lived and worked in a small but easily defended castle they built on the summit of the *Pog*.

The Cathars came to be seen as a serious threat to the church and to the kingdom of France. Pope Innocent III tried to suppress them by force. He launched the Albigensian Crusade against them, which extended from 1209 to as late as 1255.[8] Many heretics were executed without a formal hearing or trial. In one episode of this conflict, an army led by barons from northern France attacked Toulouse and Provence and massacred many of the inhabitants, Cathar and Catholic alike.

In 1224, Raymond VII, count of Toulouse, promised the king of France that he would destroy the Cathars' castle in Montségur. He failed in his first attempt but tried again in 1243–1244, methodically besieging the *Pog*. This time he was successful. After an abortive attempt to escape, the Cathars had to surrender. They were given 15 days in which to make a choice: to renounce their faith or to be burnt at the stake.

On 16 March 1244, 205 of the elite *parfaits* came down from the *Pog*, voluntarily and unarmed, and were burned alive in the *Prat dels cramants* (the field of the burned ones). The simple *croyants*, for their part, were questioned by the inquisitors and then released. After the fall of Montségur, many of the surviving Cathars sought refuge near Berga, Spain, following a trail across the Pyrenees known as the *Chemin des Bonshommes* (the Guys' Path), which is still used by hikers today. Those who chose to remain in southwestern France were forced to go underground to escape the inquisition.

BISHOP JACQUES FOURNIER V THE CATHARS OF MONTAILLOU (1318–1325)

Jacques Fournier, bishop of Pamiers from 1318 to 1325, was an exceptionally able, upwardly mobile Cistercian monk who rose from a humble background to become pope Benedict XII of Avignon. He made his mark as a gifted administrator and inquisitor in Pamiers, where he conducted a victorious, successful inquisitorial campaign against the last remaining Cathar heretics — the subsistence farmers and shepherds who lived quietly in Montaillou, a tiny village in the eastern Pyrenees, located about 25 miles southeast of Montségur. After this final defeat, the Cathar heresy disappeared from French territory.

Bishop Fournier was able to draw on a 1312 decision by the Council of Vienna, which had ordered that the powers of the local bishops should be used to support the inquisitors. Previously, the inquisitors themselves had exercised sole responsibility for cases of heresy. The council's ruling permitted Fournier to set up his own inquisitional office in 1318. Through it, he worked closely with the Dominican Jean de Beaune, a high official of the inquisition in the regional capital of Carcassonne.[9]

Fournier's *Inquisition Record* is one of the most remarkable medieval documents and a treasure-trove of interesting cases. Since he attended almost all the sittings of his own court and refused to delegate responsibility to any of his assistants, this document bears the full stamp of his own forceful personality. It shows that Fournier was so skillful and so relentless an interrogator that, as his victims wailed, he was "the very devil of an inquisitor."[10]

The *Inquisition Record* is one of the very few contemporary documents that captures at length the words of medieval peasants themselves. For this reason, it formed the basis for Emmanuel Le Roy Ladurie's pathbreaking ethnographic study, *Montaillou: village occitan de 1294 à 1324* (*Montaillou: an Occitan-speaking village from 1294 to 1324*), originally published in 1975. (The Occitan language is a Romance language still spoken by about 1.5 million people living today in southern France.)

Albi: Cathedral of Sainte-Cécile, built beginning in 1277.

Ladurie gives us such a unique glimpse into Cathar life in the eastern Pyrenees that a few points are worthy of mention. Montaillou had only about 250 inhabitants, who lived in what Ladurie calls in "an island in time." That is to say, they had few reference points either in the distant past or in the distant future. Thus, for the most part, they lived in the present. "There is no other age than ours," says Raymond de l'Aire, a local resident.[11] They measured cosmic matters by familiar local landmarks. "If you want to have an idea of Heaven," Guillaume Austatz tells us confidently, "imagine a huge *domus* [extended household] stretching from the Mérens Pass to the town of Toulouse."[12] As the crow flies, this is a distance of only 85 miles.

In the course of their own work, the muleteers and shepherds of Montaillou often traveled from France into neighboring Spain, but only one inhabitant of the town ever had a chance of getting as far as Paris. This was the Cathar heretic Guillaume Fort, who in 1321 was sentenced by Fournier to make a pilgrimage to Paris. But the next day, before Guillaume could set off on his journey, a second sentence from Fournier resulted in Guillaume being burned at the stake.[13]

According to a saying current in Montaillou, "There will never be a time in any of our lives when men don't sleep with other men's wives."[14] The swashbuckling priest Pierre Clergue, who was secretly a member of the Cathars, is a case in point. A mem-

The Cathars' *Chemin des Bonshommes* (the Guys' Path) passes through this rugged countryside.

ber of the wealthiest family of Montaillou, Pierre had more than a dozen acknowledged mistresses (see the case of Grazide Lizier, below). He would assure each one, "I love you more than any woman in the world."[15] As he grew older and less attractive, to overcome resistance to his advances Pierre would threaten to report any unwilling lady to the inquisition. Finally, after being arrested by Fournier, Pierre died in prison.

THE BEGUINS (1317)

To understand this heresy, we must begin with some background information on the Franciscan order. By the late 1270s, the order had split into two factions.[16] One, referred to as the "spirituals," wanted to follow the strict poverty exemplified by the founder of the order, St. Francis of Assisi. Some of the spirituals also cultivated an intense mysticism which to outside observers seemed suspiciously like heresy. The second group, known as the "community," favored a more moderate regime which would give Franciscans enough time and financial resources to engage in charitable works.

To end this schism, in 1317 pope John XXII decided to endorse the community. Some of the spirituals who refused to conform to this papal ruling were burned at the stake the next year. By then, however, many of the spirituals had formed close ties with the Beguins, a group of pious priests and lay worshipers. As members of an organization known as the Third Order of St. Francis, the Beguins decided to cast their lot with the spirituals. Thus, by 1319, some Beguins were being led to the stake, too.

At that time the inquisitor in Toulouse was the Dominican Bernard Gui. He wrote a famous manual for inquisitors, entitled *Practica inquisitionis heretice pravitatis (The Conduct of Inquiry Concerning Heretical Depravity)*. Finished in 1323 or 1324, this work contains invaluable details of the cases of the 930 people on whom Gui passed sentence. Although Gui himself gets no sympathy today—he was one of the villains in Umberto Eco's celebrated novel, *The Name of the Rose* (1980)—it is important to understand that, in the context of medieval life, Gui had a responsible and difficult job to do.

He was intelligent, well-educated and had successfully served as prior at several convents in southern France before being appointed an inquisitor in 1307. In this latter capacity, he discharged his duties so well that in 1324 he was rewarded with a bishopric. As David Burr, a modern scholar, reminds us, the duties of Gui and his fellow inquisitors should be quite familiar to us today:

Ruins of the Château de Montaillou, southwest France, on a rainy day. The Count of Foix, the local lord, ruled over a section of the Pyrenees which included Montaillou. Two of the count's representatives lived in Montaillou itself. One was the *châtelain*, who was the military representative and chief jailer. The other was the legal officer, the *bailli* (bailiff). The *bailli* collected rents and taxes and administered justice on the count's behalf.

They want what interrogators always want in such situations. They could be FBI agents tracking down a ring of domestic terrorists, or CIA agents trying to unravel an international espionage system. They want confessions, but they want a great deal more. They need information. There's a conspiracy out there and they want to know about it.... Genuine confession involves contrition and cooperation, and that means naming names.[17]

Illustrative Cases and Laws

Bernard Gui's Inquisitorial Techniques (1307–1323)

Gui was the inquisitor in Toulouse from 1307 to 1323. His goal was not to punish people but to extract confessions. Here is his own account, nearly verbatim, of some of the techniques he used in interrogation. The comments in parentheses are Gui's. As will be seen, the turning point in the interrogation comes when Gui insists that the accused swear an oath. If the accused refused to do so, it was highly likely that he or she would be found guilty of heresy: heretics refused to take oaths because this would violate their religious beliefs.

> When a heretic is first brought up for examination, he assumes a confident air, as though secure in his innocence. I ask him why he has been brought before me. He replies, smiling and courteous, "Sir, I would be glad to learn the cause from you."
>
> Gui: You are accused as a heretic, and that you believe and teach otherwise than the Holy Church believes.
>
> The accused: (Raising his eyes to heaven, with an air of the greatest faith) Lord, thou knowest that I am innocent of this, and that I never held any faith other than that of true Christianity.
>
> Gui: You call your faith Christian, for you consider ours as false and heretical. But I ask whether you have ever believed as true another faith than that which the Roman Church holds to be true?
>
> The accused: I believe the true faith which the Roman Church believes, and which you openly preach to us.
>
> Gui: Perhaps you have some of your sect at Rome whom you call the Roman Church. I, when I preach, say many things, some of which are common to us both, as that God liveth, and you believe some of what I preach. Nevertheless, you may be a heretic for not believing other matters which are to be believed.
>
> The accused: I believe all things that a Christian should believe.
>
> Gui: I know your tricks. What the members of your sect believe you hold to be that which a Christian should believe. But we waste time in this fencing. Say simply, do you believe in one God the Father, and the Son, and the Holy Ghost?
>
> The accused: I believe.
>
> Gui: Do you believe in Christ born of the Virgin, suffered, risen, and ascended to heaven?
>
> The accused: (Briskly) I believe.
>
> Gui: Do you believe the bread and wine in the mass performed by the priests to be changed into the body and blood of Christ by divine virtue?
>
> The accused: Ought I not to believe this?
>
> Gui: Will you then swear that you have never learned anything contrary to the faith which we hold to be true?
>
> The accused: (Growing pale) If I ought to swear, I willingly swear.
>
> Gui: If I had to swear, I would raise my hand and spread my fingers and say, "So help me God, I have never learned heresy or believed what is contrary to the true faith."
>
> Then [the accused] trembling as if he cannot repeat the form,... will stumble along as though speaking for himself or for another, so there is not an absolute form of oath and yet he may be thought to have sworn.... But a vigorous inquisitor must not allow himself to be worked upon in this way, but proceed firmly till he make these people confess their error, or at least publicly abjure heresy, so that if they are subsequently found to have sworn falsely, he can without further hearing, abandon them to the secular arm.[18]

To clarify this last point: an inquisitor did not have the power to sentence a heretic to death. A legal procedure was used to accomplish this same goal. Known as "relaxation to the secular arm," it involved formally handing over convicted heretics or relapsed heretics to the secular authorities for public execution, usually by burning at the stake. It was precisely this kind of "relaxation to the secular arm" that Henry II had wanted in his dispute with Thomas Becket over criminous clerks.

CONFESSIONS OF SIX HERETICS APPEARING BEFORE JACQUES FOURNIER, BISHOP OF PAMIERS (1318–1325)

The canonical procedure of the court at Pamiers reflects the care taken during a formal inquisition.[19] First, a person had to be denounced by one or more of his (or her) friends or neighbors. Thus accused, he was summoned to appear before the inquisition court at Pamiers. If he refused to come voluntarily, the local bailiff arrested him and brought him there.

The trial itself began when the accused appeared before Fournier's tribunal and swore an oath on the Gospels. He then had to answer Fournier's questions, at whatever length he chose. There seems to have been no limit on his right to speak: dispositions sometimes covered more than 20 big pages in the *Inquisition Record*. This process could take a great deal of time. To make sure the accused did not try to run away between dispositions, he was imprisoned or put under house arrest.

Fournier appears to have resorted to torture only on one occasion—when he was pressured into investigating spurious charges that lepers were poisoning the wells. In other cases, like a conscientious teacher he would go to enormous lengths to instruct the accused in the fallacies of their heretical views. In fact, he once spent six weeks giving the Jew Baruch (see below) detailed explanations of such complicated doctrinal matters as the nature of the Trinity, the dual nature of Christ (both man and God), and the coming of the Messiah.

Fournier's inquisition court at Pamiers was in session for 370 days between 1318 and 1325. It studied 98 cases involving 114 people, most of them Cathars. During this process, 578 interrogations were conducted. Of these, 418 were examinations of accused heretics and 160 were examinations of witnesses. When the trials were over, only five persons actually went to the stake—four Waldenses from Pamiers and one relapsed Cathar from Montaillou.

Other convicted heretics received lesser punishments from Fournier. These included imprisonment under different degrees of strictness, pilgrimages, confiscation of goods, and wearing a large yellow cross on the outer clothing as a sign of penance.[20] The servant girl Raymonde Arsen, for example, was sentenced in 1324 to wear a double yellow cross because of her ties to the heretics.[21] The muleteer Pierre Vidal was sentenced to one year in jail and the wearing of a single yellow cross.[22]

The *Inquisition Record* reflects the care taken in the inquisitorial process. This document was compiled in three stages. First, during the hearing and interrogation, which were conducted in the Occitan language, a church notary took notes and later used them to produce a clean draft in Latin. This would then be read to the accused in Occitan for his or her corrections. Later, scribes would include the corrections in a final text in Latin. Fournier was so proud of his *Inquisition Record* that he took it with him to Avignon when he became pope Benedict XII. It is now in the Vatican Library.

1. THE WIDOW NAVARRE (1319)

A medium named Arnaud Botelher assured the widow Navarre that he could get in touch with her dead husband and with other dead friends and relatives. Navarre lost faith in him, however, when he told Na Serres, a widowed friend of hers, that he had seen Na Serres' late husband. ["Na" comes from *domina*, the feminine form of the honorific *dominus*, or "master."] According to Arnaud, the deceased husband instructed him to tell Na Serres "to be prudent and that she would find a good husband." Navarre told the inquisitor that this led her to consider Arnaud "a liar and a fraud, because no husband wishes his wife to remarry or find another husband."[23]

Navarre assured Fournier and the inquisitor that

> She was ready to repent of all that precedes, and declared herself ready to do and accomplish all penance that my said lord bishop might judge to give her for that which precedes, demanding humbly to be absolved of the sentence of excommunication that she had incurred for this…. She swore on the four holy Gospels that in the future she would denounce heretics and their followers if she knew of them and have them apprehended according to her power, and that especially she would denounce all and each that she knew to have adhered to this said Arnaud in the above mentioned points or similar ones, and to have been accomplices of his.[24]

Because of her evident contrition, the widow Navarre received only a light sentence: together with Raimone Fauré, the local seamstress who had first put her in touch with Arnaud, she had to make some minor pilgrimages.

2. AGNES FRANCOU, A MEMBER OF THE WALDENSES (1320)

Arrested in Pamiers with a man from Geneva named Raymond de Sainte-Foy, who was another member of the sect, Agnes was brought before Fournier. He asked her to swear,

> On the holy Gospels given to her, to tell the truth as much concerning herself as principal as concerning those others both dead and alive as witnesses. The above-said Agnes did not wish to swear an oath on the command of my said lord bishop, even though he gave her ample opportunity to do so, but said that she would never swear an oath concerning anything, even to save her life.[25]

Later, Agnes appeared before Fournier and Brother Jean de Beaune, "inquisitor of the heretical depravity in the kingdom of France," who warned her that

> She was compelled by law to swear when she was judicially requested to do so, and by not doing so, she sinned mortally and that if she persisted obstinately in refusing to swear to tell the truth, as required by law in the case of faith, she could and would be condemned as a heretic.[26]

Since Agnes still refused to swear, she was burned at the stake, together with Raymond.

3. The German Jew Baruch (1320)

When Baruch was in Toulouse, an anti-Semitic cult known as the Shepherds went on a rampage and began to kill any Jew who would not let himself be baptized a Christian. More than 152 Jews were reportedly killed in this pogrom. In order to save their lives, two of Baruch's Jewish friends agreed to be baptized. Afterwards, they asked Baruch, who was a noted Jewish scholar, whether a baptism performed under duress was valid. Baruch said he did not know and asked a Christian monk. He was told that such a ceremony was not valid. Baruch's friends therefore returned to the practice of Judaism.

Shortly thereafter, a mob set free 24 wagon-loads of Shepherds who had been arrested by the authorities of Toulouse. The mob and the Shepherds then began to kill any Jew they could catch. Soon Baruch was in mortal danger. To save his life, he agreed to be baptized and was given the Christian name "John." Subsequently, while living with the Jews of Pamiers, he returned to the practice of Judaism, believing that his baptism had not been valid. For this apostasy, however, he was arrested on the orders of Fournier and was thrown into prison.

Unfortunately, the text does not say what punishment, if any, the inquisition ordered for Baruch. Since the inquisitor himself was not present at the trial (he sent a deputy instead), Fournier could only have imposed a maximum sentence of ordering Baruch to wear the yellow cross. It appears from the text, however, that Baruch himself ultimately decided that the best policy was simply to become a Christian. Therefore, "he abjured willingly the Jewish perfidy, its superstition and the ceremonies of the Jewish Law and all other heresy" and promised "to hold, preserve and defend the Catholic faith that the Holy Roman Church teaches and observes."[27]

4. The Widow Grazide Lizier:
Heretic and Acknowledged Mistress
of the Priest Pierre Clergue (1320)

Arrested as a suspected Cathar and as an immoral person, Grazide testified as follows:

> About seven years ago, in the summer the rector [Pierre Clergue] came to the house of my mother and demanded of me to let him know me carnally. As for me, I consented (I was then a virgin and must have been fourteen or fifteen years old, so it seems to me). He took my virginity in the grange [barn] where the straw is stored. He did not do me any violence. He knew me after that quite often,... always at my mother's house and with her knowledge and consent to this.[28]

When Grazide was sixteen, Pierre Clergue married her off to the elderly Pierre Lizier of Montaillou. A girlfriend told Grazide she should be grateful to the rector because, rather than keeping her as a concubine or simply abandoning her to become a whore, he had officiated at her wedding. We may speculate that Pierre may also have helped find a suitably complaisant husband, since with her new husband's consent Grazide continued her affair with the priest.

This does not appear to have shocked Montaillou: the remunerated complaisance of a husband (a practice known as *cognita*) was common in southwestern France at that time. Even if no payments were involved, it would not have been prudent even for an angry husband to alienate the powerful Clergue family. In any case, Grazide did not believe she was doing anything wrong in continuing the affair because, she said, the priest told her it was not a sin. She herself was convinced that if intercourse was pleasing to both parties, it could not possibly be a sin. Indeed, when she tired of Pierre Clergue as a lover, she told him that in the absence of mutual pleasure, intercourse would be a sin.

What punishment, if any, was Grazide's lot is not known. Fournier gave her instruction in the orthodox teachings of the church. A textual note, however, suggests that, on balance, her testimony was not well received. She was said to be unconsciously enunciating Cathar ideas and to have been "consciously insolent, although the trial record has the appearance of naiveté."[29]

5. Barthélemy Amilhac, Heretical Priest (1321)

The charges against this man were serious:

> Barthélemy Amilhac, priest of Lladros in the diocese of Urgel [a Spanish town near Montaillou], has been an accomplice in heresy, in giving assistance and counsel to Beatrice ... who was cited for heresy [she was accused of being a Cathar], and after appearing before the bishop, fled the bishopric of Pamiers and took herself to other secret places. This Barthélemy knew that Beatrice was a heretic and erred concerning the Christian faith, and did not denounce her to the inquisitors of heresy; because of this he is strongly suspected of heresy himself, and furthermore strongly suspected of witchcraft and casting spells. He has been denounced for putting himself into concubinage with this Beatrice ...; moreover he has committed numerous and diverse thefts in the bishopric of Pamiers.[30]

The text does not give a clear account of what ultimately happened to Barthélemy and Beatrice. Both were arrested. Barthélemy was "condemned to the Wall" as a penitential discipline. This means that he was sent to one of two kinds of inquisitional prisons: either a *murus largus* (literally, "large wall"), which resembled life in a monastery, or a *murus strictus* (literally, a "tightly-bound wall"), which was only a single cell.[31] In 1322, however, their punishments were commuted: Beatrice had to wear the yellow cross, but Barthélemy only had to do "simple penitence."

6. Jacqueline Den Carot of Ax, a Housewife (1321)

An inquisition could pardon, as well as convict, an accused heretic. Although the final disposition of this case is not clear from the text, it seems likely that Jacqueline was forgiven, or at least that she was let off with only minor penalties.

Numerous witnesses testified that she had expressed some doubt about the doctrine of the resurrection of the body after death. A local priest claimed that she had said: "There will never be another world but this one, and men and women who have died will never rise again."[32] Brought before Fournier and the inquisitor Brother Jean de Beaune, Jacqueline admitted that during a very brief conversation, "I doubted, and asked myself if men could return after death in the flesh and bones they had before. But I never at all believed there would not be a resurrection of the human body."[33]

She insisted, however, that ever since this fleeting heretical episode she had "well and firmly" believed the teachings of the church. After asking for and receiving absolution from her sentence of excommunication, she "submitted herself to the will and mercy of the said lords bishop and inquisitor and renounced and concluded the present affair." The text ends with the statement that "the said lords and bishop and inquisitor assigned her a day to hear the definitive sentence concerning the facts of her avowals, the following Sunday, the 8th of the Ides of March [8 March 1321] in the house of the Preaching Friars of Pamiers."[34]

THE MYSTICAL EXPERIENCES
OF NA PROUS BONNET (1325)

A native of Montpelier, this Beguine was arrested there and was imprisoned at Carcassonne, where she was questioned on 6 August 1325. According to the record of her interrogation, which was conducted by someone other than Fournier, Na Prous testified that about four years before her arrest, one day after mass was over and when most of the congregation had left the church,

> The Lord Jesus Christ transported her in spirit (that is, in her soul) to the first heaven. When she was there she saw Jesus Christ in the form of a man as well as in his divinity. He appeared to her and showed her his heart opened like the door of a lantern. Out of this heart came rays of the sun, but brighter than rays of the sun, which illuminated her all over.... She drew near to him and put her head beneath Christ's body, and she saw nothing but that great light which Christ gave to her in those rays....
>
> Likewise she said that every day and night and every hour she sees God in the spirit and he never leaves her; she says that Christ himself wishes to be head of the church and rule souls, and that henceforth he will not permit them to be ruled by any pope, even if another should be elected by the cardinals, since the papacy is permanently annulled....
>
> Again, she said God told her that just as Eve, the first woman, was beginning and cause of the damnation of all human nature and humankind through Adam's sin, in the same way "you shall be the beginning and cause of the salvation of all human nature or humankind through those words I make you speak, if they are believed."
>
> [Na Prous] made her deposition and confessed freely and willingly, and as many times as her testimony was read to her in the vernacular she confirmed and approved it. And having been warned, asked, and exhorted many times in judicial proceedings and on other occasions to revoke and abjure all the things reported above as erroneous and heretical, she persevered in them, claiming that in the aforesaid, as in the truth, she wishes to live and die.[35]

Given her refusal to recant, it seems virtually certain that Na Prous went to the stake.

8

A Sampler of Medieval Cases

Medieval justice was rarely boring. Here are some cases of more than average interest. They deal, for example, with judicial duels, trial by cold water in Palestine, a miraculous intercession, highway robbery, the founding of Oxford University's Balliol College, a long-running dispute between two families, a chief justice who was involved in a murder, a magnate who was both a murderer and a thief, stubbornness and caution in a dispute over a manor, an accused witch, a male transvestite prostitute, the public execution of two monks, and, finally, the protracted legal struggles of a prominent English family.

GUY V HERMAN THE IRON (1127)

When a judicial duel had to be fought to settle a lawsuit, litigants often had the right to hire a champion to fight for them. Women, the young, the old, the sick, the crippled, clerics, and Jews were those most likely to use a champion. Able-bodied men, however, might well have to fight in person, on horseback or afoot. Such a fight was not a game. This is what happened, for example, when two knights — Guy and Herman the Iron — fought each other in Flanders in 1127:

> Both sides fought bitterly. Guy had unhorsed his adversary and kept him down with his lance just he liked whenever Herman tried to get up. Then his adversary, coming closer, disemboweled Guy's horse, running him through with his sword. Guy, having slipped from his horse, rushed at his adversary with his sword drawn. Now there was a continuous and bitter struggle, with alternating thrusts of swords, until both, exhausted by the weight and burden of arms, threw away their shields and hastened to gain victory in the fight by resorting to wrestling.
>
> Herman the Iron fell prostrate on the ground, and Guy was lying on top of him, smashing the knight's face and eyes with his iron gauntlets. But Herman, prostrate, little by little regained his strength by the coolness of the earth ... and by cleverly lying quiet made Guy believe he was certain of victory. Meanwhile, gently moving his hand down to the lower edge of the cuirass where Guy was not protected, Herman seized him by the testicles, and summoning all his strength for the brief space of one moment he hurled Guy from him; by this tearing motion all the lower parts of the body were broken so that Guy, now prostrate, gave up, crying out that he was conquered and dying.[1]

PALESTINE: TRIAL BY COLD WATER (C. 1175)

The Syrian author, diplomat and warrior Usama ibn Munqidh (1095–1188) was one of the most distinguished Arabs to chronicle the Crusades. He bore the title of emir (prince) and, since he lived in Palestine, personally knew most of the leaders of Jerusalem after its capture by the Crusaders in 1099. An ambitious intriguer and an unscrupulous plotter, he was accused of arranging the assassinations of a Fatimid caliph and an Egyptian vizier to further his own ends. His autobiography, which is the source of the passage cited below, was written in about 1175. It shows him to have been a gifted observer with a fine eye for detail.

Usama ibn Munqidh tells us that on one occasion he traveled to Jerusalem with another Arab nobleman, the emir Mu'in al-Din. En route, they stopped at Nabulus, a prosperous city in central Palestine. We are told that

> There a blind man, a Muslim, who was still young and was well-dressed, presented himself before [the emir Mu'in al-Din] carrying fruits for him and asked permission to be admitted into his service in Damascus. The emir consented. I inquired about this man and was informed that his mother had been married to a Frank whom she had killed. Her son used to practice ruses against the Frankish pilgrims and cooperate with his mother in assassinating them. [The authorities] finally brought charges against him and tried his case according to the Frankish way of procedure.
>
> They installed a huge cask and filled it with water. Across it they set a board of wood. They then bound the arms of the man charged with the act, tied a rope around his shoulders and dropped him into the cask, their idea being that in case he was innocent, he would sink in the water and they would then lift him up with the rope so that he might not die in the water; and in case he was guilty, he would not sink in the water. The man did his best to sink when they dropped him into the water, but he could not do it. So he had to submit to their sentence against him — may Allah's curse be upon them! They pierced his eyeballs with red-hot awls.[2]

A MIRACULOUS INTERCESSION (C. 1221)

Wulfstan (c. 1008–1095), bishop of Worcester, was known for his preaching and ascetic life, for ending the capture and sale of slaves at Bristol, for helping to compile the Domesday Book, and for serving as an adviser to king William II Rufus of England. He was canonized in 1203 and figures prominently in the remarkable case of Thomas of Elderfield.[3]

According to a short entry in a plea roll, not long before the year 1221 a young man named Thomas wounded George of Northway on the arm. George brought suit against Thomas. The court decided that this dispute had to be resolved by a judicial duel. The outcome of the fight was clear: "Thomas was defeated, and blinded and castrated."

The chronicler William of Malmesbury, however, saw this same incident in a very different light. Writing in his *Vita Wulfstani* (*Life of Wulfstan*) in about 1240, he gives us a long, detailed account of how Thomas miraculously received new eyes and new genitals through the intercession of St. Wulfstan. William's version runs along the following lines:

Thomas found a job as a retainer in the household of the chief justiciar of England, Geoffrey FitzPeter. He did so well there that after a few years he was able to return home and set himself up as a moneylender. The wife of his lord, Robert of Northway, found Geoffrey so attractive that she frequently went out of her way to borrow money from him. As a result, we are told, she "drew him into the closer intimacy of adultery and kept him for about two years in the snares of Venus." Thomas, however, eventually tired of this relationship, broke it off and refused to marry her after her husband, Robert, died.

She then married George, "a very sly man, skilled at dissimulation." When George learned that she had committed adultery with Thomas while Robert was still alive, "he was tortured by suspicion and, inflamed by marital zeal, he came to feel an inexorable hatred for Thomas." One day, after George and Thomas had been drinking together, they began to walk home. George suddenly stopped and hit Thomas twice with a big stick. Thomas happened to be carrying an axe. To defend himself, he swung it at George. The handle bounced off George's shoulder without harming him. The blade of the axe, however, "slightly scratched George's arm just enough to draw blood." George hurried home and roused the neighborhood with the blast of a horn, claiming that Thomas had broken the king's peace and had wounded him severely.

Thomas was arrested and briefly imprisoned but then released. George, however, was not one to forgive and forget. When a new king came to power and appointed justices for the punishment of malefactors, George brought suit against Thomas.

Trial by combat was set for 5 August 1221 at Worcester. On that day, we are told,

> George stands there in the middle of the crowd trusting to his strength, nimble with the skills of dueling and ready for action. Opposite stands Thomas, putting his trust in the Lord, [and calling] devotedly to his aid Mary, the glorious mother of God, and the blessed Wulfstan, weeping copious tears for the past and promising a reformed life in the future.[4]

George turned out to be much the better fighter. Thomas was soundly thrashed, his right eye almost torn out. He was thrown to the ground, where, stripped of his fighting clothes, he lay there almost naked. Since he had lost the battle and was therefore considered to be the guilty party, he could easily have been hanged. The justices, however, "mixed mercy in their judgment" and decided he should only be blinded and castrated instead.

This sentence was enthusiastically called out by George's relatives and friends. The following description leaves little to the imagination:

> [The relatives and friends] extracted one eye at once and with ease.... But the other one, already badly injured by George, they could hardly dig out and then only with great difficulty and anguish to the suffering man. They sharpened the blinding instrument two or three times then cast it into the brain in hopes of extinguishing life along with sight ... [they then] cut off the pupils and nerves that had already been dug out but were still hanging off the front of his face and flung them down onto the field. They then tore his testicles from the scrotum and threw them even further away so that some young men kicked them to and fro to each other among the girls.[5]

Thomas was taken to St. Wulfstan's Hospital, where he lay in agony for nine days. At last he fell into a coma, during which he believed he was visited by the Virgin Mary and St. Wulfstan. "They approached his bunk," we learn, "made their benedictions over him, passed on and went on." When he regained consciousness, he found that, miraculously, he now had new, very tiny pupils in each eye socket. Unlike the color of his former eyes, they were black but they grew "from one day to the next until they were fair size." He also found that his genitals had been restored and that the wounds he had received in the duel were healed.

News of this miracle spread quickly. Bishop Benedict, passing through Worcester on a pilgrimage, visited Thomas in the hospital. To test the accuracy of the reports, Benedict ordered the monk who was his chaplain to feel Thomas' male organs. The monk did so and found that they had indeed been restored. Then the bishop himself,

> weeping tears of joy, said: "I will stroke them, not to satisfy my incredulity but in order that I may become a true and faithful witness of so great a miracle." He stroked, found matters to be as stated, and believed. Having do so, he glorified God, got back on his horse and went his way rejoicing.[6]

HIGHWAY ROBBERY AT THE PASS OF ALTON (1248]

In this context, "pass" refers to a track cleared through a forest, not a defile between the hills. Alton is located about 60 miles southwest of London. By the thirteenth century it had become a haunt of thieves, probably because it was easy for them to vanish back into the dense forest. As the following case shows, bands of robbers were attracted by a royal establishment located at or near Alton.

A trial held in 1249 revealed that during the previous year a sophisticated robbery had taken place there. It involved three ringleaders — John de Bendinges, John Barkham and Richard Bennet. The first two were knights; nothing is known about Bennet. Approximately 60 of the local inhabitants were also indicted for playing some part in this escapade. The robbers showed more resourcefulness than the average highwaymen and planned their theft quite carefully. In an age when literacy was rare and communication was usually verbal, they communicated with each other through letters written by helpful clerks.

The thieves were quite successful and made off with about 200 marks in cash, a considerable sum. To add insult to injury, they also pilfered food from the royal kitchen and probably drank deeply of the king's wine. Because they were well known locally, however, they could not escape justice. By the end of October 1248, de Bendinges and Barkham had been arrested and were imprisoned in London. The next year their lands were seized by the sheriff. In 1254, however, they were both pardoned by the king.[7] What, if anything, happened to Bennet is not known.

THE FOUNDING OF OXFORD'S BALLIOL COLLEGE (C. 1255–1260)

The nobleman John of Balliol is said to have had frequent, violent differences of opinion with Walter Kirkham, bishop of Durham.[8] Balliol was temperamentally inclined to violence. Kirkham himself, described as "little in body but great in mind," was no shrinking violet, either. Their problems came to a head sometime between 1255 and 1260, when Kirkham excommunicated a few of Balliol's men because, on Balliol's orders, they had taken over lands which Kirkham claimed belonged to the church. In revenge, Balliol waylaid the bishop and his entourage.

Legend has it that then he either assaulted Kirkham physically or otherwise subjected him to some indignities. Balliol also kidnapped a few of the bishop's men. The surviving records about this incident are very murky. The truth of the matter, if it ever could be known, might turn out to be less dramatic. It seems clear, however, that Kirkham formally complained to king Henry III about the mistreatment inflicted on him by Balliol.

The king responded with a writ condemning the attack in the strongest terms. The bishop demanded that suitable reparations be made immediately. Balliol had no choice but to surrender to the authorities. There is no hard evidence about what happened next, but rumor claimed that Balliol had to prostrate himself before the doors of Durham Cathedral, where Kirkham publicly chastised him. As a further penance, the bishop also ordered Balliol to perform a substantial act of charity.

To comply with this latter demand, Balliol founded a hostel in Oxford for 16 poor scholars and left money for this purpose in his will. It was not until 1282, however, that his widow, the Scottish princess Dervorguilla of Galloway, provided endowments and statutes for what would become Balliol College, arguably the oldest college of Oxford University. [9]

OLDCOTES V D'ARCY (1272)

This case is significant because it went on for so long (37 years, with intermissions) and because collateral evidence can be used to shed light on the extensive legal record.[10] The legal record is so convoluted and so detailed that it can be mentioned here only briefly. This is the essence of it:

On or about 1 November 1272, Ingram of Oldcotes struck a deal with the knight Roger d'Arcy. Roger, the younger son of a baronial family fallen on hard times, would himself resort to extortion, seizure of land, robbery, trickery and possibly even murder in order to climb back up the social ladder. Apparently as part of this upwardly mobile scramble, Roger agreed to make Ingram a knight by 24 June 1273. Moreover, for the rest of Ingram's life Roger would also provide food and clothing for him, as well as for an esquire (a candidate for knighthood who served as shield bearer and attendant to a knight) and for two grooms. Roger would also maintain three horses for Ingram's use.

As mentioned earlier, land was the principal source of wealth in medieval times. Thus, in return, Ingram gave Roger the use of all his lands for life. These included holdings in Oldcotes and elsewhere, to be held for an annual rent of one penny. Roger took an oath to observe this pact. He also agreed that if at any time he should fail to carry out his part of the bargain, Ingram could recover the lands. In this eventuality, Roger promised that he would not bring an assize of novel disseisin to recover the lost lands or take any other legal action.

This agreement was recorded in two separate legal documents and appeared to be clear and straight forward. In practice, however, it led to nearly four decades of litigation between the Oldcotes and d'Arcy families. A jury verdict of 1309 finally settled this protracted dispute by restoring to Robert of Oldcotes (Ingram's son) most of his father's former lands.

THOMAS WEYLAND: CHIEF JUSTICE AND ACCESSORY AFTER THE FACT (1289)

Thomas Weyland was appointed as a royal justice in 1272 and was promoted to be chief justice of the Court of the Common Bench in 1278.[11] One of the superior courts of common law in England, King's Bench derived its name from the *coram rege* court which traveled with the king. At first, King's Bench heard cases affecting only the king himself or the great lords who had the right to be tried before him. By Weyland's time, however, it dealt mainly with criminal or quasi-criminal cases.

There is contemporary evidence that Weyland was in fact guilty of some low-level corruption while he was a judge. In one case, he arranged for part of a plea roll entry to be erased. In its place was inserted a false statement asserting that the complainant had departed in contempt of court and that as a result had lost the case. Weyland's downfall, however, came about not from such petty corruption but only after two of his servants at Monewden, his Suffolk manor, murdered an Irishman named William Carwel (or Carewel le Forester) at a fair in 1289.

The reason for this killing remain unclear. It was probably the result of a drunken brawl, which were common enough at public gatherings where spirits flowed freely. In an age when every man carried a sheath knife to cut his food at the table, a few drinks could easily lead to hot words and then to knife play. Weyland failed to have the two servants arrested when he returned to Monewden, even though he knew about the murder, and may even have sheltered them from arrest. He thus became an accessory after the fact.

Special justices were named to

Balliol College, University of Oxford: an archway leading to the inner grounds.

look into this case. They arrested, tried and hanged the two servants. They also ordered Weyland's arrest. A clerk of the sheriff of Suffolk did in fact arrest him, but Weyland asked permission to spend one last night at home. He slipped away that night and took refuge at a Franciscan priory, where he donned monastic clothing.

A priory was a sanctuary, so Weyland could not be dragged out by force. He could, however, be starved into submission. The king appointed an official to take charge of this process and eventually it succeeded. Weyland surrendered early in 1290 and was taken to London. There he was offered three choices: standing trial, pleading guilty and thereby accepting the penalty of life in prison, or "abjuration of all the king's lands," i.e., exile from England. Not surprisingly, Weyland chose the third option.

He was given nine days to walk from London to Dover, his port of embarkation for France. He had to make this journey in bitter weather (it was February 1290) and had to travel barefoot and without a hat, spending the night only at specifically approved places. Medieval justice, however, was relatively kind to him: because Weyland was weak when he began this journey, it was laid out for him in easy stages. The most he would have to walk in any one day was only nine miles. Weyland managed to reach Paris safely and was still there in 1292. He was later granted a pardon and returned to England, where he died in 1297 or 1298 and was buried in a Suffolk priory.

SIR JOHN MOLYNS (1340):
MAGNATE, MURDERER AND THIEF

Molyns was simultaneously a high-ranking royal servant who undertook important missions for the king and a hardened criminal.[12] Political factors, court intrigues and his own criminal activities were responsible for his sudden fall from grace. This came about when, after a royal inquiry in 1340, Molyns was formally charged with "rebellion" and "giving false counsel."

The king ordered the Earl of Salisbury to arrest Molyns, which he did. The king then seized all Molyns' lands. With Molyns apparently securely in Salisbury's custody, the king himself looked for, and found, certain royal funds which Molyns had misappropriated. Salisbury, however, did not keep a close enough eye on the culprit, so Molyns managed to escape. He then became a fugitive and an outlaw for five years.

Molyns must have had good friends at the royal court because the king finally pardoned him in 1345 and then gave him a responsible job: steward to the queen. Not content with this unexpected improvement in his fortunes, however, Molyns could not resist trying to profit from his new office. His activities offended the queen. Still, Molyns did not desist. He stole the horse of the vicar of Stoke Poges and took two other horses as well. He also stole a huge quantity of firewood and six mute swans.

Swans were big, valuable, tasty birds. Their owners marked their beaks or feet with little nicks so they could be identified easily. Many of these birds belonged to the king. Trying vainly to cover up his latest outrage, Molyns hurriedly cut off the birds' legs and necks. The carcasses themselves he disposed of, possibly by selling them. (For some of the medieval and later laws concerning swans, see Appendix III.)

Finally convicted of felony, Molyns was imprisoned, first in Nottingham Castle and then at Cambridge, where he died in 1361 at the age of about 62. Natalie Fryde, a modern biographer, believes that "Amidst all the charges of official corruption which the royal inquiry of 1340 revealed, Molyns' case is unique. No other magnate appears who has terrorized his part of the world for such a length of time."[13]

THE LADBROKE MANOR DISPUTE (1382–1400)

During the last two decades of the fourteenth century, William Catesby and his son John repeatedly went to law to defend their ownership of Ladbroke, a manor in Warwickshire, from grasping relatives.[14] This dispute dragged on for 18 years. What is remarkable about the Ladbroke manor case is the stubbornness of the plaintiffs and the enormous caution of the defense. This single-minded dedication to the issues of the case left a broad trail of legal documents, which show that the suit was conducted on an impressive scale.

The legal trail is too long and tortuous for us to follow here. Its complexity can be seen from the fact that this dispute was heard in a wide variety of legal settings. These included the court of Common Pleas, the court of King's Bench, the Chancery, the king's council, and the seigniorial councils of magnates. Hosts of consultant lawyers and other distinguished participants were involved in this long, expensive process.

The final result was that even though the litigious relatives did their best to oust the Catesbys, they ultimately failed in their efforts. Ladbroke remained securely in Catesby hands until a later member of the family, Robert Catesby, finally sold the manor in 1597.

CHAUCER'S SERGEANT OF THE LAW (1386–1387)

As mentioned earlier, one of the great literary works of the Middle Ages was Geoffrey Chaucer's *The Canterbury Tales*, begun in 1386–1387 but never finished. Chaucer's description of a sergeant of the law gives us some insights into popular perceptions of these elite lawyers toward the end of the fourteenth century.

At one point Chaucer himself studied law, so he must have known a good deal about its practitioners. Moreover, he sometimes ran afoul of the law himself. A late sixteenth-century edition of Chaucer's work recorded that in 1564, Master Buckley (or Bulkeley), chief butler and librarian at the Inner Temple, said that "for manye yeres since ... [he] did see a record in the same howse, where Goffrye Chaucer was fined two shillings for beating a Franciscan friar in Fleet Street."[15]

By 1239, there was already in existence a band of professionally trained lawyers who were able to discharge the duties of sergeant of the law. These involved presenting a suitor's case in court, practicing law in the Court of the Common Bench, and perhaps taking on other legal duties as well.[16] By Chaucer's time, sergeants of the law were the highest-ranking lawyers, socially equal to knights. There were never very many of them. During the reign of Edward II, for example, only 22 were appointed. The chief baron of the Exchequer, the judges of the king's courts, and the judges for the circuit courts were all recruited from this elite group.

It seems possible that Chaucer's description of the sergeant of the law was actually a satire on Thomas Pynchbek, justice of Common Pleas from 1391 to 1396. Pynchbek sealed a writ in 1388 for Chaucer's arrest because of a debt the poet owed. In any case, by putting Chaucer's Middle English into modern English and editing the results, let us see what the poet wanted his readers to know.

The General Prologue to *The Canterbury Tales* tells us that:

> One of the 30 pilgrims en route to Canterbury was a sergeant of the law, wary and wise, who had often been at the Parvis [the porch of St. Paul's Cathedral in the City of London, where sergeants met their clients].
>
> He was discreet and of great reverence: he certainly seemed so because his words were so wise. He served as a circuit judge in assize courts and had been appointed by the king to exercise full judicial powers. Thanks to his knowledge and good reputation, he earned high fees and rich robes. He was also a successful speculator in land: because of his legal knowledge, his purchases could never be invalidated.
>
> There was never a busier man than he, but he seemed even busier than he had any real need to be. He knew all the cases and laws since the time of William the Conqueror. Indeed, he could draft and draw up a writ so well that no one could find any grounds to have it dismissed.
>
> He knew every statute by heart. He was conservatively dressed in a brown- and green-striped woolen gown, girt about at the waist with a silk sash reinforced by small metal bars to keep it from bunching up.[17]

In contrast to the Wife of Bath and many of Chaucer's other jolly pilgrims, the sergeant of the law comes across as a sober and pretty dull fellow. We can imagine, however, that sometimes he let his guard down and went out with his legal colleagues to a local tavern. If so, we can further speculate that he would have joined in the drinking song which in 1371 a lawyer handling Gloucestershire cases in the Court of Common Pleas jotted down on a plea roll:

> Twice two full quarts [of ale] we lawyers need,
> To fill a legal jug.
> With one, we're gay, with two, we teach,
> With three, we prophesy.
> And four good quarts it takes to bind
> Legal senses, legal tongues,
> A lawyer's hands and mind.[18]

MARGOT DE LA BARRE: PROSTITUTE
AND ACCUSED WITCH (1390)

On 30 July 1390, Margot de la Barre was tried in the Châtelet, the central courthouse and main prison of Paris. This was a very busy place. Its register of criminals shows that, in the words of Esther Cohen, a modern scholar,

The human flow passing through the Châtelet was impressive. Roughly 2,500 people were brought as prisoners within its gates during seven and a half months [between 14 June 1488 and 31 January 1489]. Not a day passed without any number of people, from two to thirty-six, being brought in. Men and women, masters and apprentices, clergymen and prostitutes, thieves, drunks, and simple debtors, all appeared briefly in the register.... Roughly one-fifth were released after short incarceration, pending a trial at the Châtelet court. All the rest were quickly tried, punished, and released within a few days.... On an everyday level authorities sought the maintenance of order, not the upholding of justice.[19]

In Margot's case, her examiners — a provost (royal judge) and nine other royal officials — clearly wanted to uphold justice. Margot was charged with "having willingly done bewitchings and made poisons given to Hainsselin Planiete and Agnesot, his wife."[20] Margot acknowledged that

she was free with her body, and gave it to all the men who wanted to take their pleasure and have their will with her, whether in the good towns of the kingdom where she went, sometimes in one, sometimes in another, or in the fields where she had gone for a long time with the other whores.[21]

She explained to the examiners that she had learned from her friends that Agnesot was suffering from a very severe headache. Remembering her mother's teachings, Margot took some dried herbs she had gathered on the previous Midsummer's Eve and, adding a fresh herb called *aumosniere*, she wove them into a hat. When she got to Agnesot's house, while putting the hat on Agnesot's head Margo said three Our Fathers, three Hail Marys, made the sign of the cross over the hat, and pronounced these words: "Two have enchanted you, three will disenchant you, in the name of the Father, the Son, and the Holy Spirit."

That same day, Agnesot's husband, Hainsselin, said he was feverish and asked Margot to give him medicine. She took some more *aumosniere*, tied it up in a small white cloth, blessed it with her hand, and gave it to Hainsselin, telling him to carry it on his person for nine days. During this period, she told him, he would notice that his fever was abating.

Asked by the examiners if she knew how a person was bewitched, she swore that she did not concern herself with such matters. She told the examiners that she never had said that Agnesot had been enchanted. She had said, however, that three or four days after receiving the hat, "one would see how Agnesot's health was improving."

This was the court's verdict:

Considering the situation, kind of life, and company of this woman who had been dissolute, her confession and denials, the herb and suspect clothing found in her house, and also the fact that, according to any man of good sense, nobody can disenchant without first knowing how to cast spells.... [I]n order to know the truth from her own mouth, she should be put to the question [that is, interrogated under torture]. She was condemned by my lord the Provost, who pronounced the sentence in the presence of the said Margot.[22]

JOHN RYKENER: A MALE
TRANSVESTITE PROSTITUTE (1395)

In 1995, two medievalists (David Lorenzo Boyd and Ruth Mazo Karras) made a
remarkable discovery, chancing upon what is apparently the only legal process document from late medieval England which deals with same-sex intercourse.[23] It comes
from a London Plea and Memoranda Roll of 1395. Regrettably, the outcome of this
case is not known, nor is it clear that a formal charge was in fact lodged against the
potential defendant, John Rykener.

What we do know is that on 11 December 1395, two men were hauled before the
mayor and aldermen of London. The first was John Britby from the county of York.
The other was John Rykener, a man dressed in woman's clothes, who called himself
"Eleanor." These two had been found "lying by a certain stall in Soper's Lane [Lon-
don], committing that detestable unmentionable and ignominious vice [anal inter-
course]."

Questioned separately, Britby confessed that while traveling through London he
had propositioned Rykener, thinking that he was a woman. Rykener had agreed to have
sex with him and had stated his price. They were caught in *flagrante delicto* by the local
authorities and were taken to prison. For his part, Rykener confirmed Britby's account.
The officials then asked Rykener how he had learned this vice. His answer is worth
quoting at some length:

> [Rykener] swore willingly on [his] soul that a certain Anna, the whore of a former
> servant of Sir Thomas Blount, first taught him to practice this detestable vice in the
> manner of a woman. [He] further said that a certain Elizabeth Bronderer first
> dressed him in women's clothing; she also brought her daughter Alice to diverse
> men for the sake of lust, placing her with those men in their beds at night without
> light, making her leave early in the morning and showing them John Rykener
> dressed up in women's clothing, calling him Eleanor and saying that they had mis-
> behaved with her.
> [He] further said that a certain Philip, rector of Theydon Garnon, had sex with
> him as a woman.... Rykener further confessed that [in Oxford] three unsuspecting
> scholars ... practiced the abominable vice with him often ... two Franciscans, one
> named Brother Michael and the other Brother John, who gave [him] a gold ring,
> and one Carmelite friar and six foreign men committed the above-said vice with
> him....
> Rykener further confessed that [he] went to Beaconsfield and there, as a man, had
> sex with a certain Joan ... and also there two Franciscans had sex with him as a
> woman.... [In addition,] after [his] last return to London a certain Sir John, once
> chaplain at the Church of St. Margaret Patens, and two other chaplains committed
> with him the aforementioned vice in the lanes behind St. Katherine's Church by the
> Tower of London.
> Rykener further said that he often had sex as a man with many nuns and also had
> sex as a man with many women, both married and otherwise, how many he did not
> know. Rykener further confessed that many priests had committed that vice with
> him as a woman, how many [he] did not know, and said that [he] accommodated
> priests more readily than other people because they wished to give [him] more than
> others.[24]

TWO MONKS COME TO GRIEF (1398)

According to the medieval *Chronique des Religieux de Saint-Denys* (*Chronicle of the Religious Community of St. Denis*), in 1398 the French king Charles VI was suffering from a bout of insanity. During his life he had 44 attacks of madness, lasting from three to nine months, interspersed with periods of sanity. Two Augustinian monks claimed to be able to cure him, thanks to their alleged supernatural healing powers.[25]

First they resorted to magic incantations and gave the king a liquid made from powdered pearls. When these remedies failed, they wanted to cut incisions in the king's head. Not being permitted to do this, they then accused both the king's barber and the Duc d'Orléans' concierge of sorcery. When these two men were acquitted, the friars accused the duke himself of having bewitched the king. Since the duke was a very powerful person (he was the king's brother), this was an exceptionally ill-advised move.

The upshot was that the friars were denounced, tried by the bishop of Paris as "idolaters, invokers of demons, apostates and sorcerers," and sentenced to death. Their carefully scripted public execution had two important objectives, in addition to simple punishment: it provided a public atonement for serious sins and it served as a warning to others. For these reasons it was designed to be a memorable occasion.

First, at sunrise the two monks were led out of the bishop's prison and were loaded into a horse-drawn cart. Their hands were tied. On their heads they wore paper miters with their names. On their backs were parchments describing their crimes. At the Place de Grève (a square located in the center of Paris), two platforms had been set up. On a high, richly decorated platform stood the bishop of Paris in all his finery, flanked by six other bishops and by distinguished citizens. On the plain lower platform across the square were the two monks.

A doctor of theology then read a long description of their crimes, whereupon the bishop ordered that they be stripped of clerical office and defrocked. After the monks' fingers had been symbolically scrubbed to remove any residual trace of the chrism used at their ordination, they were pronounced to be devoid of any ecclesiastical authority and were formally handed over to the secular arm, i.e., to the sergeants of the law.

The monks were then led through Paris to the execution spot itself. At each intersection, a herald would shout out their crimes; each time, the monks had to agree "with signs and words" that they were indeed guilty. Finally, at around three o'clock in the afternoon, the monks arrived at the place of execution. There they confessed and were beheaded. The executioner mounted their heads on lances on a high spot. Their severed arms and legs were displayed in front of the main gates of Paris, while their trunks stayed on the gibbet. The medieval chronicler concluded with evident satisfaction: "Thus these two miserable men atoned for their iniquities, serving as an example to traitors and criminals."[26]

A LYING WIFE SPARKS A
JUDICIAL DUEL (14TH CENTURY)

The *Chronique du Religieux de Saint-Denys* also moralizes that in the fourteenth century,

> The single combat of Jean de Carrouges with Jacques le Gris, accused of the rape of Jean's wife, gives plain proof to posterity how blameworthy it is to follow rumor in uncertain matters, in the way that leafy branches are bent by every breeze, so that one goes from rumor to vengeance.[27]

Both Jean (a lord) and Jacques (a knight) served in the household of the Count of Alençon in Normandy. They had been friends since youth. According to Jean's wife, however, while Jean was away, Jacques came calling. She alleged that

> In the guise of a visitor he entered the home like a thief aiming at her chastity. After dinner had been concluded, [she], unaware of his evil design, had led him about like a good friend here and there and taken him to the guest chamber. Then he was unable to conceal his savage intention. For immediately he began to confess his love, and to implore, and to mix gifts with prayers and to harass [her] spirit in every way. And when he fearfully saw her constant spirit, improper love made him bold, and throwing her down with his left arm he robbed the storehouse of her chastity and gave the victory to desire.[28]

The wife, however, did not immediately report this rape to anyone but waited until Jean returned home. Only then, the chronicler tells us, did "tears and sobs of mourning" appear. When Jean asked her if she was all right, she told him:

> No, of course not, for how can a woman be well when she has lost her chastity? There is the mark of another man in your bed, beloved husband of mine, and thus Jacques le Gris has turned from a faithful friend into an enemy. Yet although my soul is innocent, death will testify that my body has been so greatly violated, unless you give me your right hand and word that the rapist will not go unpunished.[29]

After consulting his own relatives, Jean tried to persuade her that "it is the mind that sins, not the body, and where consent is absent, so is guilt." She would not be consoled, however. Day and night, she demanded that Jacques be punished.

Jean finally decided to report this crime to the king and his barons. He told them, "If this wicked traitor denies he used deceit and violence against my most beloved wife, I cannot refuse to engage him in single combat." At length the king concurred, subject to the Parlement agreeing that Jean's demand for trial by battle was justified. After listening to the advocates for each side, the Parlement decided that "since the truth could not be known because of the problems with witnesses, so that human judgment could not ascertain the good faith of either side," a judicial duel should be held next to the walls of St. Martin-des-Champs.

As custom demanded, the king and his princes were present at the fight, as well as a huge crowd of commoners. When the marshal gave the signal for attack, both Jean and Jacques spurred their horses forward, lowered their lances and "dashed against each other courageously and with spirit." Jacques drew the first blood, spearing Jean's thigh with a lance. The chronicler tells us that

> This blow would have done [Jacques] much good if he had held the lance in that wound. But when he immediately drew it out, it was covered in blood, and the sight, rather than stunning the wounded man, made him bolder.... Jean gathered up his strength, and advancing, shouted, "This day will decide our quarrel." With his left hand he seized the top of his opponent's helmet, and drew Jacques toward him and then pulling back a little, threw Jacques to the ground where he lay weighed down by his armor. Jean then drew his sword and killed his enemy, though with great difficulty, because he was fully armored.[30]

Before Jean killed Jacques, he repeatedly demanded that Jacques confess to the rape, but "the vanquished completely denied the event." Jacques was in fact telling the truth. We learn from the chronicler that

> Afterwards everyone found out who had committed the foul rape, when someone else confessed while being condemned to death. The aforesaid lady took note of this, and thinking over the fault in her mind, after the death of her husband became a recluse and took an oath of perpetual continence."[31]

What are we to make of all this? If Jacques did not rape the wife, why then did she lie? Was she furious because she had tried to seduce him, but failed? Was she afraid that she was pregnant after an earlier affair with the unnamed man who confessed when facing death, and hoped to use Jacques as a convenient scapegoat? We shall never know.

PUNISHMENT OF PILLORY AND WHETSTONE (1412)

One of the most popular medieval pastimes was to go off on pilgrimage. Most of these travelers were genuine pilgrims but there was also a good sprinkling of rogues and conmen among the devout. Here is a case of an Englishman who was tried and convicted for pretending to be a hermit and a pilgrim:

> William Blakeney, shetilmaker [shuttlemaker], who pretended to be a hermit, was brought unto the Guildhall, before Robert Chichele, Mayor, the Aldermen, and Sheriffs, for that, whereas he was able to work for his food and raiment, the same William, went about there, barefooted and with long hair, under the guise of sanctity, and pretended to be a hermit, saying that he was such, and that he had made pilgrimage to Jerusalem, Rome, Venice, and the city of Seville, in Spain; and under colour of such falsehood he had and received many good things from divers persons, to the defrauding, and in manifest deceit, of all the people.[32]

William had no defense and had to confess that

> for the last six years he had lived by such lies, falsities, and deceits, and so invented by him, to the point of defrauding the people, under the colour of such feigned sanctity, and that he never was in the parts aforesaid. [Hearing his admission,, the

court therefore ruled] that the said William should be put upon the pillory for three market-days, there to remain for one hour each day, the reason for the same being proclaimed; and he was to have, in the meantime, whetstone [sic] hung from his neck. And precept was given to the Sheriffs to do execution thereof.[33]

JAMYS FYSCHER V THOMAS WHYTEHORNE (1456)

In 1456, Jamys Fyscher, an English fisherman and boatbuilder, claimed that Thomas Whytehorne, a convicted thief, had falsely accused him of being an accomplice in crime.[34] Their dispute had to be settled by a judicial duel. Since there were no iron-clad rules for trial by combat, local customs prevailed. According to mayor Gregory of London, in this particular case the judge, Mayster Myhelle Skylling, ordered both men to dress in white. As weapons, each was to hold, in one hand, a three-foot wooden staff made of ash; in the other, a piece of curved iron shaped like a "rammyshorne" (a ram's horn), carefully sharpened at the end.

Both Fyscher and Whytehorne fasted before the duel, "having neither meat nor drink." Mayor Gregory took a very dim view of the proceedings, stating that "it is too shameful to rehearse all the conditions of this foul conflict; and if they need any drink they must drink their own piss." A big crowd turned out for the fight. Fyscher was by far the favorite: Whytehorne was held in great contempt because he was an approver. (As mentioned earlier, an approver was a career criminal who had turned crown witness and had agreed to challenge other felons in trial by battle.)

The judicial duel began with prayers. Whytehorne jeered at Fyscher, asking him why he was spending so much time on his knees. Enraged, Fyscher jumped to his feet and attacked his opponent but only managed to break his ash staff in the process. Both parties were then disarmed by the officials and were allowed to continue the fight unarmed. This is what happened next:

Courthouse personnel: *sergeant à verge* (carrying a mace as a symbol of authority), herald (with trumpet), jailer (with keys), executioner (with flail), and the shirtless criminal himself. (Guillaume le Rouille, *Iusticie atque injusticie descriptionum compendium*, 1520. Fol. XXVIv Bibliothèque nationale de France, Paris).

[The combatants] bit with their teeth, and the leather of clothing and flesh was all rent in many places of their bodies. And then the false appealer [Whytehorne] cast that meek innocent [Fyscher] down to the ground and bit him by the member, that the poor innocent cried out ... [then] that innocent recovered up on his knees and took the false appealer by the nose with his teeth and put his thumb in his eye.[35]

This eye-gouging proved to be so painful that Whytehorne was forced to cry for mercy. Judge Skylling stopped the fight to give each man a chance to tell his side of the story one last time. Whytehorne broke down and admitted that he had wrongly accused Fyscher and twenty-eight other men as well. As a result, "then he was confessed and hanged."

LEGAL STRUGGLES OF THE PASTON FAMILY (FIFTEENTH CENTURY)

The Pastons were a prominent English family living in eastern Norfolk during the fifteenth century.[36] The Paston Letters, now preserved in the British Library in London, constitute the largest surviving collection of English correspondence from this period. These letters are of interest to us here because they reflect the trials and tribulations of a long series of lawsuits over ownership three manors in Norfolk: Caister Castle, Coton, and Hellesdon.

The rise of the Pastons shows that upward mobility was difficult but certainly possible in the Middle Ages.[37] The founding father, Clement Paston, began as a simple farmer and may even have been a bondsman. He took advantage of the labor shortage caused by the Black Death (the bubonic plague, which killed one-third of Europe's population) and earned enough to buy some land in and around the village of Paston. He then borrowed money to send his son, William, to law school.

William Paston became a lawyer, a sergeant of the law and, eventually, a judge of the Court of Common Pleas. By marrying well he acquired the manor of Oxnead. His son, John Paston Sr., was educated in the law at Cambridge and the Inner Temple. He, too, married well. His wife, Margaret, brought to their union the manors of Mautby and East Tuddenham. John Paston Sr. was both a member of Parliament for Norfolk and a justice of the peace.

As a lawyer, he spent a good deal of time in London, where he became the close friend and lawyer of Sir John Fastolf, the Norfolk knight and landowner who was the model for Shakespeare's famous character, Sir John Falstaff. Fastolf himself had won fame and fortune in the later phase of the Hundred Years War between England and France. Although childless and unmarried, he used his war booty to build a gigantic pile known as Caister Castle, which was completed in about 1432.

When Fastolf died, it turned out that the main beneficiary of the old knight's will was none other than his lawyer, John Paston Sr. He thus inherited Caister Castle. Fastolf's descendents, however, bitterly contested the will. When John Paston Sr. himself died in 1466, the legal wrangle was still going on. The baton then passed to John Paston's two sons, John Paston the Elder and John Paston the Younger. Their letters to and from their mother Margaret give many details of the unsettled conditions of that era.

Fastolf's executors — Sir William Yelverton, Thomas Howes and possibly also the De la Pole family (the dukes of Suffolk) — still refused to accept the fact that the Pastons owned Caister Castle. Their implacable hostility even forced Margaret to move into the castle for a time. She complained to John the Elder, however, that the castle was much less comfortable and much colder than her former home at Oxnead. Probably because of this, John the Younger sent her back to Oxnead and moved into the castle himself. At about the same time, Yelverton and Howes sold their alleged rights to the castle to the Duke of Norfolk, who had always coveted it.

In 1469 — a time of civil war — the Duke of Norfolk surrounded Caister Castle with 3,000 soldiers and eventually forced it to capitulate. The siege lasted five weeks. Only 30 Paston soldiers had been available to defend the castle. In a letter written in late September 1469, John the Younger, who had fought there himself, explained that the odds against the Pastons had been insurmountable:

> As for the surrender of Caister, John Chapman can tell you as well as myself how we were forced to it.... We were sore lacking in victuals, gunpowder and men's hearts, and the lack of certainty of rescue drove us to the treaty [of surrender].[38]

Unlike his warlike younger brother, John the Elder was a dilettante. A Paston letter reveals that his own father had complained that John the Elder was "a drone among bees, which labour for gathering honey in the fields, and the drone doth naught but taketh his part of it."[39] Perhaps it was the loss of Caister Castle that finally spurred John the Elder into action. The upshot was that he spent the next 11 years pursuing the Duke of Norfolk through the courts. When the Duke died in 1476, John the Elder quickly moved into the castle himself.

At this point he got some good advice from his younger brother, who warned him that unless the Pastons obtained a patent from the king, the castle would revert to the duke's wife. John the Elder moved quickly and the king granted a patent to him. As a result, the duke's widow gave up her husband's claim, leaving the Pastons masters of the field. Ironically, however, John the Elder was to enjoy Caister Castle for only three years. He died of the plague in 1479.

It should be mentioned that during his years in London, John the Elder, like other litigants involved in complex, protracted cases, had to hire a number of professional lawyers. Such men were among the earliest literate laity. As the first well-trained secular administrators, they would later become key agents in the slow political unification of medieval states.

9

Medieval Crime

The Middle Ages were dangerous times. The rule of law was still in its infancy throughout much of Western Europe. Violence was common: as we have seen, in 1024–1025 bishop Burchard of Worms was appalled by "the murders which arise daily in the familia of St. Peter, as though among beasts." Judicial archives reveal that murders constituted between 50 and 75 percent of the recorded crimes.[1]

New methods of criminal procedure were introduced after 1215 as ordeals were gradually abandoned, but law and order was still very shaky in thirteenth-century England, where only one in 100 murderers was ever brought to trial and convicted. The rest often fled to the thick forests, where they joined the bands of outlaws symbolized by the fictional Robin Hood. The cities, for their part, were full of beggars, thieves and prostitutes. The poet François Villon knew some of them in fifteenth-century Paris and chronicled their lives in verse.

Trying to Maintain Law and Order

The French scholar Marc Bloch believed that medieval men "were emotionally insensitive to the spectacle of pain, and they had small regard for human life, which they saw only as a transitory state before Eternity."[2] Such men were quick to resort to violence. If they did, they were likely to escape unpunished. Only a small proportion of those who committed murder or less serious crimes were actually brought to justice. The basic reason was that there was no such thing as a police force.

As a result, collective responsibility had to be used instead. This meant that all males over the age of twelve were organized into of small groups of ten or twelve men, which were known as tithings. Every commoner over the age of twelve had to swear to the lord's steward:

> Hear this, Sir steward, that I will not be a thief nor the fellow of a thief, nor will I conceal a theft nor a thief but will reveal it to those to whom it should be revealed; and I will bear faith to the lord King of England and more especially to my [own] lord, and will be obedient to the orders of his bailiffs.[3]

If the men of a tithing captured a thief, who then escaped, they either had to recapture him or pay a stiff fine. After Norman rule began in 1066, these tithings were required to join larger groups known as *frankpledge*. The oath they took on this occasion required them to refrain from committing crimes themselves and make sure that any suspected criminal in their own group appeared in court.

THE SHERIFF

Maintaining law and order in the English countryside was a difficult task which fell on the local sheriff, who was the king's representative in the county. After the Norman Conquest, the position of sheriff gained additional importance because the previous powers of the Anglo-Saxon shire-reeves were linked to the much greater powers traditionally exercised by the Norman *vice comites* (vice or deputy counts).[4] The sheriff thus became the most powerful secular official in the county.

Twice a year, a ceremony known as "view of *frankpledge*" was organized at the hundred court. Presided over by the sheriff himself, this event was also referred to as the sheriff's tourn. The sheriff collected taxes, administered the local courts (except for the courts dispensing feudalized justice) and tried to keep the king's peace. He was president of the county court, executed all the writs and presided at both criminal and civil cases.

The sheriff could, if necessary, call out the *posse comitatus*, i.e. "the force of the county." This summoning of armed private citizens to help restore the peace was the model for the sheriff's posse of the nineteenth-century American West. Not surprisingly, as we will see below in the section on Robin Hood, the "proud sheriff" was an important figure in fiction as well as in fact. He has been aptly described as "the chief pillar of the medieval monarchy."[5] It is important to remember, however, that this state of affairs was true only for England: no other medieval European country had such a powerful local official.

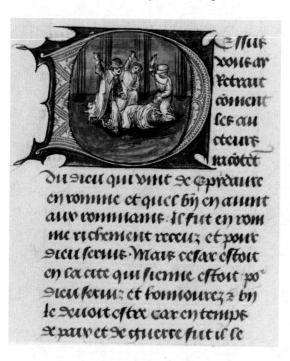

Murder was a common crime in the Middle Ages. (Ovidius, *Metamorphoses*, MS.fr.137, fol. 234r. Bibliothèque nationale de France, Paris.)

The influence of the sheriff varied considerably over time. As the jurisdiction of the *curia regis* (king's court) expanded during the reign of Henry II (1154–1189), the role of the sheriff shrank. His remaining duties, however, were still considerable. He had to investigate crimes in his county, interrogate accused men and try minor offenses. If someone was accused of a major crime, the sheriff was required to keep him in custody until the next visit of the king's itinerant justices. Usually there was one sheriff per county. London would eventually have two sheriffs, and one of the capital's privileges was to elect them.[6]

The sheriffs' stock rose in 1166 when in the Assize of Clarendon Henry II gave them full responsibility for maintaining law and order in their respective counties, subject only to the visits of the king's justices. This grant of power, however, led to further corruption. Sheriffs were not paid by the king; indeed, they themselves had to pay a yearly sum to the king in order to keep their own positions. What, then, were their sources of income?

A British scholar, William Morris, who painstakingly studied this issue in the 1920s, concluded that "the sources of a regular income from the office [of sheriff] are not obvious."[7] What seems clear is that the sheriffs had to resort to different forms of exaction to make ends meet. As late as 1260, for example, the men of Nottingham had to pay their sheriff 100 shillings not to invade their liberty. (As mentioned earlier, a "liberty" was a right or immunity enjoyed by prescription or by grant.)

The sheriffs also demanded high "ferms." These were fixed annual payments owed by the bailiffs to the sheriffs in return for holding their offices. The bailiffs, in turn, got from the public whatever income they could earn or were entitled to, but they were always required to pay ferms to the sheriff if they wanted to keep their jobs.[8]

The sheriffs held other aces as well. Some sheriffs seized the property of criminals or used the threat of imprisonment to extort money from innocent people. Unscrupulous sheriffs could make a man pay twice for a single offense. They could also demand payment from several persons with the same name, when a fine had been imposed on only one of them. They could compel people to pay higher taxes than were legally required. In 1274 there were many cases of a sheriff taking a bribe at the tourn, i.e.,

---

La quarte nouuelle.

dit tout hault que ſſecy et ſe bon hom/
me de ſoy ſauluer et deſſoubz ſe lit ſe
boute pour eſtre plus ſeurement beau/
coup plus eſbahy que par auant. La da
me fut repzinſe et de rechief enſerree a
ſon beau loiſir et en ſa faꝛon que deſſus
touſiours ſeſpee au plus pres de lui.
Apzes ceſte rencharge et pluſieurs lon
gues deuiſes dentre leſcoſſois et la da
me ſeure vint de partir/ſi lui donna ſa
bonne nupt et picque et ſen va. Le poure
martir eſtant deſſoubz ſe lit a peu ſil ſe
oſoit tirer de la doubtât ſe retour de ſõ
aduerſaire ou pour mieulx dire ſon cõ
paignon. A chief de pechie il pzint cou/
raige, et a ſayde de ſa ſéme la dieu mer
cy il fut remis ſur pies. Sil auoit bien
tenſe ſa femme au par auant encores
recommenca il plus dure legende. Car
elle auoit conſenti apzes ſa deffenſe ſe
deſhonneur de luy et delle. Helas dit el
ſe et ou eſt la ſéme ſi aſſeuree qui oſaſt
deſdire vng homme ainſi eſchauffe et
enraige comme ceſtup eſtoit quât vous
qui eſtes arme embaſtonne et ſi baillât
a qui il a trop plus meſfait que a moy
ne ſauois pas oſe aſſaillir ne moy deſ
fendre. Ce neſt pas reſpõſe dit il dame
ſe vous neuſſiez voulu iamais ne fuſt
venu a ſes attainctes vous eſtes mau
uaiſe et deſſeaſe. Mais vous dit elle
laſche meſchant et reprouchie homme
pour qui ie ſuis deſhõnouree. car pour
vous obezr ie aſſignay ſe maulditſ tout
a ſeſcoſſois. Et encozes naues eu en vo⁹
tant de couraige détrepézdre la deſſéſe

de ceſte en qui giſt tout voſtre bien et vo
ſtre hõneur. Et ne penſez pas que ieuſ
ſe trop mieulx apme la mort ꝗ dauoir
de moy meſmes conſenty ne accorde ce
meſchief. Et dieu ſcait ſe doeul que ien
pozte et pozteray tât ꝗ ie viuray. quât ce
ſuy de ꝗ ie dois auoir a tout ſecours at
tédre en ſa pzeſéce ma bien ſouffert deſ
honnouter. Il fait aſſez a croire et pé
ſer quelle ne ſouffrit pas la vouſéte de
ſeſcoſſois pour plaiſir quelle y pzint.
mais elle fut a ce contrainte et forcee
par non reſiſter laiſſant la reſiſtéce en
la pzoueſſe de ſon mary ꝗ ſen eſtoit treſ
bien chargie. Donc chaſcun deulx laiſ/
ſa ſon dire et ſa querelle apzes pluſieurs
argumés et repliques dung coſte et dau
tre. mais en ſon cas euident fut ſe ma
ry deceu et demoura trõpe de ſeſcoſſois
en la faꝛon quauez oupe.

In the back streets of a city, a man was not safe from robbers. (*Les cent nouvelles nouvelles* [sic], 1486, fol.b8v Bibliothèque nationale de France, Paris.)

when he presided over the hundred court, but doing nothing in return to help those accused of offenses.

The list of exactions does not end here. Sheriffs and bailiffs could summon excessive numbers of jurors, including those who could not possibly serve for reasons of age, poor health or because they lived in another jurisdiction. These unfortunate men would be forced to pay bribes if they wanted to be excused from the onerous task of jury duty. Sheriffs could pocket money offered by their prisoners in hopes of better treatment. Suspected criminals (that is, accused or indicted persons) could be encouraged to pay up to avoid arrest.

INQUEST OF SHERIFFS (1170)

Henry II tried to deal with the problem of corruption through his Inquest of Sheriffs (1170). This was an effort to uncover misconduct by sheriffs and other local officials. It provided that:

> In the first place the barons shall require security and pledge from all sheriffs who have been sheriffs since the lord king last crossed into Normandy, and from all who have been bailiffs or ministers of these [sheriffs], whatever bailiwick they have held from them; also from all those who since that time have held hundreds of the barons which they [the barons] have in the county, whether they have held them at firm or in custody: that they will be before the lord king on the day which they [the barons] shall set for them for the purpose of doing right and redressing to him and his men what they ought to redress.
>
> Afterward they [the barons] shall take oath from all the barons and knights and free men of the county that they will tell the truth concerning that which shall be asked of them on behalf of the lord king; and that they will not conceal the truth for love of anyone or for hatred or for money or reward or fear or promise or for anything else.[9]

This sonorous edict, however, was not enough to stem the tide of corruption. We learn that many years after this inquest, the sheriff of Cambridgeshire, together with his wife and a large number of retainers, frequently stayed, free-of-charge, at the priory of Barnwell. In 1287, for example, he spent three days and two nights there with his family, his followers and their 22 horses. He even became angry when the prior would not lend him the monastery's cart to carry a cask of wine up to his manor.[10]

The powers of the sheriff were gradually lessened by the rise of other English officials responsible for keeping the peace. These included the coroners (c. 1194), the local constables (c. 1242), the *custodes pacis* ("keepers of the peace," c. 1263), the commissioners of trailbaston (1305), and the justices of the peace (1361). We shall look briefly at the last three institutions because they are the most important and the most important.

CUSTODES PACIS (C. 1263)

In medieval England, collective responsibility proved to be a weak tool at best, even when well-known criminals were involved. This system was quite incapable of handling any widespread emergency. When such a danger threatened, special *ad pacem conservandam* (peacekeeping) commissions were issued to selected local knights. These men later came to be called *custodes pacis* (keepers of the peace).

Thus when faced with an invasion from Wales, in 1263 the barons named one *custos* (keeper) for each county. His job was to police his area independently of the sheriff and not to get involved in the sheriff's fiscal and administrative duties.[11] The role of the *custodes pacis* was later formally defined by the Statute of Westminster (1327), which ordered that "For the better keeping and maintenance of the peace the King wills that in every county good men and lawful ... shall be assigned to keep the peace."[12]

COMMISSIONERS OF TRAILBASTON (1305)

"Trailbaston" means "one who trails or carries a club or cudgel," i.e., a club-wielding criminal. There was so little law and order in England toward the end of Edward I's reign that special commissioners of trailbaston had to be set up (in 1305, 1306 and 1307) to try these offenders. In one case, three local landowners — Edmund Deincourt, Robert Willoughby and Thomas Burnham — were ordered to hold inquests in Lincolnshire, Nottinghamshire and Derbyshire. The problem they faced was that "malefactors and peace-breakers" were roaming unchecked through the woods and parks, committing arson, theft and murder. These commissioners of trailbaston were charged with arresting the criminals themselves and anyone who was helping or sheltering them.[13]

The "malefactors and peace-breakers" were often desperate men with nothing to lose, so they were quick to resort to violence. An excellent example of this is *The Outlaw's Song of Trailbaston*, a poem written in Norman French between 1305 and 1307. In it, an outlaw who is hiding "in the woods under fresh cool shade/Where there's no treachery nor twisting of laws" tells us what he would like to do to the commissioners of trailbaston:

> If these lousy jurors don't get things under control
> So I can ride or go as I please back where I belong,
> If I get my hands on them their heads are going to roll.
> They think threats scare me, they couldn't be more wrong.
>
> Judge Martin, Judge Knowville, they're nice enough guys,
> They pray for poor folks and hope they do well –
> But those sadists Spigurnel and Belfou I do despise -
> If I had them in my power there'd be no more to tell.
>
> I'll teach them the game of Trailbaston all right –
> I'll break their backs and hand them their ass in a sling,
> Arms and legs too, it's no more than right —
> I'll cut out their tongues and hear how they sing.[14]

JUSTICES OF THE PEACE (1361)

In 1361 the Statute of Westminster broadened the responsibilities of the *custodes pacis* by creating an important new office known as the justices of the peace. Also called lay magistrates, these were unpaid officials appointed on behalf of the king from the ranks of important landowners or other local dignitaries whose reputation and loyalty to the crown was beyond challenge. In court procedures, these men ultimately displaced the sheriff.

The sheriff continued to be a powerful official in England until the Tudor reorganization of local government in the fifteenth and sixteenth centuries. He was ultimately responsible for maintaining law and order in the whole county. In 1461, however, a statute decreed that henceforth all indictments and presentments taken at the tourn should be taken before a justice of the peace, not before the sheriff. The justices thus gradually replaced the older English courts which had administered communal and feudalized justice.

METHODS OF CRIMINAL PROCEDURE

In 1199 pope Innocent III had authorized canon law judges, for the first time, to use force to extract information to determine a person's guilt or innocence.[15] This new type of criminal procedure, known as *per inquisitionem*, formed part of the pope's campaign against clerical concubinage, fornication, and simony. It permitted a judge to begin proceedings against a suspected offender without any formal accusation or denunciation. The judge thus became both the investigator and the prosecutor, as well as the official who imposed sentence.

This concentration of power in the hands of the man on the bench put defendants at a great disadvantage. Law professors and academically inclined lawyers felt that this new procedure was patently unfair. They argued that action *per inquisitionem* did grave damage to the legal safeguards built into the *ordo iudiciarius*, the fusion of Roman law and canon law which was discussed earlier. Remarkably, as a result of their beliefs they even taught young lawyers to modify or even to ignore this particular aspect of canon law.[16]

In 1070, pope Alexander II had forbidden the ordeal to be used in the case of ecclesiastics, since it was, he said, simply a popular invention entirely unsupported by any canonical authority.[17] As we have seen, at Fourth Lateran Council in 1215 pope Innocent III forbade clerics to take part in any ordeals. This prohibition effectively removed the "holy" element from the ordeals and officially ended them as a legitimate mode of proof. Thus the ordeals gradually fell into disuse. The sole exception was trial by battle, which survived until the fourteenth and fifteenth centuries and which technically remained in force in England until as late as 1819.

After the Fourth Lateran Council, confession — often extracted by torture — became the preferred method of obtaining what was considered to be reliable proof. Trial by jury was still in its infancy. Since an accused person could not at that time be *forced* to submit to a jury trial, justices tried to persuade every accused person to ask

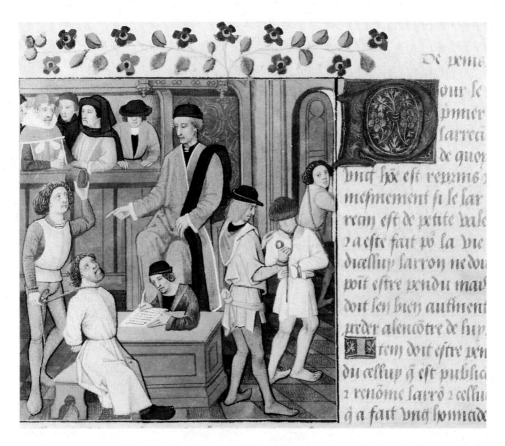

In the fifteenth century, a modest amount of force could be used in court to persuade suspects to answer the judge's questions. (MS. fr.4367.fol.55v. Bibliothèque nationale de France, Paris.)

for such a trial; if he or she refused, they had to be released.[18] What, then, could justices do with a suspect they had good reason to believe was guilty?

A clever legal solution to this conundrum was found in the procedure known as *peine forte et dure*—that is, "heavy and hard punishment."[19] A "contumacious felon," i.e., a stubbornly disobedient person willfully demonstrating contempt of court, could not be convicted if he refused to ask for a jury trial—but he could be stripped of his clothing and tied to a stone floor with a wooden plank laid across his chest. Heavy rocks could then be piled upon the plank until he either agreed to plead or was crushed to death. Understandably, the threat of *peine forte et dure* made jury trials more popular, with one notable exception.

This exception arose when valuable property was at stake. When a man (or a woman) was convicted of a felony, his or her property and possessions were subject to seizure. In order to make sure they would pass instead to the next of kin and thus not impoverish a family, a courageous person might accept what Shakespeare calls "pressing to death" to escape trial and conviction. Surviving records show that a lady named Juliana Quick was pressed to death by weights in 1442. Other people met the same fate in 1598, 1605, 1657 and 1741. This procedure was not abolished in England until 1772.[20]

Regulating the Pleasures of the Flesh

Taverns and prostitutes enjoyed a mutually beneficial relationship in medieval France.[21] Both were popular diversions: "Everyone to the taverns and the girls!", the poet François Villon urges his readers.[22] For religious and law-and-order reasons, however, taverns and *filles de joie* (literally, "girls of joy," i.e., prostitutes) invariably attracted the attentions of regulators. These agents of public morality, however, met with only limited and short-lived successes.

Taverns

The French of all classes liked to drink. They drank a great deal of wine, not only at meals and festivals but also at other times. By the end of the Middle Ages there were more than 4,000 taverns in Paris alone. Every day these dispensed, either cup by cup or *en vrac* (in bulk), 700 barrels of wine. This total does not include the numerous duty-free and thus unrecorded barrels of wine reserved for nobles, landlords, and the staffs of secondary schools in Paris.

The authorities tried in vain to hold down the number of taverns. In fifteenth-century Flanders, civil authorities believed there were too many inns, which of course sold wine as well. The city of Ypres decreed that there should be no more than one inn for every eight households. Religious establishments sold wine as well — to such an extent that Pius II, who became pope in 1458, forbade this practice under pain of excommunication. He made an exception, however, for one religious order, the Carthusians, who were allowed to retail 30 *muids* of wine (about 8,040 liters or 1,768 gallons) from their monastery in Paris.

Prostitutes

French legislation on prostitution dates from the reign of Louis IX (1226–1270). A law of 1254, for example, ordered the expulsion of prostitutes from cities and villages and the seizure of their goods. An ordinance of 1256 shows that the authorities tried to move the girls away from "honorable" streets in the center of Paris and to ban them from soliciting near churches, convents and cemeteries. The authorities were instructed to make them move outside the city walls. It is unlikely, of course, that the girls stayed away from their urban customers for very long.

As a modern French medievalist explains, there was an inherent ambiguity in medieval laws against prostitution: "the fight against prostitution coexisted with a tolerance which formed a tempting framework for it."[23] In Paris, the prostitutes could legally ply their trade only in red-light districts. They did so, however, under the direct surveillance of the public authorities. Hugues Aubriot is a good example.

He was the *prévôt* of Paris, that is, he was both a royal judge and the senior administrative officer of the city. He took strict measures to limit the spread of the red-light districts. Indeed, he supervised them personally. Under his draconian regime, the girls were allowed to receive clients only during the day. If they did so after 6 p.m. in winter or 7 p.m. in summer, they could be fined.

Regulation seemed necessary because prostitution had an inherent tendency to expand beyond its approved boundaries. A Paris law of 1420 indicates that the girls had moved into "good" neighborhoods, where they bought houses and turned them into taverns, or owned boutiques where they entertained their clients, most of whom were laborers or artisans. The *filles de joie* were not supposed to receive clients at home but this rule was frequently ignored. When it was, however, if two neighbors complained to the authorities, a prostitute could be forced to leave.

A prostitute empties her chamber pot on a group of rowdies to encourage them to move on. (Sebastian Brant, *La nef des floz du monde*, 1497, fol. LII. Bibliothèque nationale de France, Paris.)

Since it was apparent that prostitution could never be suppressed entirely, the practical solution was allow it to be practiced only in certain areas, subject to restrictions. Thus municipal laws in fourteenth- and fifteenth-century France approved certain streets and certain hours for this trade. Moreover, in some cities prostitutes were supposed to dress in a style which visibly set them apart from "honest women."

In Toulouse, for example, the approved trademark was a bonnet trimmed with white ribbons. In Paris at the beginning of the fifteenth century, prostitutes were forbidden to pin silver or gold decorations on their dresses or wear them in their hair. Pearls, daring tunics and gold or silver belts were prohibited, too, along with many other kinds of finery, such as long flowing cloaks trimmed with squirrel fur, and silver buckles on their shoes.

Since these regulations were frequently ignored, they had to be reissued from time to time but with no more lasting results. When some Parisian prostitutes went to church, they were so well turned-out that it was impossible to distinguish them from the upper class women in the pews. Even though these elegant prostitutes were completely illiterate, they made a point of ostentatiously carrying large prayer books into church, just like their more respectable sisters.

Where there were prostitutes, there were also pimps and madams. Pimps recruited country and village girls, promising these innocents a wonderful life in the city. When they got there, they were installed in whorehouses and the pimps lived off their earnings. Lawmakers were especially worried that the wives and daughters of "good families" might be lured into the trade by madams working at respectable jobs. In one case in point, a woman named Katherine who worked as an embroiderer hired her 18-year-old sister-in-law as an apprentice. Katherine was later convicted of having sold this young woman to a great lord.[24]

Illustrative Cases and Laws

THE FOLK HERO HEREWARD (1070–1071)

One of the very few medieval outlaw-heroes who can claim a documented history is Hereward the Wake, i.e., "the watchful one."[25] He is familiar to British readers because Charles Kingsley, one of the most successful nineteenth-century novelists, immortalized him in a romantically illustrated book entitled *Hereward the Wake: Last of the English*. Kingsley drew his material from a long, highly dramatized thirteenth-century account in Latin, the *Gesta Herewardi*, i.e., *The Deeds of Hereward*, an excerpt from which appears below. This manuscript in turn echoes an earlier work, the *Anglo-Saxon Chronicle*.

The Norman Conquest of England in 1066 had such profound political and economic consequences that Michael Swanton, an expert in Anglo-Saxon history, has likened them to what might have happened in Britain had the Germans invaded it during World War II.[26] The heaviest burdens fell on the established citizens of the old order, that is, the Anglo-Saxon landowners, many of whom lost their land and their leadership positions. Most had no choice but to submit to the Normans. A few, however, retreated to the forests and swamps and waged guerrilla raids in hopes of driving out the invaders.

The hopes of the rebels in eastern England were raised in 1070 when the Danish king Swein Estrithson led a raiding party into the area. He was expected to make a bid for the English crown. Swein set up his base of operations on the Isle of Ely, a patch of dry fertile ground in the middle of boggy lands, located roughly 70 miles north of London. Ely was a good base because it could be reached from the sea by ships but it was protected from landward assault by meandering steams and treacherous swamps which could be crossed safely only with local knowledge.

The Anglo-Saxons of the Ely region, many of them of Danish descent, eagerly joined Swein's forces. One of these men was Hereward, a small-scale squire holding lands from the abbeys of Peterborough and Crowland. After the abbot of Peterborough died, Hereward and his men marched to remove the monastery's valuables before a new Norman abbot could be installed there. The monks resisted as best they could but were no match for armed men. Hereward and his men set Peterborough on fire, looted the monastery and turned over the spoils to the Danes, who returned to Denmark not long thereafter.

Ely became a refuge for outlaws, i.e., anti-Norman dissidents. Finally William the Conqueror himself arrived to take matters in hand. Not a man to be content with half-hearted measures, in 1071 he imposed a naval blockade on the seaward side and built a long causeway which allowed his army to cross the swamps on the landward side. His campaign was successful: the insurgents were surrounded and had to give up. A contemporary chronicler says that some of these guerrillas he imprisoned. Others he let go free — but only after having their hands cut off or their eyes gouged out.

Hereward himself managed to escape with some of his followers and soon became a folk hero in the eyes of the conquered Anglo-Saxons. At this point, he disappears from the official record. Other reports suggest, however, that later on he made peace with William. Hereford may even have led troops on William's behalf. For this reason, it was rumored that he was killed by a group of jealous Norman knights.

AN EXCERPT FROM THE DEEDS OF HEREWARD

Now when those who lived in the Isle of Ely, then beginning to hold out against King William who had gained England in battle, heard of the return of such a man as Hereward, they directly sent to him and negotiated through messengers for him to join them with all his men....

Concealing his troops near the river bank, Hereward himself with three knights and four archers well equipped with arms drew close to the edge of the river opposite to where [his enemies] the earl and his men had just arrived.... [T]he earl immediately approached and, catching sight of Hereward, urged all his men to swim across the water with him [to attack the outlaw band]....

[But the earl's men refused to do so, fearing an ambush.] And leaning forward a little, Hereward stretched his bow and shot an arrow with force against the earl's breast. Although it rebounded from the protecting mailcoat, the earl was rendered almost lifeless by the blow. Whereupon his men, very anxious on their lord's account because he had fallen from his horse at the blow, quickly carried him away in their arms. Hereward went away and that very day withdrew his men into the Isle of Ely, where he was now received with the greatest respect by the abbot and monks of the place.[27]

A BLIND, IRON-FINGERED MURDERER (C. 1115)

An Anglo-Norman chronicler, the twelfth-century monk Orderic Vitalis, tells us how the first-born child of King David of Scotland and Countess Judith, his wife, "was cruelly murdered by the iron fingers of a certain wretched clerk."[28] Orderic records that

This man was punished for an appalling crime which he had committed in Norway by having his eyes put out and his hands and feet cut off.... Afterwards Earl David took him into his care in England for the love of God, and provided him and his small daughter with food and clothing. Using the iron fingers with which he was fitted, being maimed, he cruelly stabbed his benefactor's two-year-old son, while pretending to caress him, and so at the prompting of the devil he suddenly tore out the bowels of the suckling in his nurse's arms.... The murderer was bound to the tails of four wild horses, and torn to pieces by them, as a terrible warning to evil-doers.[29]

Unjustly Convicted, Bricstan Is
Miraculously Freed (1115 or 1116)

Orderic records another interesting case. It comes from a letter from bishop Hervey of Ely which gives an unusually full account of the trial, punishment and divine vindication of a man who was unjustly charged with theft, usury, and failure to surrender treasure-trove to the king.[30] Treasure-trove consists of coins, bullion, or gold or silver articles discovered hidden in the earth and for which no owner can be found. In England, the king had a right to all treasure-trove; concealing it was an indictable offense.

This is some of what the bishop, who clearly believed Bricstan was innocent, wrote:

> A certain man named Bricstan lived in an estate of our church, in a village called Chatteris.... Believing that he was at peace with all men and without a single enemy, he was inspired by divine grace ... to seek to be bound by the rule of St. Benedict and clothed in the habit [of a monk].
> But, sad to relate, ... a certain minister of King Henry, who was more particularly a servant of the devil with wolf-like fangs, appeared on the scene.... His name was Robert and he was nicknamed "Malarteis," from the Latin meaning "ill-doer"....
> [Robert] said to us: "Know that this man, Bricstan, is a thief, who has seized the king's money by larceny and hidden it, and is trying to take the habit to escape judgment and punishment for his crime, not for any other kind of salvation. For he found hidden treasure, and by secretly stealing from it has become a usurer....
> Therefore I have been sent here to you at the king's command, and I forbid you to receive him into your community." We, therefore, hearing the king's prohibition and fearing to incur his wrath, refused to receive the man among us.[31]

Bricstan was then sent to the shire court, presided over by the royal justice Ralph Basset. The court condemned Bricstan, even though his wife had volunteered to carry the hot iron to support his oath that he was telling the whole truth. Bricstan was then cast into prison in London. He languished there for five months but never ceased praying for deliverance. At last his prayers were answered. One night, says the good bishop,

> St. Benedict and St. Etheldreda, with her sister St. Sexburga, appeared to the supplicant.... The venerable Benedict placed his hand on the ring fetters and broke them on both sides.... When he had pulled them off he tossed them aside almost contemptuously and struck the beam which supported the room above the dungeon with such violence that he made a great crack in it.[32]

The guards were sleeping in the room above. The saint's blow jolted them awake. Terrified and fearing that their prisoner had escaped, they rushed down to his cell. There they found the doors undamaged and still locked. Upon entering the cell, when "they saw that the man they had thrown into fetters was freed, they marveled greatly." They immediately reported this event to the queen, who sent Ralph Basset to investigate. The justice reported that there had been no witchcraft and that a miracle had indeed occurred. So, "rejoicing and weeping," Basset escorted Bricstan to meet the queen and her barons.[33]

ENTRAPMENT BY A MATRON (C. 1170S?)

Ada de Morville was the mother of Hugh de Morville, one of the knights who murdered archbishop Thomas Becket in 1170. At the time of the incident described below (it
is not clear precisely when it occurred), Ada was still an attractive woman. She also had
a reputation for being licentious and treacherous. The following lawsuit explains why:

> [Ada], so it is said, was ardently in love with a young man called Litulf, who
> rejected adultery. She asked by some extraordinary female trickery that, with drawn
> sword, he should bring her horse forward, as if playing a game.
>
> As he did this, she in the language of the country [Norman French, spoken by the
> upper classes in England], exclaimed to her husband who was in front of her: "Hugh
> de Morville, beware, beware, beware. Litulf has drawn his sword."
>
> Therefore the innocent young man was [tried and] condemned to death, boiled in
> hot water and underwent martyrdom as if he had stretched out his hand to spill the
> blood of his lord.[34]

A FATAL DISPUTE OVER ONE PENNY (EARLY 1170S)

The case of Ailward, a peasant at the king's manor of Westoning, has a conclusion similar to that of the case of Thomas of Elderfield, discussed earlier. It also has
two very unique features.[35]

First, Ailward was baptized on Whitsun (Pentecost) evening. According to local
folklore, this made him immune either from sinking in water or being burned by fire. As
a result, if he were ever put to the ordeal by cold water, he would surely be proved guilty
because he would float. On the other hand, the ordeal by hot iron would prove him innocent beyond the shadow of any doubt because he would not be burned. The second
unique feature was that St. Thomas Becket miraculously came to Ailward's assistance, if
only very belatedly and at the end of a very painful process. The story is as follows:

A neighbor owed Ailward one penny (see Appendix II on the difficulty of establishing what a medieval penny was worth) but refused to pay up, claiming that he did
not have the money. At first, Ailward was not very demanding. On a certain feast day,
however, he asked his neighbor to pay him a half-penny so he could buy some ale. If
the neighbor did this, Ailward said, he would forget about the remaining half-penny.
This generous offer was refused. Ailward must have had a little money in his pocket,
though, because he went to the local tavern and promptly got drunk. He then broke
into the neighbor's house and confiscated a whetstone, a gimlet and some gloves as security for the one penny debt.

The neighbor's children witnessed the break-in and ran to tell their father. He
chased Ailward, grabbed the whetstone from him and hurled it at Ailward's head,

> thus breaking whetstone on his head and his head with the whetstone. Drawing also
> the sharp knife that he was carrying, he pierced [Ailward's] arm, got the better of
> him and took the miserable man in fetters as a thief, robber, and burglar to the
> house into which he had broken....[36]

A crowd quickly gathered. The general overseer of the manor, Fulk the reeve, appeared on the scene, too. He came up with a creative if illegal idea:

> Since the theft of goods worth one penny does not justify mutilation, [Fulk] sug-
> gested augmenting the importance of the theft by pretending that more goods had
> been stolen. This was done and beside the fettered man was placed a package con-
> taining hides, wool, linen cloth, a garment, and a ... pruning knife.[37]

Ailward and all these goods were brought before the sheriff. His case was sus-
pended for a month but was taken up again at a meeting of judges in a nearby town.
Ailward testified that he had taken only the whetstone, gimlet and gloves as security
for the unpaid debt. He asked for trial by battle or by hot iron. Fulk, however, had
been bribed by the gift of an ox. Accordingly, it was decided that in view of Ailward's
baptism on Whitsun eve, he should undergo the ordeal of cold water: since he would
not sink, he would certainly be found guilty.

After spending another month in prison, Ailward was sent to this ordeal. As
expected, he floated and was immediately led away for punishment. Before "a not incon-
siderable crowd of people," he was mutilated: Fulk and the neighbor put out Ailward's
eyes and castrated him. Ailward was so devoted to St. Thomas, however, that he was
eventually made whole again — but his new testicles were tiny and one of his eyes was
not its former color but was jet black.

ANOTHER HISTORICAL OUTLAW:
EUSTACHE THE MONK (1170–1217)

A manuscript of 1284 describes the adventures of Eustache the Monk. These are
loosely based on the life of a real person, Eustache Busquet, who lived from about 1170
to 1284.[38] This is his story:

Originally trained in France as a knight, Eustache later learned seamanship, per-
haps in Italy. At the age of about 20 he became a monk at a Benedictine abbey in
Boulogne and stayed there until his father was murdered by a local landowner named
Hainfrois de Heresinghen. Eustache went to the count of Boulogne to demand justice.
The count decided that this dispute had to be settled through trial by battle.

Because Hainfrois was an old man of about 60 and Eustache was a monk, the combatants were authorized to hire champions to fight for them. Eustache's champion was
killed. Even though this proved that Hainfrois had been in the right, when the count
left Boulogne in 1203 to join the French king's expedition to reconquer lands in Normandy held by the English, the count made Eustache his seneschal. When the count
came back home the next year, however, Hainfrois falsely accused Eustache of financial mismanagement. To escape what he feared would be an unfair trial, Eustache took
refuge in the forest. The count thereupon declared him an outlaw and burned his fields.

With no other means of support, Eustache remained an outlaw from 1204 to 1205.
Later, putting his nautical skills to good use, he turned pirate and entered into King
John's service. He did so well at this new calling that, as a reward for capturing the

island of Sark, John gave him lands in Norfolk. Eustache's star continued to rise. By 1209 he was an English ambassador to the count of Boulogne. Three years later he was in London, helping the count negotiate a charter of allegiance with John.

Fearing treachery for some reason, Eustache then returned to France, where he switched sides and joined the forces of King Philip. When the English barons rebelled against John in 1214, Eustache supplied them with weapons; in retaliation, John seized his lands in Norfolk. In 1216, Eustache and a French fleet of 800 ships delivered King Louis to the Isle of Thanet to support the barons. After returning to France, Eustache was en route back to England in 1217 to help Louis when his ship was attacked and captured by four English ships. Taken prisoner, Eustache was beheaded immediately.

The manuscript itself runs to 2,307 verses. Here we will cite only the story of how Eustache burned the mills of the count of Boulogne and was outlawed as a result:

> One day Eustache came upon two mills which the count had built just outside the city of Boulogne. While his men stayed back he found a miller in one of the mills. He threatened to cut off the poor man's head unless he accepted to go at once to the city, where they were celebrating Simon of Boulogne's wedding feast.
>
> The miller was instructed as follows: "When you get there, you shall say that Eustache the Monk has come to enlighten them, for they don't have enough light to see what they are eating. I'm going to set fire to the count's two mills so that they'll have two nice, bright candles to light up their festivities."
>
> The miller set off. As instructed, he gave the monk's message to the count. The count leapt up from the table and had great difficulty shouting instructions: "Eustache the Monk ... everyone ... after him!" The mayor and the provost both jumped up too and in no time had the alarm bell ringing to signal Eustache's banishment as an outlaw. When Eustache heard the bell ringing, he began his flight. The count's men began the chase but couldn't catch up with him.[39]

LOW-LIFE PARIS (C. 1205–1210)

The French priest Jacques de Vitry was the greatest preacher of his time. Ordained in 1210, he later reminisced about the Paris of his student days:

> The city of Paris, like many others, drifted in the shadows enveloped in many crimes and perverted by innumerable abject [events].... Like a scabious she-goat and like a soft ewe, it corrupted many of the newcomers who flowed in from all parts with its ruinous example.... Simple fornication was held to be no sin. Everywhere, publicly, close to their brothels, prostitutes attracted the students who were walking by on the streets and squares of the city with immodest and aggressive invitations. And if there were some who refused to go [into the brothels], they called them sodomites, loudly and behind their backs.[40]

A FACE-SAVING SETTLEMENT: CHAMBERLAIN V HERBERT OF PATSLEY (1207)

According to the records of a court convened in Norfolk in the autumn of 1207 a man named Herbert of Patsley violently struck another Englishman, Drew Chamberlain, on the head with a bow.[41] This blow was so ferocious that Drew's skull broke open and his brains poured out. Still, Herbert, "not content" with this, then drew his knife and stabbed Drew in the heart, "so that he died."

The next year Drew's brother, John, appealed Herbert of the homicide (i.e., formally charged him with this crime). It was agreed that the dispute would be settled by a judicial duel. Both sides began to prepare for this event but Thomas of Ingoldisthorp, a local dignitary, intervened. He was an experienced man who had already served on several grand juries together with a Patsley kinsman and was apparently a friend of the Patsley family.

Thomas accepted responsibility for seeing that Herbert would be on his good behavior before the duel and would turn up for it at the appointed time and place. He also paid the 40 marks needed for a royal license to settle this issue. More importantly, however, thanks to Thomas a face-saving settlement was hammered out just before the trial by battle.

This agreement provided that within the next 40 days Herbert would start on a pilgrimage to Jerusalem and would serve God there for seven years, praying for the repose of Drew's soul. If Herbert returned home before the end of that period, he would be liable to execution as a convicted murderer. Thomas also undertook to finance the cost of one of Drew's relatives joining a religious order and to pay Drew's family 40 marks in installments. Eight local knights agreed to stand surety for these arrangements.

A "PERFECT" RAPE (THIRD QUARTER OF THE THIRTEENTH CENTURY)

The *Placita Corone* was a collection of cases which were either made up for purposes of instruction or were chosen because they provided useful precedents for procedures in royal courts. They sometimes included highly dramatized and memorable details which, from a legal point of view, were not only comprehensive but were also definitive. In other words, they showed students or prosecutors precisely what kind of information they would need to win a case of this kind. In this sense, because of its wealth of specific details the following case represents, according to Kim Phillips, a feminist scholar, a "perfect" crime of rape.[42] The context makes it clear that in this hypothetical case the rape victim was a virgin:

> Alice de C, who is here, appeals [charges] H de P, who is there, that whereas she was in the peace of God and in the peace of our lord the king, the day after the Annunciation of Our Lady in March, at the hour of *prime* [6 a.m.], in such a year from the coronation, in such a wood, or elsewhere: namely in such a place called N, where she went seeking her mare to carry her grain to be ground at the mill of A de C: there came this same H, who is there, feloniously as a felon and in premeditated attack, and called her vile names in that he called her, namely, whore, thief, and anything but her proper name, and said; "I have wanted you for a long time — and here you are!" and then he seized her, feloniously as a felon, and laid her down beneath an oak tree, tied her hands together with the cord of his yew bow; with his

left hand he held her so feloniously by the throat that she could no wise escape from him nor make a noise, and with his right hand he forced open her legs and thighs, and, by violence and against her free will, he raped her in such a way as to make a thorough job of it.[43]

SIR WILLIAM WALLACE (1305): DRAWN AND QUARTERED

In 1296, the English king Edward I invaded Scotland. He carted away many of its national treasures, including the famous Stone of Scone, on which every king of Scotland had been crowned.[44] The English occupation of Scotland infuriated Scottish separatists. A leader of these men was William Wallace, one of Scotland's greatest national heroes. He became an outlaw and a rebel both to avenge the death of his girl-friend, Marion Bradfute, who had been murdered by Sheriff Hazelrig of Lanark, and to drive the English out of Scotland. In 1297 he and a band of about thirty followers burned Lanark and killed the sheriff.

A long 10,877-line poem about this outlaw, entitled *The Acts and Deeds of Sir William Wallace*, was written between 1476 and 1478. It retains the unique syntax of the Middle Scots and gives us an idealized version of Wallace's deeds as an outlaw in the then-dense forests of Scotland. Like the fictional Robin Hood, he is depicted as an expert archer and deer-slayer but, unlike Robin, his own way of life in the woods was far from easy.

AN EXCERPT FROM THE ACTS AND DEEDS OF SIR WILLIAM WALLACE

> [Wallace] bore a large and well-equipped bow as well as arrows that were long and sharp. There was no man who could draw Wallace's bow.... He slew a great hart with one shot, and his men made preparations for fresh venison....
>
> Sometimes he had a great sufficiency within: now want, now has, now loss, now win, now happy, now sad, now blissful, now in torment. In haste, now hurt; now sorrowful, now healthy. Now faring well; now cold weather, now hot. Now moist, now drought, now changeable wind, now wet weather.[45]

Although Wallace's guerrilla war against the English lasted for only two years, the poem suggests that, quite literally, he cut a wide swath through his enemies:

> Whoever [Wallace and his men] met who owed fealty to England they slew immediately. They spared no one who was of English blood; such a one immediately met his death regardless of how valiant he was. They saved neither knight, squire, nor knave.... By virtue of war, they slew all from that party that could wield bow or spear. Some they slew through cunning, some through force, but Wallace thought they destroyed not half enough. They took silver and also gold that they found, and other good gear they casually took to hand. They cut throats and cast the bodies out of sight into caves, for they thought that best.

> At Blackfurd [in south-east Perthshire] as they prepared to pass, a squire came
> and with him four barons who were riding to Doune castle. Thinking Wallace and
> his men Englishmen, he tarried among them to hear the news. Wallace quickly
> swung his sword and struck upon the head with such great ire that he cut the neck
> asunder through bone and brain. The other four were soon taken and boldly
> stabbed to death before the Scots would stop. They took their horses and what of
> their gear they liked best, plundered [the bodies of the slain men] bare and cast
> them into the brook.[46]

Wallace was a bold fighter who succeeded in rallying the Scots. He defeated the
English at the Battle of Stirling Bridge in 1297. For this achievement he was knighted
and elected as guardian of the Kingdom of Scotland. The next year, however, the
English defeated him at the Battle of Falkirk. Wallace then resigned his office and
escaped to France in 1299. He returned to Scotland not long thereafter and became a
guerrilla leader again.

In 1305 he was betrayed by Ralph Rae, a fellow Scotsman who had been captured
by the English and released on condition that he find Wallace for them. Arrested near
Glasgow, Wallace was taken to London, where he was put on trial before a bench of
nobles in Westminster Hall.

A long indictment was read against him, accusing him of treason and other crimes.
Wallace was not allowed to defend himself. He did, however, manage to shout out that
he could not be guilty of treason because he had never sworn allegiance to the English
king. Nevertheless, the court's verdict was a foregone conclusion: death by drawing and
quartering. Here is how the English chronicler Matthew of Westminster describes Wallace's subsequent execution:

> He was hung in a noose, and afterwards let down half-living; next his genitals were
> cut off and his bowels torn out and burned in a fire; then, and not until then, his
> head was cut off and his trunk cut into four pieces.[47]

As grim warnings to other potential rebels, the four pieces of Wallace's body were
sent to four cities in England, where they were put on public display. His head was
impaled on a metal spike on London Bridge.[48]

ROBIN HOOD V THE "PROUD SHERIFF"
OF NOTTINGHAM (C. 1330S-1340S)

Derived from the Latin *gesta*, meaning "deeds" or "exploits," a gest is a story of
adventures and achievements. Unlike a ballad, which was sung, a gest was recited or
chanted by a minstrel.

Of the thirty-eight medieval accounts of the fictional outlaw Robin Hood, one of
the earliest is the 1,824-line work, *A Gest of Robyn Hod*. Not printed until about 1510,
it draws on earlier traditions and is set in the England of the 1330s and 1340s.[49] Robin's
adventures with the sheriff of Nottingham make good reading even today.

Westminster Hall, the only surviving part of the original Palace of Westminster, was built in 1097–1099 by King William II Rufus as an extension of Edward the Confessor's palace. First used as a banqueting hall, it was also the meeting place for the king's Great Council and, later, for some of the early Parliaments. For more than 700 years (from 1178 to 1882) this building housed the Courts of Justice. With its many shops and stalls selling wigs, pens, books and other necessities, Westminster Hall became a center of London legal life. It is now part of the House of Commons. In 2002, several hundred thousand people queued here to pay their respects to Queen Elizabeth, the late Queen Mother, as she lay in state.

AN EXCERPT FROM A GEST OF ROBYN HOD

Attend and listen, gentlemen, who are of freeborn blood. I shall tell you about a good yeoman, whose name was Robin Hood. While he was alive, he was a proud outlaw, and no outlaw was found who was as courteous....

Because Robin was free to roam in the forest under the green leaves, the proud sheriff of Nottingham was greatly vexed. Although the sheriff waited for Robin both day and night, he missed him and could not take his prey....

[Later, when Robin and his men] arrived in Nottingham, they walked through the streets and soon met up with the proud sheriff.... All at once Robin shot an arrow from his bow and hit the proud sheriff so that he fell still on the ground. And before he could get up and stand on his feet, Robin struck off his head with his bright sword. "Lie there, proud sheriff," Robin said, "badly may you end! No man could trust you while you were alive." Robin's men drew out their sharp swords, attacked the sheriff's men, and chased them out without delay.[50]

THE STATUTE OF WESTMINSTER
CREATES JUSTICES OF THE PEACE (1361):

The preamble of the Statute of Westminster first asks "What sort of Persons shall be Justices of the Peace, and what Authority shall they have." It then goes on to say:

That in every shire of England shall be assigned for the keeping of the peace one lord, and with him, three or four of the most worthy in the shire, with some learned in the law; and they shall have power to restrain the offenders, rioters, and all other barrators [i.e., those who bought or sold offices or preferment in church or state], and to pursue, take, and chastise them according to their trespass or offence; and to cause them to be imprisoned and duly punished according to the laws and customs of the realm....

and also to inform themselves and to inquire of all those who have been pillagers and robbers in the parts beyond the sea, and have now returned and go wandering and will not labour as they were wont to do in times past; and to take and arrest all those that they may find by indictment or by suspicion and to put them in prison....

and they are to punish [offenders] duly, to the intent that the people shall not be troubled or injured by such rioters and rebels, nor the peace endangered, nor merchants or others passing on the king's highway be disturbed....[51]

FRANÇOIS VILLON (D. AFTER 1463): A LIFE OF CRIMINAL EXCESS

Villon was one of the greatest French lyric poets and the one who most often found himself on the wrong side of the law. He spent a good bit of time in prison or in banishment from Paris.

Villon's first crime occurred in 1455. He had graduated from the faculty of arts at the University of Paris with a master of arts degree three years before. By virtue of this degree he was a junior member of the clergy. The lure of the roistering life of Paris was so great, however, that he stayed on there after graduating, though without any visible means of support, and in the process fell into bad company.

On 5 June 1455, while drinking with two friends (who were later hanged) at the cloisters of Saint-Benoît, Villon killed a priest, Philippe Sermoise, with a sword thrust. As a result, he was banished from the city. But because the priest, just before he died, publicly forgave Villon, the poet obtained a royal pardon in 1456 and returned to his beloved Paris.

He was soon involved in a theft of 500 gold coins from the Collège de Navarre and was banished again. He first drifted to Angers and then to Blois, where he was the house guest of another but far more powerful poet — Charles, duke of Orléans. Villon earned another prison sentence during his stay there but it was remitted in 1457, thanks to a general amnesty proclaimed on the birth of Charles' daughter.

Villon then continued his wanderings throughout France. Imprisoned again in 1461 in Meung-sur-Loire, he was freed because of another amnesty — King Louis XI happened to be passing through the region. In 1462 he was arrested for robbery and was held at the Châtelet in Paris. Released later that year, he was in jail once more in 1463 — for taking part in a street brawl. The authorities decided that this was the last straw: Villon was condemned to be *pendu et étranglé* (hanged and strangled).

His luck held, however, and in 1463 the Parlement granted his appeal that the death sentence be commuted to banishment from Paris for 10 years. At this point Villon disappears from history. His ribald poems, however, are still with us today. They vividly depict the excesses and tribulations of the life of the French underclass in fifteenth century Paris.

Villon could poke fun at himself and others. He jokes to the reader:

> I am François, a man without hope
> Born in Paris not far from Pontoise,
> And with a six-foot length of hemp rope,
> My neck will know the weight of my ass.[52]

One of Villon's jailers, a man named Garnier, held a very low opinion of Villon personally and of his chances in winning any appeal. As we have seen, Villon did appeal and managed to escape the noose. He teases Garnier:

> What think you now of my appeals,
> Garnier? Was that mere vanity?...
> Was that a time to hold my peace?...
>
> Thought you that 'twixt my head and heel
> Was not enough philosophy
> To find the words for: "I appeal!"?
> Aye, aye, there was, I certify;
> My wits are scarce, but not awry.
> What, in full court, I heard that voice:
> "Thou shall be hang'd!" pray testify,
> Was that a time to hold my peace?

[Villon now addresses the prince who granted his appeal.]

> Prince, if the pip [Garnier] had hush'd my cry,
> I'd be today in Clotaire's [one of his friends] place,
> Strung in the meadows like a spy:
> Was that a time to hold my peace?[53]

Villon had numerous flings with *filles de joie*. One of his favorites was a girl named Macee. She was from Orléans. Macee eagerly made love with Villon but one night when he was asleep she stole his money belt and vanished. He never managed to track her down but he got a lasting revenge in verse:

> And as for little Macee
> From Orléans, who took my money belt,
> May her penalty be heavy
> For she's a rotten scum.[54]

Many of Villon's criminal acquaintances came to a bad end. He pays an ironic tribute to them in the opening stanza of his famous *Ballade des Pendus* (*Ballad of the Hanged Men*):

Brother humans who live on after us,
Harden not your hearts against us,
For if you can pity us, poor devils,
God will pardon you the sooner.
You see us hanging here—five, six –
We who have overindulged our flesh,
Our flesh which is now shredded and rotten
While we, the bones, can only turn to dust.
Let no one laugh at our sad plight,
But pray to God that he forgive us all.[55]

SIR THOMAS MALORY (D. 1471): A "KNIGHT-PRISONER" WRITES ONE OF THE WORLD'S GREAT ROMANCES

Sir Thomas Malory of Newbold Revel, Warwickshire, was a violent, lawless English knight who spent most of the last 20 years of his life in jail. There he wrote *Le Morte d'Arthur* (*The Death of Arthur*), the last medieval English work based on "the matter of Britain," i.e., the body of accounts and romances dealing with the legendary King Arthur. Malory's epic narrative and his simple but moving language have made this work an indispensable companion for all later versions of the legend, including T.H. White's well-loved modern classic, *The Once and Future King* (1958), and Frederick Loewe and Alan Jay Lerner's musical *Camelot* (1960).[56]

Incarcerated in London by 1452, Malory recorded that his book "was drawyn by a knyght presoner, Sir Thomas Malleorre, that God sende hym good recover. Amen." His first brush with the law occurred in 1443, when he was charged with wounding and imprisoning one Thomas Smith and stealing his goods.[57] This charge fell through and Malory was subsequently elected as a member of Parliament for Warwickshire and also served on tax commissions for that county. Civil war was brewing in England, however, and this conflict appeared to trigger a fundamental change in Malory's behavior.

On 4 January 1450, Malory and 26 other armed men laid an ambush for the duke of Buckingham in the woods near Newbold Revel. On 23 May of the same year, Malory was accused of raping Joan Smith at Coventry. The charge was not simply abduction or elopement, but rape in the modern sense: *cum ea carnaliter concubuit* ("he carnally lay with her").

Malory continued his depredations. By using threats, he extorted money from two residents of Monks Kirby on 31 May 1450. On 6 August 1450, he raped Joan Smith again and stole £40 of goods from her husband. Twenty-five days later he extorted money from a third resident of Monks Kirby. A warrant was issued for Malory's arrest on 15 March 1451, but a few weeks later he and his accomplices stole seven cows, two calves, 335 sheep, and a cart worth £22 at Cosford. The Duke of Buckingham formed a posse of sixty men and tried to catch Malory but failed to do so. Adding insult to injury, Malory then raided the duke's hunting lodge, killed his deer and did £500 worth of damage.

Finally arrested and imprisoned at Coleshill, our villain managed to escape by swimming across the moat at night. He then led a band of 100 men on two raids on Combe Abbey, assaulting the monks there and stealing a good deal of money. Malory was recaptured, however, and by January 1452 he was in prison in London, where he waited for eight years for a trial that was never held. Bailed out several times, on one occasion he and a comrade went to East Anglia to steal horses—an episode which landed Malory back in jail. By using swords, daggers and halberds, however, he escaped again, only to be recaptured and imprisoned in London once more.

The changing tides of civil war led to a new round of pardons and prison terms for Malory. Finally released in 1470, he died in London six months later, never having been tried for any of the crimes he had committed. His tombstone bore only the charitable description that he was *valens miles* ("a valiant knight") of Monks Kirby. Since then, his literary abilities have far eclipsed his criminal propensities.

The gallows. (François Villon. *Le Grand Testament. Codicille. Ballades. Petit Testament.* 1497. Fol. E8r. Bibliothèque nationale de France, Paris.)

10

Justice in Medieval Germany

Early Germanic laws have already been discussed in this book, as have the legal achievements of bishop Burchard of Worms. Medieval Germany as a whole, however, is arguably of more interest to the historian or political scientist than to the legal scholar. Many innovative legal developments were taking place in England and France during the Middle Ages. The legal institutions of Germany were fully adequate for their time and place but, in comparison with England and France, what was going on in Germany seems in retrospect to be mainly of local interest.[1]

It is true that German legal antiquarians have found much subject matter in the medieval era. Between 1971 and 1978 a five-volume dictionary of the history of German law was published. It runs to about 5,000 pages. A three-volume compilation covering German laws between about 920 and 1290 contains nearly 2,000 pages of legislation.[2] Nevertheless, from the nonspecialist's point of view, legal developments in medieval Germany were less noteworthy than those in England, France, Italy or even Spain.

SOME LEGAL HIGHLIGHTS

There were, however, two legal highlights which deserve our attention. The first of these were the *landfrieden* (peacekeeping associations) of the early twelfth century. These were German associations pledged under oath to enforce the peace and bring criminals to justice. A British expert on German history has praised these institutions as being "one of the most sophisticated of all medieval legal devices."[3]

The second highlight was the *Sachsenspiegel* (*Mirror of the Saxons*) of 1224–1225, the most important of the medieval compilations of German law. An early thirteenth-century document, the *Sachsenspiegel* was used by many towns in Germany and in Eastern Europe as a model for their own constitutions and statutes. Beginning in 1300, it was also produced with colorful illustrations which, visually, took precedence over the text itself and appealed to a much wider audience.

A BRIEF OVERVIEW OF MEDIEVAL GERMANY

Despite the relative paucity of legal highlights, developments in medieval Germany are still worth reviewing. By using a highly simplified overview which will doubtless appall professional historians, we can trace briefly some of events there during the thousand years of the Middle Ages.

Here we will refer to as "Germany" what contemporaries usually knew as "the empire," that is, the Holy Roman Empire — a term which was not invented until the fourteenth century. This empire lasted for more than 1,000 years: from Charlemagne's coronation as Holy Roman Emperor in 800 until the final renunciation of the imperial title in 1806. The Holy Roman Empire embraced a diverse collection of lands in western and central Europe. Administered first by Frankish and then by German kings, it was fragmented into a disparate congregation of lands and political systems traditionally known as *Alamannia*.[4]

After the Roman Empire in the West came to an end in 476, the Franks were not politically united. They did, however, share a common language, a common culture and similar laws. These qualities enabled them to expand to the east. King Clovis and his successors brought much of Germany under Frankish control and gave the local people a law code based on both Frankish traditions and on local customs.

The emperor Charlemagne (742–814) greatly extended Frankish power by conquering the Lombard kingdom in Italy, subduing the Saxons, annexing Bavaria, and fighting campaigns in Spain and Hungary. The net result was that with only a few exceptions — Britain, southern Italy and part of Spain — he forged most of Western Europe into a single superstate, at least temporarily. Law played an important role in this process. For example, Charlemagne issued stern royal ordinances — the *Capitulatio de partibus Saxoniae* (*Capitulary for the Saxon Regions*) and the *Capitulare Saxonicum* (*Capitulary for the Saxons*) — in c. 785 and in 797, respectively. Their purpose was to force the Saxons to submit to the Franks and accept Christianity.

Charlemagne himself did not attempt to unify Germany. Instead, he left each region under the control of the counts and bishops he appointed. However, after the death in 840 of Louis the Pious, Charlemagne's sole surviving son and his successor, three of Louis' sons vied for the throne. Under the terms of the Treaty of Verdun (843), they agreed to split up the empire into three parts. The western section (France) went to Charles II the Bald; the eastern section (Germany) to Louis II the German; and the central section (which included the northern half of Italy) to Lothar I, who also inherited the title of emperor.

Louis II the German (804–876) extended his sway over the whole of Germany. Under his reign, the German peoples had, for the first time, a ruler whose authority was coterminous to their own lands. Louis encouraged the use of the German language and the development of German literature. The Gospels were translated into Germanic dialects and a start was made at writing Germanic poetry. Louis was described by his contemporaries as being "the Frankish king of the eastern Carolingian kingdom." Gradually, however, this part of the kingdom was becoming "Germany," while the western part was becoming "France."

Modern historians of medieval German law believe that "the very concept of royal legislation was extremely restricted before the gradual revival of Roman jurisprudential ideas about imperial law-giving in the twelfth century."[5] Law was seen as a treasured gift, carefully handed down from the tribal past: it was not something to be tampered with lightly. The royal court was expected to settle civil cases on the basis of consultation, memory and discussion, not by making bold new laws. When criminal cases had to be decided, until the appearance of peace-keeping associations (the *Land-frieden*) at the end of the eleventh century, it was usually up to angry kinsmen to exact retribution for any wrongs done to their tribal group.[6]

The king was conceived of as the supreme magistrate of his domains; the royal court was the official guardian of justice and the seat of government.[7] To keep the fractious duchies in line, the king had to travel constantly. Wherever he went, his court went with him. It had jurisdiction over the regional nobles, which permitted him to collect the revenues from local justice and to exert some influence over it.

Since there was no system of assizes or lesser courts, the royal cases on record do not reflect the problems of the average man or woman but only those of the nobles and prelates who could obtain a hearing at the itinerant royal court. In one case, for example, when king Conrad I reigned in East Francia from 911–918, bishop Erchanbald of Eichstätt appeared in his court asking for royal protection for the bishop's see, which was apparently being jeopardized by another party. The king arranged a *placitum* (court meeting), attended by three bishops and nine counts, to review this matter. Similarly, the Otto the Great (German king from 936 and Holy Roman emperor from 962–973) used a public court and the judgments by his magistrates to redistribute rights and property by royal authority.

The kingdom of Germany occupied a dominant political position in Europe for much of three centuries — between about 900 to 1200 — but it was prone to violent oscillations between kingly solidarity and princely regionalism.[8] Otto the Great was hailed as emperor after his victory over the Magyars in 962 but it was the fate of Germany to remain more fragmented than united. Ironically, the more monarchy tried to assert itself, the more it offended powerful regional leaders. The net result was a weakened kingship.

As centralized control began to ebb, *de facto* military, political and economic power passed from the king to the regional dukes, the only men who could defend their own lands against hostile forces. Germany gradually became a loose federation of princes aligned under a purely elective monarchy.[9] Like France, though to a much lesser degree, imperial Germany was bound together by feudal ties of lordship and vassalage. However, the existence of powerful, semi-autonomous tribal duchies acted as a brake on the development of these classic feudal relationships.[10] Not surprisingly, these duchies were also strongholds of customary law.

During the Middle Ages, the three biggest German cities were Cologne, Augsburg, and Nuremberg. At various times, these had respective populations of 60,000, 40,000 and 30,000 people. Strict laws had to be passed to deal with the growing problem of able-bodied beggars in the cities. But it was thanks to the cities that Germans became the source of the later saying, "City air makes man free." Municipal legal jurisdictions extended to a city's limits; beyond that, the countryside was ruled, often harshly, by feudal, territorial or landed lords.

THE KAISERCHRONIK (C. 1150)

A long epic German poem of the twelfth century, the *Kaiserchronik* (*Chronicle of the Emperors*) was probably the work of an ecclesiastic in Regensburg. It gives a good snapshot of conditions in the countryside and the customary law in force there. We learn that a peasant is legally permitted to wear only black or gray clothes. Moreover,

> He is to spend six days at the plow. On Sunday he is to go to church, carrying his animal goad openly in his hand. If a sword is found on a peasant, he is to be tied up in the churchyard and flayed, hide and hair. If enemies threaten him, let him defend himself with a pitchfork.[11]

THE GROWTH OF LEGAL AUTONOMY (C. 1250)

Frederick I Barbarossa (1152–1190), Henry VI (1190–1197) and Frederick II (1212–1250) were universally recognized as the most powerful monarchs of Europe. The German duchies, however, still carried on relatively independently as separate areas of customary law. Regional aristocrats — dukes, margraves (German nobles corresponding in rank to a British marquess) and counts — enriched themselves at the expense of the king and the church and took over most of the rights of local government.

In 1152, Frederick I Barbarossa had issued a "land-peace ordinance" which tried to stop private wars and feuds. It offered imperial help in enforcing local laws against such violence. Nobles who broke the peace were supposed to surrender their lands to the emperor, who would then give them to more law-abiding counts.[12]

This well-meant if somewhat naive law appears to have had little effect. Frederick II's rupture with pope Innocent IV in 1245 and his own death five years later marked the end of the imperial system in Italy and left a power vacuum. As Kenneth Pennington, a legal historian, explains, "German political institutions fell into complete disarray after the death of Emperor Frederick II in 1250."[13] Thus by 1250 no effective central authority existed in the Holy Roman Empire. In its place were only endless petty feuds and disorders between the territorial princes. Regional legal autonomy was most strongly evident in Saxony and in Swabia.

THE GOLDEN BULL (1356)

The basic constitutional document of medieval Germany was known as the Golden Bull because of its pendant gold seal (*bulla*). It was promulgated in 1356 by the king of Bohemia, Charles IV, after he had been crowned emperor by the pope. Issued with the approval of the Diet, the assembly of German states, the Golden Bull endorsed and extended further the powers of the seven "great electors."

These secular and lay nobles were the archbishops of Mainz, Cologne, and Trier; the count palatine of the Rhine (a count palatine was a count of the Holy Roman Empire having imperial powers in his own domain); the king of Bohemia (Charles IV himself); the margrave of Brandenburg; and the duke of Saxony.

These seven electors were the only people permitted to vote for an emperor, who was elected by their votes. The Golden Bull also confirmed the sweeping legal powers of the electors, from which there was no appeal save to the Diet:

> We decree also that no count, baron, noble, vassal, burgrave [a man appointed to command a fortified town], knight, client, citizen, burgher, or other subject of the churches of Cologne, Mainz, or Trier, of whatever status, condition, or rank, shall be cited, haled, or summoned to any authority, except [by the electors]....
>
> We refuse to hear appeals based upon the authority of others over the subjects of these princes; if these princes are accused by their subjects of injustice, appeal shall lie to the imperial Diet, and shall be heard there and nowhere else....[14]

The electors were also the supreme advisory council on affairs of state. Plots or rebellion against them constituted high treason. The Golden Bull, however, did nothing to unify Germany. Indeed, as the British historian Lord Bryce (1838–1922) remarked wryly, the Golden Bull simply "codified anarchy and called it a constitution."[15] By the same token, this document has also been called the Magna Carta of German territorialism. It failed to address, let alone resolve, any of the major problems facing imperial Germany. These included the loss of crown lands, shortfalls in revenues, and the absence of a reliable army or a well-trained bureaucracy.

KEEPING THE PEACE (C. 1378)

The maintenance of law and order was not in the hands of the German king. There were no royal officials in Germany with powers similar to those of the English sheriffs or justices of the peace. Stepping into this breach, regional associations of cities and princely territories tried to keep the peace but without much effect. When Charles IV died in 1378, Germany had been effectively partitioned into a number of loosely defined territorial principalities.

Without the national focal point which a strong monarchy would have provided, German law — and, indeed, German culture as a whole — was regional and diverse. The country remained badly splintered until the Prussian chancellor Otto von Bismarck finally managed to unify it in 1871 as the German Empire.

THE LEGISTS
(FOURTEENTH AND FIFTEENTH CENTURIES)

A legist was a specialist in law, especially one trained in Roman law. As the administration of the territorial states became more complicated and more demanding, professional bodies of full-time legal councilors appeared. These men were legists usually trained in Italy or in the newly founded universities: Prague (1348), Vienna (1365), Heidelberg (1385), Rostock (1419) and Tübingen (1477). Well-tuned to the centralized, authoritarian aspects of Roman law, they worked hard and successfully to increase the powers of their territorial princes. The major exceptions were Saxony and Schleswig-Holstein, where customary law was too firmly entrenched to be displaced easily.

FEHMIC COURTS (FOURTEENTH CENTURY)

A fehmic court (*Fehmgericht*) was a medieval institution which originated in West-phalia.[16] In every county, the count's agent judged minor cases himself. Three times a year, however, the count would hold an "open assembly" (*offenes Ding*) for all his free men. Those who attended regularly came to be seen as the count's permanent repre-sentatives. By the thirteenth century, there were so many of them that their number had to be reduced. Each county was thereafter limited to having only two or three "seats of justice" (*Freistühlen*).

In the fourteenth century, the emperor had cases from all over Germany assigned to the fehmic courts in Westphalia and elsewhere. They thus became royal institutions. These courts held two kinds of sessions. The first was the *offenes Ding*, which judged minor crimes and property disputes. The second type was the "secret assembly" (*Stilld-ing*), at which only the judge, the aldermen and the parties to a case were admitted.

Probably because it was efficient, secret and severe, the "secret assembly" had entirely displaced the "open assembly" by 1500. These very qualities, however, also brought the fehmic courts into direct conflict with the territorial princes, who jealously guarded their own jurisdictions. The result was that by the end of the fifteenth cen-tury, the few fehmic courts that remained were found only in Westphalia.

GERMANY ADOPTS ROMAN LAW (1495)

In Germany, as we have seen, political fragmentation prevented the development of a uniform legal code. Such a code was needed because of the plethora of overlapping customary law jurisdictions. Although customary law had been adequate for settling dis-putes between individual tribesmen, a more broadly based law was necessary to keep the territorial peace. In belated recognition of this fact, during the reign of the emperor Maximilian I, Germany formally "received" (that is, adopted) Roman civil law in 1495.

This measure did not have any immediate or far-reaching practical consequences. It did, however, permit the establishment of an Imperial Court of Justice (*Reichskam-mergericht*), which became the final legal authority in Germany.[17] This tribunal con-sisted of two branches.

The first was the "learned bench," which was composed of legal scholars (*doctores in iure*). The second was the "noble bench," staffed by aristocrats and by experts in judicial procedures. The court's decisions were based on the *ius commune*. If one of the parties to a legal action requested it, the Imperial Court of Justice could consider local customary law, too, provided that it did not conflict with the *ius commune*.

Despite the obvious advantages of ending Germany's legal disarray, this newly revived Roman law was not at first greeted with universal applause. Indeed, opposition was inevitable: by displacing customary law, Roman law was striking at the roots of feudalized justice and thus at the feudal structure on which it was based. As hostility toward this new type law grew stronger, it trickled down through the social structure, to the extent that average folk in rural areas sometimes shouted the insult, "*Juristen böse Christen!*" (Lawyers are bad Christians!)[18]

Full recognition of the beneficial effects of "received" Roman law as the ultimate law of the land, and of a legal system staffed by professionals (*Juristenrecht*), had to wait until a later German jurist, Samuel Stryk (1640–1710), wrote a famous study entitled *Usus modernus Pandectarum* (roughly, *Practices of Roman Law Brought into Line with the Needs of the Times.*)[19] It was this Roman law which provided the intellectual underpinnings for the impressive work of German legal scholars in the nineteenth century.

Illustrative Cases and Laws

A CAPITULARY OF THE EMPEROR CHARLEMAGNE (802)

In 802, one of Charlemagne's capitularies became the foundation charter of the Holy Roman Empire. In it, he put a clear premium on the pursuit of justice. Here are some excerpts from the capitulary's first chapter:

> The most serene and most Christian emperor Charles did choose from among his nobles the most prudent and the wisest men — archbishops, as well as other bishops, and venerable abbots, and pious laymen — and did send them over his whole kingdom; and did grant through them, by means of all the following provisions, that men should live according to law and right.
>
> He did order them, moreover, that, where anything is contained in the law that is otherwise than according to right and justice, they should inquire into this most diligently and make it known to him; and he, God granting, hopes to better it....
>
> And let the messengers diligently investigate all cases where any man claims that injustice has been to him by any one.... Let them fully administer law and justice according to the will and to the fear of God. And if there should be any matter such that they themselves, with the counts of the province, could not better it and render justice with regard to it: without any ambiguity they shall refer it, together with their reports, to the emperor's court.[20]

GUNDHART V AN UNNAMED COUNT (C. 814)

The use or threat of force played an important role in medieval disputes in Germany. Here is a case in point:

A man named Gundhart was a retainer of Hraban, abbot of the German monastery of Fulda.[21] Gundhart, however, lived in fear for his life due to a potentially lethal feud with an unnamed count. Einhard, a powerful patron who had been Charlemagne's court scholar and his biographer, agreed to help Gundhart. He wrote to abbot Hraban on Gundhart's behalf.

Using technical legal terms signifying a formally declared state of hostility, Einhard explained in his letter to the abbot that Gundhart was terrified because somehow he had aroused the *ira* (anger) and *inimicia* (hostility) of the count. This was indeed a serious problem because in the near future Gundhart was required to accompany the count on a military expedition which the count was leading. He was afraid to do so, however, because of the *faidosus* (feud) which existed between them.

The text of the letter is not entirely clear but it suggests that when a feud had been formally declared, a limited use of violence was considered legitimate, or was at least tolerated, to resolve it. Gundhart, then, probably had good reason to worry about what the count or his men might do to him during the military expedition once they were beyond the protection of the monastery. The final outcome of this case is not recorded but given Einhard's great prestige it seems a reasonable guess that Gundhart managed to escape unharmed.

COUNT GERO V THE SAXON WALDO (979)

An important judicial duty of the German royal court was to oversee trial by combat.[22] In 979, Count Gero of Alsleben was arrested on a charge, the details of which are now lost, brought by a Saxon named Waldo. The case came to Otto II's court, where it was decided that it had to be resolved by a judicial duel.

Both Gero and Waldo were doughty warriors. During the fight, Gero gave Waldo two deep cuts on the neck. Nevertheless, despite these severe wounds Waldo was still able to deliver so heavy a blow to Gero's head that the count was, by his own later admission, too dizzy to continue to fight. Since Gero could not go on, Waldo left the site and disarmed. But as he rested and refreshed himself after the duel, he suddenly dropped down dead from his neck wounds.

Despite Waldo's death, the judges decided that it was *Gero* who had lost the duel and who was therefore the guilty party. As a result, on the emperor's orders Gero was decapitated at sundown, despite protests by a duke and a count that the charges against him were too thin to warrant the death penalty. This remarkable outcome was long remembered in medieval Germany; indeed, many years later the count's innocence was still being asserted.

LANDFRIEDEN (1103)

Landfrieden were German associations pledged under oath to enforce the peace and bring criminals to justice. At a time when peace could not be established simply by a king's edict, the peace-keeping declarations of the *Landfrieden* functioned as a kind of royal legislation by specifying church-approved truces, as well as the scope and duration of regional conflicts.[23]

A cleric at Augsburg has left us a vivid description of these peace-keeping associations in 1103 and of the crimes which fell within their purview. This example is important because under its terms the three ducal dynasties of southern Germany, which had been feuding since 1079, agreed to lay down their arms. Participants swore this oath:

> No one shall violently enter anyone's house nor devastate it by fire, and no one shall kidnap anyone for money, nor wound, nor beat up nor kill them. And if anyone

should do this, then he shall lose his eyes or a hand. If someone protects him, he shall suffer the same penalty. If he flees to a castle, it shall be destroyed in a three-day siege by those who have sworn to the peace....

If anyone steals to the value of five shillings or more, he shall lose his eyes or a hand. If he commits a robbery worth less than five shillings, he shall have his hair torn from his head and shall be scourged and shall restore the theft. And if he should commit this sort of robbery or theft three times, then he shall lose his eyes or a hand. If your enemy should run into you on the open road, you may injure him if you can. If he flees into a house or some other building, he must remain unharmed.[24]

THE SACHSENSPIEGEL (1224–1225)

The most important codification of Saxon customary law, the *Sachsenspiegel* (*Mirror of the Saxons*), was used by many German and east European cities as a legislative model. This was a sizeable text, consisting of four "books" (chapters) with a total of 321 legal entries. It was written in Latin by the knight Eike von Repgowe, who tried to bring order to the confusing range of regional, municipal, feudal and seigniorial laws then in use in Saxony. His purpose was, as he explains in the prologue, to help the Saxons themselves see what they otherwise could not see as a whole — "like a woman looking at her face in the mirror."[25]

Eike succeeded so well that, translated into German, his *Sachsenspiegel* soon became the foundation on which many German judges based their findings. He opposed any standardization of the law, emphasizing instead that the German peoples had inherited valuable laws from their ancestors. There was thus no need to change them. In his view, the diversity of laws among the German tribes was a good thing, being hallowed by the passage of time. Eike's own literary style was verbose and riddled with exceptions but the numerous illustrations used in post-1300 manuscripts made the *Sachsenspiegel* a much more user-friendly book.[26]

The *Sachsenspiegel* generated numerous glosses and gave rise to a number of lesser works.[27] It consisted of two sections. The first, known as *Landrecht* (territorial law), included procedures for what we would call constitutional law, criminal law and civil law. These procedures applied to Austria, Bavaria and other lands. The second section, *Lehnrecht*, consisted of feudal regulations for the management of fiefs.

TWO EXCERPTS FROM THE SACHSENSPIEGEL

At the beginning of his book, Eike gives the reader a calm, even-handed interpretation of the contentious "Doctrine of the Two Swords," i.e., the proper relationship between church and state:

> The Pope has been given the spiritual sword, the Emperor the secular one.... Any force which opposes the Pope beyond his power to subdue it with spiritual law should be brought under control by the Emperor with the secular law. The spiritual power should also support the efforts of worldly justice when it is needed.[28]

The second excerpt from the *Sachsenspiegel* explains an interesting custom known as the "morning gift":

> Now hear what each man of knightly birth is permitted to give his wife as a morning gift [that is, on the morning after their wedding night]. In the morning when he goes to table with her before breakfast, he may without prior oath or agreement of the heirs give her a servant boy or girl who is not yet of age, also a house and enclosed garden, and grazing stock.
>
> [A this point there are a number of detailed provisions discussing what happens to this property if the husband should die before the wife.]
>
> All those not of knightly birth may give their wives as a morning gift nothing more than the best horse or livestock they own.[29]

"THE HOLE": THE DUNGEONS OF NUREMBERG (1332)

In about 1050, the German emperor Henry III, duke of Saxony and Bavaria, built a castle in southern Germany at what is now Nuremberg. A settlement grew up around the castle; in 1219 the city was granted its first charter. It soon gained full independence as a free imperial city. By the latter half of the thirteenth century, Nuremberg had become a thriving commercial center of artisans and aristocrats. But as its prosperity and population increased, so did the crime rate. Thus it was that when Nuremberg built a new city hall in 1332, it was designed to serve both as a law court and as a prison.

The city hall was built on the site of a former Cistercian bakery. Because of the danger of flooding from the Pegnitz River, the ground level of the new building had to be raised by about 3 meters. The bakery, which had been located on the old ground floor, now became a cellar which housed the notorious Nuremberg dungeons and torture chamber. These were known as "the Hole" and are preserved today as one of the city's museums.[30]

A criminal's progress toward the Hole was marked with "crime calls." When a crime was committed, the victim or the victim's family had to raise the "court cry"—"Murder!" or "Catch thief!" Neighbors then helped to capture the accused and bind him. If a murder had been committed, the *Handhafte*, that is, a hand or finger of the murdered person, was tied to the criminal's back. If goods had been stolen, they were tied to him instead. He was then taken to the judge at the city hall, accompanied by the appropriate crime calls.

Even prominent citizens could find themselves in the Hole. The most famous felon was the sculptor Veit Stoss, who was jailed because he had forged a borrower's note. He received a pardon, however, so instead of being executed he was only branded.

MACHIAVELLI ON CONDITIONS IN GERMANY (LATE FIFTEENTH CENTURY)

In *The Prince*, Machiavelli gives us a vivid picture of the remarkable legal and military autonomy of Germany's city-states towards the end of the Middle Ages:

The cities of Germany are wholly independent, they control only limited territory, and they obey the emperor only when they want to. They fear neither him nor any neighboring power, because they are so fortified that everyone knows it would be a protracted, difficult operation to reduce them. This is because they all have excellent moats and walls; they have adequate artillery; they always lay in public stocks of drink, food, and fuel to last a year.

Over and above this, every German city, making provision for the common people without public loss, always keeps a year's supply of the wherewithal for them to work at those trades which give them their livelihood and are the sinews of the city itself. Military exercises always enjoy a high standing, and they have many laws and institutions providing for them.[31]

11

Where Medieval Law and Politics Meet

In the medieval world as well as in our own, law and politics were closely related. Anthony Musson, a modern scholar, has noted that "The very expression of royal authority and administration in terms of law meant that law became inextricably linked with politics and a key aspect of royal government."[1] This is especially evident in the evolution of England's Parliament.

By the beginning of the fourteenth century, it had been agreed that old laws could be changed or canceled, and new ones created, by parliamentary actions. Parliament was also the place where the king's dealings with his nobles and common subjects could be adjusted. The medievalist G.L. Harriss concludes that "Such work was largely judicial in character, though with a strong political flavour."[2] In addition to the rise of Parliament, certain medieval cases also show politics at play. Three good examples here are Scotland's "Great Cause" (1291–1292), the dispute between Robert of Naples and Henry VII (1312–1314), and the two trials of Joan of Arc (1431 and 1455–1456).

THE RISE OF PARLIAMENT (1258)

On this subject it can be difficult to separate fact from fiction. We need to remember that, according to the legal historian Paul Brand,

> Parliamentary history has been a great battlefield over the centuries for historians, lawyers and politicians. It has been the subject of more than the usual quantities of mythology and wishful thinking. Some of it has survived in [standard reference works] but needs to be corrected.[3]

What seems clear is that "parliament" meant a meeting where men parleyed, or spoke. Other terms — for example, "colloquium" or "council" — were used at first. The word "parliament" appears in its Latin, French or English forms (the three official languages of the day) on the English plea rolls in 1237 and in the 1240s. Formal recognition of the term, however, dates from 1258, when King Henry III agreed to accept the Provisions of Oxford.

The provisions were a plan for governmental reform, forced upon Henry III by

159

Parliament meeting in Westminster in the fifteenth century. (MS. Harley 1319, fol. 57. By permission of the British Library.)

his barons. In return, the barons held out their promise of financial support. No official text of the provisions exists. The unofficial texts containing the decisions of the provisions do not refer to the meeting where they were approved as a "parliament." Instead, they reflect agreement that regular meetings of parliament should be held three times a year to consult on further reforms and on the desired attendance at these meetings.[4]

At the heart of each early parliament was a meeting of the king's council: *concilium regis in parliamento* (the king's council in parliament), which was composed of royal administrators and judges, major magnates, and bishops and other royal advisers. Later, Parliament would consist of the House of Lords and the House of Commons. Technically speaking, there were and still are three houses of parliament: the sovereign (the king or queen); the Lords Spiritual and Temporal, i.e., the ecclesiastical and lay magnates who formed the House of Lords; and the House of Commons, consisting of knights and landowners from the counties and freemen representing the cities and boroughs.

During the parliamentary process, the king tried to gain his subjects' support on the foreign or domestic issues of the day. His subjects, in return, got the chance to express their own views on these issues. The British legal historian Maitland found that the work of the early parliaments fell into five categories:

(1) the discussion of affairs of state, more especially foreign affairs; (2) legislation; (3) taxation or supply; (4) the audience of petitions; and (5) judicial business, the determination of causes criminal and civil.[5]

Judicial business included the difficult cases sent forward from the lower courts (the common law courts) to the king's council in parliament. These could involve technical points of law which were without any legal precedent and were thus difficult to adjudicate. Cases of treason were sometimes tried at a parliament, too, as were cases against cities — for example, against Salisbury and Winchester, which had let a hostage from Bayonne escape.[6] Parliament also dealt with petitions submitted by men and women who were having legal problems which the lower courts could not satisfactorily resolve. Moreover, it legislated general answers to difficulties and responded to demands for taxation.

The king was the final judicial authority of medieval England. Parliament was his high court, i.e., the supreme court of England. Only his writ could summon it. The first written reference to the role of Parliament as the high court appears in 1384, when the chancellor, Michael de la Pole, referred to "parliament which is the high court of the realm."[7] Even earlier, however, the legal treatise known as *Fleta* (1290) had outlined Parliament's judicial duties. Ironically, *Fleta* was probably written by a semi-professional lawyer who was then behind bars in London's Fleet Prison. Although this man had a very unsavory background (he had been an *agent provocateur* in the mass trials of the Jews in 1278), he did know about the function of Parliament as a high court. This is what he tells us:

> The king also has his court in his council in his parliaments ... [where] are terminated doubts concerning judgements, and new remedies are devised for new wrongs which have arisen, and justice is done to each one according to his deserts.[8]

The issues which parliaments took up varied according to their urgency but virtually all of them had a direct or indirect political component. This is not surprising because Parliament itself was a highly politicized institution. Thanks to his battery of sheriffs, justices and financial advisors, the king would have been able to handle most of England's judicial and fiscal matters on his own. Only Parliament, however, could give him both the financial backing he needed to pay for his policies and the moral (political) support which was essential if these policies were going to be put into practice. Indeed, after Richard II was deposed in 1399, the medieval parliament was increasingly driven by politics.

Over the subsequent years, Parliament's overall importance waxed and waned but it was always a bully pulpit for contending factions and always the court of last resort on contentious national issues. It became the venue for state trials and, by extension, the place where the heirs of those convicted at such trials could seek a reversal of their fortunes. It also judged disputes between lords when these quarrels threatened the peace.[9]

In 1485, Henry Tudor, earl of Richmond, seized the throne and Parliament acknowledged him as Henry VII, "our new sovereign lord." His era would mark the end of England's medieval parliament. The next Tudor, Henry VIII (1509–1547), would use the Reformation Parliament, which first met in 1529, to assert his own sovereign authority as "King-in-Parliament."

SCOTLAND'S "GREAT CAUSE"(1291–1292)

Edward I wanted to rule Scotland as well as England. When the Scottish throne became vacant, he chose John of Balliol (not the same man who founded Oxford's Balliol College) as the rightful heir. Edward I claimed the right to hear cases on appeal from Scotland for failure of justice. The Scots rebelled, setting in motion 250 years of bloody strife, including a Scottish alliance with France, England's archenemy. The "Great Cause" is a case which offers a good mixture of medieval law and politics.

DEATH OF THE MAID OF NORWAY (1290)

The story begins in 1286, when the king of Scotland, Alexander III, fell off his horse onto the sands of Kinghorn (on the Firth of Forth, north of Edinburgh) and broke his neck. After his death, Scotland was ruled by a collection of lay magnates and bishops who were known as the Guardians of Scotland. The crown was supposed to pass to Alexander's granddaughter, Margaret, called the Maid of Norway because she was the daughter of Eric II, king of Norway. III. Young Margaret, however, died in 1290.

Before Margaret's death, in the Treaty of Birgham the Guardians had agreed with Edward I that she should marry his heir, Edward of Caernarvon. Under this plan, Scotland would have been preserved as a separate kingdom. With Margaret gone, 13 candidates, most of them Scottish magnates, rapidly came forward to claim the throne. Because it was not at all clear who the rightful heir was, Scotland trembled on the brink of civil war. The Scots therefore asked Edward I to pick the next king.

EDWARD'S MACHINATIONS

Edward I saw this as a way to get control of Scotland.[10] While Margaret was still alive, he had never tried to resurrect the old, shaky English claims over Scotland. Indeed, he had made a treaty with Scotland on a basis of equality, not as its feudal overlord. Now, as a first step to power, under feudal law he required "seisin" of Scotland. In this context, seisin was the act of an overlord taking possession of land held of him on a temporary basis, pending surrender of it to an heir.

Through an elaborate legal strategy involving several steps, Edward I became the legal possessor of Scotland. In his capacity as one of the contenders for the throne, he arranged for the royal castles in Scotland to be handed over to him by their keepers. These castles were then formally entrusted to him by the other contenders, who wanted to stay on good terms with the English king because he was their feudal lord.

However, the Guardians declined to commit themselves on the thorny issue of who should be the next king. On behalf of the Guardians, bishop Wishart of Glasgow told Edward I that in light of the fact there was presently no Scottish king, the Guardians could not surrender Scottish sovereignty to the English: only the rightful king of Scotland could do so.

JOHN OF BALLIOL'S WORDS OF HOMAGE

Lauded by his own countrymen later on as the "English Justinian," Edward I was not an expert in legal matters but he was willing to take advice from those around him. Because pope Boniface and the Guardians did not accept him as the feudal lord of Scotland, he realized he had to find some authoritative legal backing for his claim. He therefore ordered that the monastic and the royal archives be carefully searched. University professors learned in Roman law were summoned to Parliament.

A key piece of evidence was found at last: a copy of John of Balliol's words of homage and of feudal recognition to Edward I. Because these words had been formally drawn up by a notary public, they constituted firm and not-readily controvertible evidence. The medievalist Anthony Musson offers a revealing comment:

> It appears that the particular notary had to alter the document because he had omitted an acknowledgement by Balliol that the English king should direct the affairs of Scotland. It did not matter, however, whether this statement was the truth, since the document itself provided the legal evidence ... and so was more important than pure historical fact.[11]

THE SCOTS REBEL

Two men — John of Balliol and Robert the Bruce — had emerged as the leading contenders for the throne. In 1292, on the advice of his legal experts, Edward I chose Balliol as king. But then he overreached himself on two counts. First, Edward I tried to exercise overlordship by insisting on jurisdiction over legal cases on appeal from Scotland for failure of justice. Second, he called on Balliol and his soldiers to perform military service for him in France.

These steps were too much for the Scots. They rebelled and made an alliance with France (the Auld Alliance) in 1295, in effect declaring war on England. Edward I, however, proved to be the stronger party. He forced Balliol to submit to him in 1296. Balliol's crown was stripped from him and his royal insignia torn off his coat. The English seized two much-revered Scottish relics — the Stone of Scone (also known as the Stone of Destiny), on which Scottish kings were inaugurated, and the Black Rood of St. Margaret (believed to be a fragment of the True Cross) — and carted them away to Westminster.

The Scots, however, were not ones to give up easily. William Wallace led a revolt against the English in 1297, for which, as we have seen, he was drawn and quartered in 1305. Then Robert the Bruce, the grandson of Balliol's co-contender for the throne, staged another uprising. In 1307, Edward I, by this time known as the "Hammer of the Scots," went north again to crush the revolt but he died en route. Subjugating Scotland had become so important to him that he decreed he should never be buried until the Scots had been brought to heel. Today, visitors to Westminster Abbey will see that he still lies there in a simple lead casket.

ROBERT OF NAPLES V HENRY VII (1312–1314)

Let us turn now to a more technical and more difficult legal subject: summary judicial procedure, as seen in the dispute between Robert of Naples and the Holy Roman emperor Henry VII. This is, according to the legal scholar Kenneth Pennington,

> an event of the first rank in legal history…. The dispute is a splendid example of politics and legal theory swirling about and creating unpredictable turbulence…. [I]t introduced the ideas of due process and the relationship of natural law [law derived from nature, not made by humans] into a wider political arena and into the *ius commune*.[12]

Henry VII was the German king from 1308 until his death in 1313. One of his goals was to revive the ancient imperial policy of Rome by assuming power in Italy. At that time, France controlled both the papacy and southern Italy; the northern Italian towns were autonomous. Pope Clement V and others welcomed Henry VII's policy as a way to end the factional struggles in Italy between the rival factions of the Guelphs and the Ghibellines. At first, however, this policy only precipitated further fighting between the two camps.

Once relative peace was restored, Henry VII was crowned Holy Roman emperor by the pope in Rome in 1312. The next year he declared war against king Robert of Naples, who opposed his policies in Italy. Pope Clement V initially backed Henry VII but under French pressure to support king Robert, he changed sides and in 1313 threatened Henry VII with excommunication. As Henry VII was getting ready to attack Robert, however, he died of a fever. With the throne vacant, Clement V assumed rule and soon gave Robert the title of imperial vicar in Italy.

The political struggle between Henry VII and Robert generated many *concilia* (detailed analyses of the law relevant to specific cases) and a fair amount of papal and imperial legislation as well. The most important document produced in the process was Clement V's "constitution," known from its first word as *Saepe* ("Often"), which was issued sometime between 1312 and 1314.[13]

In it, the pope clarified the rules of summary judicial procedure, which had been unclear in the clause, *simpliciter et de plano, ac sine strepitu et figura iudicii* ("simply and plainly, without clamor and the [normal] forms of procedure"). This clause was a common legal phrase and one which Henry VII had used in his letters condemning Robert.

Summary judicial procedure was a much-abbreviated form of procedure for use in canon law courts. It cut down on the number of statutes and the length of time it took to reach a definitive decision. *Saepe* was important because it gave an authoritative explanation of what summary justice meant in procedural terms, that is, where the balance should be struck between the right to a fair trial and the desirability of speed in resolving disputes.[14] According to the famous canon law scholar Stephan Kuttner, *Saepe* was "the most important single piece of medieval legislation in the history of summary judicial procedure."[15]

THE TWO TRIALS OF JOAN OF ARC: (1431 AND 1455–1456)

Joan of Arc, a peasant girl known as *La Pucelle* (the Maid), is the national heroine of France. She was canonized in 1920. A festival in her honor is held every year on the second Sunday in May. Acting under what she believed was heavenly guidance, she led the French army to victory at Orléans and thus defeated an English attempt to conquer France during the Hundred Years War.

Captured by the French allies of the English, Joan was tried in 1431 before bishop Cauchon of Beauvais and Jean Lemaître, vice-inquisitor of France; was condemned to death as a relapsed heretic; and was burned at the stake. This first trial is now known as the condemnation trial. Twenty-five years later, a second trial (the nullification trial), ordered by pope Calixtus III, revoked and annulled the sentence of 1431.

To understand these two events, we need to review Joan's era and her story in some detail. It is a tragedy but is not without a flicker of humor. As the Irish comic dramatist George Bernard Shaw (1856–1950) put it in the preface to his splendid play, *Saint Joan*, she was "judicially burnt for what we call unwomanly and insufferable presumption ... there were only two opinions of her. One was that she was miraculous: the other was that she was unbearable."[16]

THE HUNDRED YEARS WAR

The phrase "Hundred Years War" is a nineteenth-century coinage which covers a series of struggles which went on intermittently between England and France for 116 years. This conflict began in 1337 when Philip VI, the French king, seized the extensive lands in southwestern France held by the English king, Edward III, as in his capacity as duke of Gascony. This prompted Edward III to intervene militarily. The struggle ended in 1453 when the French, aided by their new *culverins* (cannons) and *batons-à-feu* (primitive handguns), routed the English army at Bordeaux.

During the Hundred Years War, the two sides were not evenly matched. The English had more combat experience than the French because of their constant skirmishes with the Scots. The English were also better disciplined, better paid and better armed. They were experts in the use of the powerful Welsh longbow, which at close range would drive an iron arrowhead through the oak door of a church. At long range, as the battle of Crécy proved in 1346, the arrow-storms unleashed by English archers could darken the sky, killing or wounding French knights and driving their horses mad. Many decades later, by the time Joan of Arc appeared on the scene, there seemed to be a good chance that England would win the Hundred Years War.

An incident during the Hundred Years War: Guillaume Sans, lord of Pommiers, is executed in Bordeaux on the orders of Thomas Felton, the city's English seneschal. (Chroniques de Froissart, No. 2644. Bibliothèque nationale de France, Paris.)

The other side of the coin was that as a nation France was much richer, more populous and much stronger militarily than England. The thirteenth-century English chronicler Matthew Paris was obliged to admit that "The king of France is the king of all earthly kings."[17] The heavy cavalry of France was the best in the world and its elegant, well-mounted knights were available "in great abundance." Moreover, France only had to defend its own territory; the English had to invade and occupy it.

The English strategy was initially based on bloody *chavauchées* (intense raids of limited duration). Calais was the only French city permanently occupied by the English. When the English and their Burgundian allies tried to conquer and hold down not only Normandy but also all the rest of France, this proved to be a financially ruinous policy.[18] Joan of Arc's successful campaign to have the dauphin Charles ("dauphin" means heir apparent) crowned as king of France in 1429 greatly boosted French morale. The 1435 defection of Philip the Good of Burgundy weakened the English. In retrospect, it is not surprising that France ultimately won the Hundred Years War.

ENTER JOAN OF ARC

The Hundred Years War had been rumbling on for 77 years when Joan was born at Domrémy in eastern France in about 1412. The daughter of a tenant farmer, she came to believe that she was instructed by the heavenly voices of St. Michael, St. Catherine and St. Margaret to drive the English and their French allies (the Burgundians) out of the Valois kingdom of France.[19]

At that time the crown of France was claimed by two men. One was the dauphin Charles, son of the late Charles VI, the Valois king. But five years after Charles VI's death, the dauphin had still not been crowned. Reims, where French kings were traditionally crowned, was in the hands of his enemies. As long as he remained uncrowned, his claim to the throne of France was shaky. The other claimant was the Lancastrian English king Henry VI, who under the terms of the Treaty of Troyes (1420) had a good claim to the French throne. His forces, allied with those of the duke of Burgundy, Philip the Good, already held much of northern France.

Domrémy, Joan's village, lay on the border between the lands held by the English and Burgundians, on one hand, and by the dauphin's forces, on the other. The inhabitants of this village were forced to abandon their homes because of Burgundian threats. Inspired by her voices, at the age of sixteen Joan made her way to the nearest fort which was loyal to the dauphin and asked permission to join his forces. Rebuffed, she went back home but tried again the next year. This time she was successful. Dressed in men's clothes and accompanied by French men-at-arms, she traveled for eleven days across enemy-held territory before reaching the dauphin at the city of Chinon.

The dauphin decided to grant her an audience but concealed himself among his courtiers to see if she would be able to identify him, sight unseen. She did so at once and told him that she wanted to fight the English and that she would have him crowned at Reims. Because of the ever-present fear of heresy, the dauphin first had her interrogated for three weeks by church authorities friendly to his cause. She promised them that she would give proof of her mission at Orléans, which the English and their allies had been besieging for months by means of a ring of fortifications. With no other hope in sight, the churchmen recommended that the dauphin see what Joan could do.

Thanks in large part to the inspiration they derived from Joan's own heroism (she was wounded but quickly returned to the thick of battle), the dauphin's troops liberated Orléans. After other victories, Reims opened its gates to the Maid and her forces. The dauphin was crowned there in 1429 as Charles VII.

The war with the English still ground on. In 1430, when Joan learned that Compiège was besieged she led her forces there to protect the inhabitants. While fighting a rear-guard action to protect French troops who were forced to withdraw from Compiège by crossing a river on a bridge of boats, Joan was captured by the duke of Burgundy's forces. According to an eyewitness account,

> The Maid ... performed a great feat and took much pain to save her company from loss, staying behind like a chief and like the most valiant member of the flock.... An archer, a stiff and very harsh man, angry that a woman of whom one had heard so much should have surpassed so many valiant men ... laid hold of her from the side by her cloth-of-gold doublet and pulled her from her horse flat upon the ground.[20]

When news of her capture reached Paris, the University of Paris, which was on the English side, insisted that she be tried as a heretic and asked the duke to turn her over either to the chief inquisitor or to the bishop of Beauvais, Pierre Cauchon, in whose diocese she had been captured. By January 1431 she was in the bishop's hands and was facing trial before a church court.

Illustrative Cases and Laws

THE FIRST TRIAL OF JOAN OF ARC (1431)

The legal proceedings culminating in Joan's conviction stretched out for more than four months — from 9 January to 30 May 1431. A complete, authentic report of this trial, conducted by bishop Cauchon, has fortunately survived. Seventy charges were drawn up against her. Of the many remarkable passages which could be cited here, here is one in which Joan testifies about the voices she heard. According to the record of the trial,

> She further confessed that when she was thirteen years old she had a voice from God to aid her in self-discipline. And the first time she was greatly afraid. And this voice came about noon in summer in her father's garden, and she had fasted the day before. And she heard the voice on her right hand toward the church, and she seldom heard it without a light. Which light usually comes from the same side as the voice, but it is usually great. And when she came to France she often heard this voice....
>
> She also said that the voice seemed to her worthy, and she believes it was sent by God; and after she had heard it three times she knew it was the voice of an angel. She said that it always guarded her well, and that she knew it well.... She also said that her voice had told her that she should raise the siege of Orléans.... She also said that when she entered [the dauphin's] chamber she knew him from the rest by the revelation of her voice. And she told her king [the dauphin] that she wished to go making war against the English....[21]

HER CONVICTION AND EXECUTION (1431)

In May 1431, Bishop Cauchon and his assistants threatened Joan with torture to get certain points of her testimony clarified. But since she assured them that she would later deny anything she had said under torture, they decided, by a vote of 10 to 3, that torture would be useless. As a result, the University of Paris ordered that she be turned over to the secular arm (the lay authorities) because only they, and not the church, could execute a condemned heretic.

Now, for the first time, her courage ebbed: she signed a document abjuring her acts. She was then condemned to "perpetual imprisonment." Shortly thereafter, however, she told her inquisitors that her voices had criticized her for "treason" in signing such a document:

> God has expressed through St. Catherine and St. Margaret His great sorrow at the strong treason to which I consented in abjuring and making a revocation to save my life, and said that I was damning myself to save my life.[22]

The cleric who recorded these words wrote in the margin of his manuscript: "A deadly reply."[23] Her judges and 39 assessors unanimously agreed she was a relapsed heretic who must be handed over to the secular arm. This was immediately done. At the age of 19, Joan was burned at the stake in the public marketplace at Rouen on 30 May 1341. Her ashes were collected and thrown into the Seine to make sure that no remains survived and could be venerated later on as relics. To the very end, Joan maintained that her voices came from God and were not delusions.

Friar Isambart de La Pierre, who had found in a nearby church a cross which he held up before Joan's eyes as she died, reports that Joan,

> Being already surrounded by the flame, never ceased up to the end to proclaim and profess in a high voice the holy name of Jesus, imploring and invoking without cease the aid of the saints of paradise, and again, which is more, while surrendering her spirit and letting her head fall, she uttered the name of Jesus as a sign that she was fervent in the faith of God.[24]

THE SECOND TRIAL OF JOAN OF ARC (1455–1456)

The Hundred Years War continued. In 1449, the inhabitants of Rouen revolted against the English and Charles VII entered the city unopposed. To show his gratitude to the people of Rouen, he decided to order an inquiry into Joan's trial. After time-consuming and thorough preparations, the new trial opened in Paris in 1455 and ended in Rouen in 1456. The court interviewed 115 witnesses, many of whom had been involved in the first trial. Twenty-seven articles were drawn up and served as the basis for the whole process of interrogation.[25] Because these articles give such a good insight into Joan's case, they are listed in Appendix IV.

The second trial found that the condemnation trial had been procedurally flawed from the outset. It was thereupon nullified: Joan, now dead for twenty-five years, was fully acquitted. Edward Peters, a student of the inquisition, tells us why the first trial fell so far short of late medieval judicial standards.[26] There had been grave irregularities in this case from its very onset. Joan had been put into an English military prison run by men, rather than into an ecclesiastical prison guarded by women. The interrogation procedures used and the evidence amassed against her were much below par. Thanks to a serious procedural flaw, Joan was condemned solely on the basis of her interrogation in Rouen: nothing was ever actually *proven* against her.[27]

There were many other abuses of medieval justice, too. A common sentence for reformed heretics was three years in jail, followed by release. By denying her any legal or other counsel and then sentencing her to death as a relapsed heretic, the authorities were being unjustly harsh. Another serious irregularity was that, in his haste to get rid of Joan, bishop Cauchon failed to obtain the necessary sentence of a secular court. He simply sent her from his own ecclesiastical court directly to the stake.

Finally, the reasons for her conviction and subsequent surrender to the secular arm were visibly political, not religious. Although political considerations were in fact involved in the second trial, too, (both Charles VII and the pope wanted to clear Joan's name) the trial itself carefully followed well-established inquisitorial procedures. If these had been adhered to in the first trial, Joan might well have escaped the stake.

At least she was finally vindicated. She has been called "the most phenomenal and attractive personage of the Hundred Years War on either side."[28] Joan of Arc remains for most French citizens today — and for many foreigners, as well — a dramatic symbol of personal courage and integrity.

12

Modern Legacies of Medieval Justice

Taken in their entirety, the Middle Ages have left a strong imprint on modern life. Medieval legacies include many of the urban, village and rural landscapes of Western Europe; the historical conflicts and compromises between faith and reason; the relationships between church and state; the setting up and maintenance of mercantile and civic standards through crafts guilds and merchant guilds; and the establishment of universities at Bologna, Oxford, Cambridge, Paris and other cities. This last achievement, dating from about 1200, must surely rank as one of the West's most important and most long-lasting contributions to world culture. There can be little argument with the conclusion of Jacques Verger, a French medievalist, who concludes that the university was "one of the greatest creations of the Middle Ages."[1]

A number of lesser items can be added to the above list. These include the artistic and literary sensitivities stimulated by the paintings, illustrations, music and writings of the Middle Ages; the physical format of the book itself (the *codex*, or manuscript book, gradually replaced the earlier rolls); the novel; some types of men's clothing (the shirt and trousers replaced the Roman toga); the generally supportive social attitudes toward the poor; and the organized public responses to epidemics and other calamities.[2]

MEDIEVAL JUSTICE: ITS LEGACIES

Medieval justice, for its part, has left us some impressive legal legacies. In this last chapter we will look at a number of them, beginning with the jurisprudential ideas of St. Augustine of Hippo (354–430), which dominated medieval thought until the midthirteenth century, and ending with continental Western Europe's widespread acceptance of the *ordo iudiciarius* (Romano-canonical) procedure by the end of the Middle Ages. A final section will attempt a summing-up of medieval justice as a whole.

ST. AUGUSTINE ON THE ROLE OF LAW

The most important legacy of medieval justice is the conviction that the true purpose of law is to prevent or at least restrain the arbitrary exercise of power by secular or religious authorities. During the Middle Ages, this belief owed a great debt to St. Augustine, who described law as operating on three interrelated levels.

For Augustine, the first and most exalted level was the divine law. This sprang directly from God's will and from God's reason. It was eternal and was binding on all human beings at all times. The second level of law was the unchangeable natural law, that is, the divine law as manifest in nature and as understood, however imperfectly, by individual men and women. The third and lowest level was positive law or man-made law — for example, the Roman law of the Christian Roman Empire, as practiced during St. Augustine's own lifetime.

According to Augustine, positive law (and, by extension, customary law as well) necessarily varied from one country to another and from one time to another. Provided that they did not conflict with natural law and divine law, these positive and customary laws had to be obeyed. The reason was that all men and women, including kings, were subject to them.

When secular rulers obeyed these laws, they could be said to be ruling legitimately. By thus giving legitimacy to the idea of secular power, Augustine laid the groundwork for the concept of government under law. His implicit line of thought — that no man, not even the king — is above the law would later be embedded in Magna Carta and would become a cornerstone of Western constitutional thought.

LAW SCHOOLS

The role of law and lawyers in modern life, especially in such highly litigious societies as the United States, hardly needs to be emphasized. In medieval times, law school was not the only way to become a lawyer, but since the Middle Ages it has been one of the best ways. By the late 1180s or early 1190s Oxford had began to offer students a university education in canon law and in Roman law. By 1274, a recognizable legal profession was taking shape in England.[3]

Even earlier on the continent, in the late eleventh century the teacher Irnerius reportedly drew crowds of students to the law school at the University of Bologna. As the demand for trained judges and administrators increased, Bologna became the center of legal scholarship in Europe. It produced the famous "four doctors" of the medieval study of Roman law: Bulgarus, Martinus Gosia, Hugo da Porta Ravennate, and Jacobus de Voragine. Legend has it that all four of them studied under Irnerius, but this was probably only true of Bulgarus. He later became an advisor to the Holy Roman emperor Frederick I Barbarossa and wrote De regulis iuris (On the Rules of Law), the earliest legal gloss from the law school at Bologna.

Civil law and canon law were at first the only courses of study offered at Bologna, which tended to attract men employed in these fields. The typical student was a mature man who already had a job with church or state. Since facilities for students were very limited, these legal students banded together and formed voluntary associations (guilds) to protect their interests. Such guilds became models for the universities themselves to follow.

Many graduates of medieval law schools eventually became royal judges. By the end of the Middle Ages, there was widespread agreement that a man who was not

Ceiling of the Divinity School, Bodleian Library, University of Oxford (1488). This is one of the masterpieces of Late Gothic architecture. The intricately sculpted stonework of its fan-vaulted ceiling, with its 455 carved bosses featuring the coats of arms of subscribers, reflects Oxford's importance both to the king and to the church as the place where some of the realm's most illustrious lawyers and prelates were trained.

"learned in the law" was not qualified to be a senior judge. Learned judges gradually displaced their unlearned feudal counterparts. Rigorous legal training thus became a necessity and helped improve the administration of justice.

There were at least three other legacies of medieval law schools:

First, from the twelfth century on, more attention was paid to legal documents and other forms of written evidence because these were important and familiar tools for the newly minted lawyers.

Second, these schools endorsed the practice of English courts that "the burden of proof falls on him who brings the action," that is, on the plaintiff.[4] In other words, the defendant no longer had to prove that he was in the right. This was a step toward our own doctrine that a person is presumed innocent until proven guilty.

Finally, the *ius commune*— the common law of continental Europe — attracted some of the finest minds of the Middle Ages. The Italian scholar Manlio Bellomo concludes that "for the keenest intellects and the greatest jurists in Europe of the Middle Ages, the *ius commune* turned out to be a formidable unifying force. It lay at the center of the law and was the symbol of its unity."[5]

It affected England, too. The legal historian Richard Helmholz has pointed out that while the *ius commune* did not exert the same degree of influence on English law as it did on continental European law,

> It was the *ius commune* that long governed practice in the courts of the church, the Admiralty, the universities, and (to some extent) the courts of equity. Chancery procedure, for example, drew heavily upon it.... These courts, which stood outside the

common law, exercised an extensive jurisdiction over the economic and social lives of virtually all men and women in the land, and they affected the overall shape of the English legal system in myriad ways.[6]

COMMON LAW AND THE ROYAL COURTS

The common law of England has evolved into the legal systems now found in the United States and in many member states of the British Commonwealth of Nations. Royal courts were an important legacy, too. It has been noted that by 1400 these courts were being run

> on bureaucratic lines by legal experts and they were already organized into a judicial hierarchy. It was also the royal courts which did most to create a single common law for the whole of England between c. 1150 and c. 1250.... A national legal system, a national law, and the capacity to legislate on a national basis are all important constituent elements of the modern European state. In England, at least, they are part of the medieval legacy of that state.[7]

THE JURY SYSTEM

The jury existed in Anglo-Saxon England in the form of the jury of presentment (indictment). The Normans had a similar institution in France before they conquered England in 1066. Indeed, the Normans may have used the jury system in post-conquest England more readily precisely because it was an indigenous institution with which they were already familiar. Only in the century after the Assize of Clarendon (1166), however, did the jury emerge as a common and frequently used element in the English system.[8]

As mentioned earlier, this assize called on twelve men of the hundred and four men of each township to testify under oath "that they will tell the truth, whether in their hundred or in their vill there is any man who is accused or said to be a robber or a murderer." There was at first, however, no trial by jury. It was not until the thirteenth century that most of the nonrational modes of trial (i.e., most of the ordeals) were replaced by the jury trial, which subsequently became the approved form of trial in both criminal and civil cases at common law in England. (Trial by battle, however, continued in some criminal trials through the thirteenth century and beyond.)

The jury was not unique to England: juries had existed in various forms in northern France, the Netherlands, parts of Germany and in Sweden. It was the English jury, however, which has left the most important mark on the Constitution of the United States. The Sixth Amendment, for example, provides that "In all criminal prosecutions, the accused shall enjoy the right to a speedy and public trial, by an impartial jury of the state and district wherein the crime shall have been committed." The Seventh Amendment states that "In suits at common law, where the value in controversy shall exceed twenty dollars, the right of trial by jury shall be preserved...."

Moreover, in 1967 the U.S. Supreme Court held that the Fourteenth Amendment guarantees the right to a jury in state criminal trials. This amendment, which dates from 1868, states that

> No state shall make or enforce any law which shall abridge the privileges or immunities of citizens of the United States; nor shall any state deprive any person of life, liberty, or property, without due process of law; nor deny to any person within its jurisdiction the equal protection of the laws.

The Supreme Court has ruled that a jury trial is a constitutional right in all criminal cases in which the penalty may exceed six months' imprisonment. Most American courts use jury trials for a variety of civil cases. In the United Kingdom today, however, jury trials are used only in civil cases where community attitudes are very important — in defamation and fraud cases, for example.

LEGISLATIVE ASSEMBLIES

Another medieval legacy springs from the willingness of European rulers to consult with the different "estates" (interest groups) of their kingdoms to get approval for important royal policies, such as the imposition of taxes. Magna Carta (1215) was the first clear statement of the principle that those who have to pay taxes also have the right to approve them. This consultative practice gave rise to both the French Parlement, which functioned from 1250 until it was abolished in 1789 by the French Revolution, and the English Parliament, which dates from 1258 and is still very much in business.

JUSTICES OF THE PEACE

As we have seen, in 1361 the Statute of Westminster created a new office known as the justice of the peace. These justices, also known as lay magistrates, continue to play an important role in the Anglo-American legal system today.

In the United Kingdom today, more than 30,000 justices of the peace dispense justice at the grassroots level of the court system. (See Appendix VI for a description of justices of the peace in the United Kingdom.) In the United States, a magistrates' court is sometimes referred to as a police court. Such courts are empowered to adjudicate minor criminal or civil cases. In certain jurisdictions, they can also administer oaths, authenticate documents, issue arrest warrants, deal with traffic violations, hold inquests, and officiate at marriages.

INTERNATIONAL LAW

International law has been heavily influenced by the work of medieval canon lawyers. As James Brundage, a specialist in canon law, reports,

While most legal systems [in the Middle Ages] were confined to a particular region or locality, canon law emerged as a working and quite often effective international law. With relatively few exceptions, the same canonical rules applied to everyone in Latin Christendom.[9]

A good case in point is Giovanni de Legnano (ca. 1320–1383), a canonist of the fourteenth century. He studied law at Bologna and wrote *Tractatus de bello, de repre-salis et de duello* (*A treatise on war, reprisals, and the duel*) and *De pace* (*On Peace*). These influential works laid the foundations on which later legal thinkers, most notably the Dutchman Hugo Grotius (1583–1645), began to build the structure of modern international law. Giovanni da Legnano himself dealt not only with war and peace but also with the legal basis for relationships between sovereigns. He was thus a pathfinder of international public law.[10]

THE INVESTIGATIVE AUTHORITY OF THE JUDGE

With the notable exception of England (which relied on juries), by the end of the Middle Ages most Western European countries had adopted the *ordo iudiciarius* (Romano-canonical) procedure of the church courts.[11] This gave considerable "inqui-sitional" (investigative) authority to the judge. It is the bedrock on which modern civil law procedure rests.

MEDIEVAL JUSTICE: A SUMMING-UP

Medieval men and women had no doubt that they lived "under the gaze of and in the company of angels."[12] If so, rushing in where these angels would certainly fear to tread, we can try to distill all of the foregoing into three main points.

NO SHORTAGE OF MEDIEVAL JUSTICE

The first point is that despite the common perception today that there was no such thing as "medieval justice," the reverse is true: there in fact was a great deal of medieval justice. If we remember the late fourteenth-century French jurist Jean Boutillier's definition that "Justice ... is a constant and perpetual determination to give everyone his due," we can conclude that most, if not all, medieval people did indeed get what they were due —*according to the prevailing customs and the secular and ecclesiastical laws of their times.*

The fact that not all these customs and laws meet with our approval today is beside the point. What is important is that, as stated early in this book, they were widely accepted at the time and their potency cannot be denied. It should be added that there were sometimes miscarriages of justice. But, in general, when legal errors were detected and when it was important to correct them for political or religious reasons, they could indeed be corrected by the legal system — even, if necessary, posthumously, as in the case of Joan of Arc.

Restraining Political Power

The second point is that, as stated earlier, the most important legacy of medieval justice is the conviction that the ultimate function of law is to prevent or at least restrain the arbitrary exercise of political power by royal, civil or church authorities. The great principle of Magna Carta is that no man, not even the king, is above the law.

Case Studies

The third point is that the case studies cited here are only a tiny fraction of those which still exist. Taken collectively, they are an excellent way — perhaps, in fact, the very best way — to get to know medieval men and women on an intimate basis, warts and all. Over all these centuries, the minor triumphs and tragedies of the individuals participating in the legal system come across to us loud and clear, filtered only by the formal language of the courtroom and its law clerks. We are indeed fortunate that so many of these legal records have survived.

Selected Chronology

430	Death of St. Augustine of Hippo, whose jurisprudential ideas dominated medieval thought until the mid-thirteenth century.
438	*Codex Theodosianus* (Theodosian Code) preserves and transmits Roman law.
476	Barbarian chieftain Odoacer deposes Romulus Augustulus, the last Roman emperor, thus bringing to an end the Roman Empire in Western Europe.
c. 500	A raider who kidnaps a slave is denounced as a "werewolf."
502	Burgundian king Gundobad condemns perjury by Burgundian oath-takers.
c. 507–510	*Pactus Legis Salicae* (Salic Law), one of the most important barbarian laws, is written down during the reign of Clovis I, king of the Franks.
mid–520s	Clermont formulary shows how to file a claim for restitution.
527–533	Byzantine emperor Justinian I revises and codifies Roman law through his *Institutiones* (a basic textbook); *Codex Iustianus* (a collection of past legislation); *Digesta* (a summary of previous authorities); and the *Novellae* (collection of recent legislation).
Late sixth century	St. Gregory of Tours on oath taking and peacekeeping.
c. 605	First *dooms* (Anglo-Saxon laws), attributed to King Æthelbert of Kent, are drafted.
c. 692	Abbot Ermenoald loses his case, involving 1,500 pounds of oil and 100 barrels of good wine.
800	Charlemagne's coronation as emperor marks the beginning of the Holy Roman Empire, which will last more than 1,000 years.
802	A capitulary by Charlemagne becomes the foundation charter of the Holy Roman Empire.
806	Willibert is forced to transfer land for the repose of Waltolf's soul.
c. 814	The case of Gundhart v an unnamed count reveals the threat or use of force in medieval disputes.
828	King Pippin I settles a dispute over monastic rent in Aquitaine.
820s–830s	French documents describe the interlocking feudal ceremonies of vassalage, i.e., commendation and the oath of fealty.

179

843	Under the terms of the Treaty of Verdun, the Holy Roman Empire is divided into three parts.
c. 850	A pious forgery: the Pseudo-Isidorian Decretals, written to enhance the power of bishops and popes.
893	Welsh scholar Asser describes the personal involvement of king Alfred the Great in Anglo-Saxon justice.
c. 897	Anglo-Saxon thief Helmstan wins his case, thanks to his influential patron, Ealdorman Ordlaf.
Ninth century	A Carolingian capitulary (royal ordinance) is issued against sorcerers and witches.
966	Swans are already considered to be the property of the crown.
978	King Æthelred the Unræform tries to suppress counterfeiters.
979	Trial by combat: Count Gero v the Saxon Waldo.
c. 990	A resourceful abbot bribes the English king and queen to win his case.
c. 1015	Bishop Burchard's *Decretum*, covering the whole span of canon law, is a useful guidebook for the clergy. The section known as the *Corrector* lists the questions which priests are to put to women making their confessions.
1020	King Canute orders the Danes and English to abide by the laws they agreed on at Oxford.
1024–1025	Bishop Burchard's *Lex Familie Wormatiensis* (*Law of the Retainers of the Bishop of Worms*) tries to keep his dependents in line.
1064	French abbots prevent a battle between their monks.
1066	Normans conquer England.
1070	Pope Alexander II forbids use of the ordeal in the case of ecclesiastics.
1071–1071	Deeds of the outlaw-hero Hereward
1072	William the Conqueror establishes church courts in England, which use the Romanized canon law.
1084	Irnerius, "the lamp of the law," reportedly draws law students to Bologna.
1086	The *Anglo-Saxon Chronicle* analyzes William the Conqueror from a quasi-legal point of view.
1086	Domesday Book records all the properties in England.
1091	King William II Rufus orders that if a man wants to kill an enemy in Normandy, he must first give him fair warning by blowing a horn.
1098	Champions for two monasteries fight a judicial duel over ownership of a marsh.
c. 1100	A judicial battle is fought over mills along the Seine.
1103	A cleric at Augsburg explains the scope of Germany's *Landfrieden* (peace-keeping associations).
1108	King Henry I puts his personal stamp of approval on the four most important lay courts in England — the royal court, the shire court, the hundred court and the lord's court.
c. 1115	A blind, iron-fingered cleric murders a royal child.

1115 or 1116	Bricstan, unjustly punished, is miraculously freed and made whole.
1127	Trial by battle: Guy v Herman the Iron.
c. 1140	Gratian's *Decretum* marks the beginning of the classical period of canon law.
1150	A navigation code is established for the port of Arles.
1150	An epic poem, the *Kaiserchronik*, shows the role of customary law in the German countryside.
1158	Mabel de Francheville loses her lands when she loses in a case in the papal and the king's courts.
1164	In the Constitutions of Clarendon, king Henry II redefines the relations between church and state, sharply tilting the balance toward the king.
c. 1165	Roman law and canon law are fused in the *ordo iudiciarius*.
1166	In the Assize of Clarendon, Henry II establishes the jury of presentment, an institution which will eventually evolve into the grand jury, and gives sheriffs full responsibility for maintaining law and order in their respective counties.
1170	Murder in the cathedral: archbishop Thomas Becket is assassinated by four of Henry II's knights.
1170	Henry II arranges the inquest of sheriffs to uncover misconduct by them and other local officials.
1170(?)	Ada de Morville, a matron, causes the death of Litwulf, an innocent young man.
Early 1170s	A dispute over one penny leads to Ailward's mutilation and miraculous healing.
1170–1217	The historical outlaw Eustache the Monk.
1175	Beginnings of England's General Eyre (county visits by the king's itinerant judges).
1176	In the Assize of Northampton, Henry II divides England into six judicial circuits and sets up a possessory action (*mort d'ancestor*, or "death of an ancestor") so that an heir can get what is rightfully his.
1184	Pope Lucius III bans the Waldenses as an heretical sect. His decretal *Ad abolendum* directs lay authorities to cooperate with ecclesiastics to root out and punish all heretics. This decretal is considered the founding charter of the inquisition.
c. 1188	*Glanvill*, the first treatise on English common law, is finished.
1189	Limit of legal memory in England is the accession of King Richard I on 3 September 1189.
Late 1180s– early 1190s	Oxford offers students a university education in canon law and Roman law.
1199	Pope Innocent authorizes canon law judges to use force to extract information to determine a person's guilt or innocence. His decretal *Bergentis in senium* links heresy, for the first time, with the Roman doctrine of treason.

c. 1200	Royal writs are compiled in a register of writs.
1202	French king Philip II Augustus confiscates all the French fiefs of his vassal, king John of England, because John refuses to answer a feudal summons to Philip's court.
c. 1205–1210	Jacques de Vitry chronicles his student days in low-life Paris.
1207	A face-saving settlement: Chamberlain v Herbert of Patsley.
1207	In his decretal *Cum ex officii nostri*, pope Innocent III orders that heretics shall be punished severely.
1215	Canon 18 of the Fourth Lateran Council forbids clerics from participating in the ordeal, thus effectively ending it as a method of proof. The ordeal is gradually replaced by the threat of *peine forte et dure* (heavy and hard punishment).
1215	Magna Carta, known as the "Great Charter" of English liberties, is drafted by English ecclesiastical and lay magnates to make sure that King John acknowledges their customary feudal rights.
c. 1220–1250s	*Bracton*, the greatest legal treatise of the Middle Ages, is written.
1221	Defeated in a judicial duel, Thomas of Elderfield miraculously gets new testicles and new eyes, thanks to St. Wulfstan.
1224	In an edict for Lombardy (Germany), Frederick III orders that heretics "shall, on imperial authority, suffer death by fire."
1224–1225	The *Sachsenspiegel* (*Mirror of the Saxons*) codifies Saxon customary law.
1234	Pope Gregory IX's collection of laws, the *Liber Extra*, affirms two important concepts of canon law: exclusivity and textuality.
1244	French forces capture and demolish the castle of Montségur, forcing the Cathars to disperse.
1248	Highway robbery at the pass of Alton.
c. 1250	Growth of legal autonomy in Germany.
1252	Pope Innocent IV's bull (a solemn papal letter) *Ad extirpanda* authorizes the use of torture to wring confessions from heretics.
1254–1256	French legislation attempts to regulate prostitution.
c. 1255–1260	Founding of Oxford's Balliol College.
1256	Charter of the customary laws of the *bastide* of Monflanquin.
1258	Formal recognition of the word "parliament" as Henry III agrees to accept the Provisions of Oxford.
1263	Advent of the *custodes pacis* (keepers of the peace).
1272	Start of a 37-year-long legal battle: Oldcotes v d'Arcy.
Late 13th century	A "perfect" rape.
1274	Many sheriffs take bribes at the tourn but do nothing to help those accused of offenses.
1274	Death of St. Thomas Aquinas, who held that both natural law and positive law reflected divine law.
1275–1290	King Edward I reshapes the unwritten common law of England with new enactments which for many centuries will constitute the basic statue law of England.

1283	*Coutumes de Beauvaisis* (*Customary Laws of Beauvaisis*) — one of the best early collections of French legal customs and the first to include actual cases.
1289	Chief justice and accessory after the fact: Thomas Weyland.
1290	Legal treatise *Fleta* outlines Parliament's judicial duties.
1291–1292	Scotland's "Great Cause," i.e., the question of who is the rightful claimant of Scotland's throne.
13th century	French bailiffs become the principal agents of the king's efforts to build up an effective central administration to replace feudalism.
1305	Commissioners of trailbaston are named to help restore law and order.
1306	The Scottish patriot William Wallace is drawn and quartered.
1307	A Paris ordinance of king Philip the Fair describes how trial by combat should be conducted.
1307–1323	Bernard Gui is the inquisitor in Toulouse.
1312–1314	Dispute between Robert of Naples and Henry VII leads to a papal clarification of the rules of summary judicial procedure.
1317	To resolve a schism in the Franciscan order, pope John XXII endorses the faction known as the community. Members of a rival faction, the spirituals, form close ties with the heretical Beguins.
1318–1325	Jacques Fournier is bishop of Pamiers.
1327	Statue of Westminster formally defines the role of the *custodes pacis*.
c. 1330s–1340s	The era depicted in the fictional adventures of Robin Hood v the sheriff of Nottingham.
1340	Sir John Molyns: magnate, murderer and thief.
1341	First trial of Joan of Arc results in her condemnation and execution.
1340s	Inns of Court are set up in London to provide a focal point for legal studies.
c. 1350	Oldradus da Ponte uses case studies, e.g., involving a marriage made under duress and a knight's responsibility for losing a castle.
1356	Promulgation of the Golden Bull, the basic constitutional document of medieval Germany.
1361	Statute of Westminster creates the new office of justices of the peace.
1368–1380	A protracted Parlementary suit is conducted over a castle in Normandy.
1382–1400	A weighty legal dispute over Ladbroke Manor.
1386–1387	Geoffrey Chaucer begins *The Canterbury Tales*.
1390	Prostitute and accused witch: Margot de la Barre.
1395	A male transvestite prostitute: John Rykener.
1397	French king Charles VI decrees that a repeated blasphemer will have his tongue cut out.
1398	Sentenced to death as "idolaters, invokers of demons, apostates and sorcerers," two monks are publicly executed in Paris.
14th century	Fehmic courts begin to handle cases from all over Germany.
14th century	A lying wife causes a judicial duel.
1420	A Paris law complains that prostitutes have moved into "good" neighborhoods.

1455–1456	Second trial of Joan of Arc nullifies the first trial.
1456	Trial by battle between Jamys Fyscher and Thomas Whytehorne.
1461	The justice of the peace becomes more important after a statute decrees that indictments and presentments taken at the tourn shall be taken before a justice of the peace, not before the sheriff.
c. 1463	Death of François Villon ends a life of criminal excess.
1478	Pope Sixtus IV authorizes the Spanish Inquisition.
1482–1483	Royal legislation on "The Lawes, Orders and Customs for Swans."
1483	Tomás de Torquemada is appointed the first grand inquisitor of Spain.
1495	Germany adopts Roman law.
1498	Savonarola, a famous Dominican theologian and preacher, is tortured, hanged and burned for heresy.
15th century	Legal struggles of the Paston family over the ownership of manors in Norfolk.

Appendix I

A Brief Overview of the Inquisition

In about 1000, the Cathars and other neo-Manichean sects gradually spread from the Middle East into Italy, Spain, France and Germany.[1] Manicheanism itself was a dualistic religion founded in Iraq in the third century CE. Neo-Manichean heresies in Europe resulted in occasional persecutions by local Christians.

Emperor Henry II hanged several heretics in Goslar, Germany, in 1051-1052 to prevent the further growth of heresy. In northern France, the bishop of Cambrai condemned a Cathar heretic to the stake in 1076 or 1077. Also in northern France, in 1114 the "believing folk" (parishioners) of the bishop of Soissons stormed the prison where heretics were held, took them outside of the town, and burned them.

The French king Robert the Pious had thirteen distinguished ecclesiastic and lay citizens burned at Orléans in 1122 because, it was said, "he feared for the safety of the kingdom and the salvation of souls." In 1129 the Synod of Toulouse installed three inquisitors (one priest and two laymen) in every parish to denounce heretics.

A mob in Cologne, Germany, snatched heretics from the custody of the clergy and burned them at the stake in about 1144. In Flanders, duke William, together with William of the White Hand (the archbishop of Reims), caused nobles and commoners, clerics, knights, peasants, spinsters, widows and married women to be burnt alive in 1183. The two Williams then confiscated the heretics' properties and divided the spoils between them.

Between 1183 and 1206, bishop Hugo of Auxerre, France, seized the property of neo-Manicheans, exiling some and sending others to the stake. The year 1184 marked a major turning-point: pope Lucius III's decretal *Ad abolendum*, promulgated with the agreement of the emperor Frederick Barbarossa, denounced the "insolence" of heretics and "their attempts to promote falsehood." The most elaborate juridical statement on heretics issued to that date by the church, *Ad abolendum* required lay authorities to cooperate fully with ecclesiastics to root out and punish heretics. This decretal has been called "the founding charter of the inquisition."[2]

In 1197, Peter II, king of Aragon and count of Barcelona, expelled Waldenses and other heretics from his lands, ordaining that any who were still there a year later would have their goods confiscated and would be burned at the stake. In 1199, pope Innocent III issued the decretal *Vergentis in senium*, which for the first time linked heresy with the Roman doctrine of treason.[3] King Philip Augustus of France had eight Cathars burned at Troyes in 1200, one at Nevers in 1201, several at Braisne-sur-Vesle in 1204, and a good many in Paris. The victims included priests, clerics, and men and women belonging to the sect.

In his 1207 decretal *Cum ex officii nostri*, Innocent III ordered that heretics be punished severely:

> In order altogether to remove from the patrimony of St. Peter the defilement of heretics, we decree as a perpetual law, that whatsoever heretic... shall be found therein, shall immediately be taken to the secular court to be punished according to law. All his goods shall also be sold [and the proceeds shared, equally, between by the man who captured the heretics, the court, and the prison service.][4]

St. Francis of Assisi founded the order of Friar Minor (known as the Franciscans) in 1209 to preach and to lead lives of holy poverty. Later, together with the Dominicans these men would serve the inquisitions.

In 1211, French soldiers, carrying out a law issued by count Raymond of Toulouse, boasted that they had burned alive many heretics, and would continue to do so. At first, the church thought that torture was so terrible a process that clerics were strictly forbidden to be present when it was being used, under pain of what was known "irregularity." In 1220, however, pope Alexander IV gave clerics permission to absolve each other of such irregularity.

That same year, St. Dominic founded the order of Preachers (the Dominicans) to teach doctrine and suppress heresy. The first law in which death by fire was mandated appears to be an edict for Lombardy (Germany), issued in 1224. At that time, Frederick III ordered that heretics duly convicted by an ecclesiastical court "shall, on imperial authority, suffer death by fire."

The French king, Louis IX, issued a law, *Cupientes*, in 1229, ordering royal officials to seek out and prosecute heretics in their jurisdictions. Pope Gregory IX established a papal inquisition in 1231 to deal with the Cathars and Waldenses. He also sent a priest to Germany to investigate reports of heresy there.[5] Heretics who confessed and repented were to be sentenced to life imprisonment; unrepentant heretics would go to the stake. An inquisition was set up in Languedoc (south-central France) in 1233 to root out the Cathars. Six years later, in Champagne, Robert Le Bougre, a Cathar convert to Christianity who became a Dominican monk, deliberately arranged mass executions, committing to the flames up to 180 people at one time.

The Council of Tarragone (Spain) used canon law in 1242 to arrive at slight but legally vital distinctions between accused persons. In a series of canons, the council announced that:

> *Heretics* are those who remain obstinate in error.
> *Believers* are those who put faith in the errors of heretics, and are assimilated to them.
> *Those suspect of heresy* are those who are present at the preaching and participate, however little, in their ceremonies.
> *Those simply suspected* have done such things only once.
> *Those vehemently suspected* have done this frequently.
> *Concealers* are those who know heretics but do not denounce them.
> *Hiders* are those who prevent heretics from being discovered.
> *Receivers* are those who have twice received heretics on their property.

Favorers are all of the above to a greater or lesser degree.

Relapsed are those who return to their former heretical errors after having formally renounced them.[6]

In 1249, count Raymond VII of Toulouse caused 80 confessed heretics to be burned in his presence, without giving them any opportunity to recant. Pope Innocent IV's bull *Ad extirpanda* of 1252 authorized the use of torture to get confessions and the names of suspected heretics. This document also provided that

> When those adjudged guilty of heresy have been given up to the civil power by the bishop or his representative, or the inquisition, the [chief magistrate] of the city shall take them at once, and shall, within five days at the most, execute the laws made against them.[7]

In 1262 Urban IV renewed the permission for priests to absolve each other of the irregularity of being present when torture was used. This was soon interpreted as papal permission for priests to continue their interrogations in the torture chamber itself. Philippe de Beaumanoir's 1283 work *Coutumes de Beauvaisis* (*Customary Laws of Beauvaisis*) made it clear that while the church passed judgment on a heretic, only the secular authorities could carry out punishment:

> After questioning the suspect, the [ecclesiastical] judge, if he finds him to be a bad fellow, will send him to the secular justice system, which will subject him to torture to make him confess."[8]

There were not many checks on the excesses of inquisitors. In 1286, however, the officials of Carcassonne complained to the pope, the king of France and the vicars of the local bishops about the inquisitor Jean Garland. He was, they protested, inflicting torture in an absolutely inhumane manner. The fate of convicted heretics was not always death. At Toulouse from 1308–1324, out of 930 convicted persons, only 42 were handed over to the secular authorities to be burned. At Pamiers from 1318–1324, out of 24 persons convicted, only 5 were actually sent to the stake.

In 1310, the Beguine Marguerite Porete was burned in Paris for heresy. Her mystical book *Miroir des simples âmes* (*The Mirror of Simple Souls*) is considered to be the greatest religious tract written in Old French. In 1478, pope Sixtus IV authorized the Spanish Inquisition and in 1483 the Dominican Tomás de Torquemada was appointed the first grand inquisitor of Spain.

Torquemada reorganized and greatly expanded the Spanish Inquisition. In 1484 he issued 28 articles for the guidance of inquisitors, who were charged with rooting out not only heresy and apostasy but also sorcery, sodomy, polygamy, blasphemy and usury. Under Torquemada's tenure, arbitrary arrest and torture were in frequent use. He caused about 2,000 people to be burned at the stake.

At the very end of the Middle Ages, Girolamo Savonarola, a celebrated Dominican theologian and preacher, was accused of heresy. His prophetic and denunciatory preaching had won him a large following but had also aroused virulent opposition. Savonarola's open defiance of the church ultimately led pope Alexander VI to excommunicate him. In 1498, Savonarola was imprisoned, tortured, and finally publicly hanged and burned in the Piazza della Signoria, the main square of Florence.[9]

Appendix II

What Was One Penny Worth in the Middle Ages?

At first glance, it would appear easy enough to answer this question, at least in general terms. We might guess, for example, that a laborer earned about a penny a day. It turns out, however, that this is an extremely complicated question which cannot be answered satisfactorily. A slightly different version of this question, reflecting the case of the peasant Ailward (discussed in the chapter on medieval crime), was put to J.L. Bolton, a British scholar who is a specialist in medieval economics. The revised question was: "What was one penny worth in the 1170s?" Dr. Bolton replied[1]:

"There is no reliable answer to the question, "How much was a penny worth in the 1170s?" Wage/price evidence is very limited indeed before the early thirteenth century, and even then most of our information is drawn from two sources only — the pipe rolls and the records of the estates of the bishops of Winchester. Both have severe limitations.

"The problem is compounded by other factors. Both wages and prices were influenced by changes in the value of money, e.g. due to fluctuations in the money supply. If the silver from which pennies were made was in short supply, the intrinsic value of the coins, i.e., of the silver they contained, increased. As a result, a penny would buy more. If silver was in plentiful supply, as it was after about 1180, then the purchasing power of the penny fell, although it is also true that prices fell, too.

"Prices were also severely affected in the short term by harvest fluctuations and by outbreaks of cattle and sheep disease. Wheat might cost 2 shillings a quarter [a quarter was a unit of measure equal to about 291 liters] one year and 8 shillings a quarter the next. The cost of wheat per quarter in 1175–1176 was four times what it had been in 1168–1169. Prices were also likely to be higher in towns than in the countryside. Wheat had to pass through the hands of dealers and bakers before it was finally sold to the consumer as bread.

"Wages also responded to the labor supply. A rising population meant that more men and women were looking for work, so wages fell. It should be remembered, too, that in 1180 the main form of exchange was probably still barter. A money economy did not emerge until the thirteenth century.

"Having said all that, wheat cost on average about 1 shilling 7 pennies a quarter between 1160 and 1170, so 1 penny would buy 1/18th of a quarter, which is just under

188

half a bushel (36.37 liters). Many wages were paid in kind, but between 1208–1220 a carpenter working alone, or a thatcher with his helper, were paid at the rate of about 2 shillings _ penny per day, without food. An unskilled laborer, however, might express far less, if there was any work for him.

"Evidence for rents is equally limited. Rents varied from region to region and according to social status and the amount of land held. An unfree virgater [the tenant of a piece of land averaging 30 acres] on the estates of the Abbey of Holy Trinity in Caen [France], paid 6 pennies a year in rent, in addition to the labor he had to provide, in the early twelfth century, and that is unlikely to have changed by 1170. Every year, a smallholder on the same estates might have to pay 2 pennies a head for himself, his wife and any servant, plus another 2 pennies for a cow in milk. Many labor services were commuted for money payments in the twelfth century, and so money payments from peasant to lord increased. Given all these variables, it should be clear why a satisfactory answer to the question cannot be given."

Appendix III

Medieval and Later Laws Concerning Swans

The mute swan (Cygnus olor) is not in fact mute.[1] It can make soft snorting noises and can even grunt sharply. By 966, this bird was already considered to be the property of the crown: it was then that king Edgar gave the abbots of Croyland the rights to "stray" swans in their area.

Unmarked swans "flying at liberty" traditionally belonged to the crown, but at times the right of capturing such birds was granted in a certain area and for a limited time. During the reign of Edward III, for example, on 20 June 1356 such a grant was made for seven years "to the Warden and College of the King's Free Chapel of Wyndesore [Windsor] of all swans flying, not marked, within the water of the Thames between Oxford and London Bridge, as fully as these should pertain to the king by reason of his right and prerogative."[2] Similar rights were granted in 1390, 1398 and 1400.

The office of "keeper of the king's swans" existed before 1378. A document of 1482–1483, entitled "The Lawes, Orders and Customs for Swans," states that all swans owned by those who held freehold property worth five marks were forfeit to the king. Not only were swans a status symbol but they were also very good eating. They provided a tasty ceremonial or Christmas dish for hundreds of years, until edged aside by the turkey early in the twentieth century.

During the reign of Elizabeth I (1558–1603), gamekeepers along the River Thames were required to mark the swans each year. This ceremony, known as "swan upping," involved the "taking up" of them, i.e., capturing the swans, for marking their cygnets (young swans). Some of the cygnets were removed and were fattened up for the kitchen. Swan-upping is still performed on the Thames today, though without the culinary aspect.

To indicate ownership, the beaks of the cygnets used to be cut with the same mark as their parents; now, the legs of the birds are banded with stainless steel rings instead. In the past, there were many private owners of swans, so there was a great variety of marks. These were approved by the king's swan master and were noted in a registration book.

Swans were strictly regulated. The right of marking swans cost one third of a pound, paid into the royal exchequer. A man caught driving swans away during their breeding season or stealing their eggs was subject to one year's imprisonment, plus a

190

fine. If someone who was not a swan-herd was caught carrying a swan hook (a metal hook used to pull swans out of the river), he was fined two-thirds of a pound.

Today the owners of swans on the Thames are the crown and two City of London livery companies, the Worshipful Company of Dyers and the Worshipful Company of Vintners. The dyers' swans are marked with a nick on one side of the beak; the vintners' swans have a nick on each side. Royal swans are now marked with rings.

Because these birds are bottom feeders, they can take the bait of anglers who fish close to them and can also get entangled in fishing lines. In the past, many were poisoned by lead weights lost by fishermen. Most lead weights are now illegal and, as a result, the number of swans is increasing. They are a common sight on the Thames, where in summer their numbers may approach 1,000 birds, including cygnets. The queen's swan warden, currently a University of Oxford ornithologist, professor Christopher Perrins, is officially responsible for their well-being.

Appendix IV

Joan of Arc: The Twenty-Seven Articles

Witnesses at the second (nullification) trial of Joan of Arc were asked to confirm or deny the truth of each of the following articles. They have been lightly edited by removing the formulaic sentence, "And so it was and that is the truth," which appears at the end of each of them.[1]

1. That because she had come with the aid of the most Christian king of France and fought with the army against the English, Joan was pursued by a mortal hatred and was hated by the English, and that they sought her death by every means.
2. As Joan had inflicted numerous defeats on the said English in the war, they greatly feared her, and therefore sought by every way possible to deliver her to death and to put an end to her days so that she could harm them no longer.
3. That in order to give this an appearance of virtue, they brought her to this city of Rouen, then held in the tyrannical power of the English; and that they imprisoned her in the castle and caused to be brought against her a false prosecution for heresy, and this under fear and pressure.
4. That neither judges, confessors, or consultants, nor the promoter and others intervening in the trial, dared to exercise free judgment because of the severe threats made against them by the terrorizing English; but that they were forced to suit their actions to their fear and to the pressure of the English if they wished to avoid grave perils and even the peril of death.
5. That the notaries recording this trial, because the English caused them the same fear and directed threats against them, could not report the truth or faithfully set down the true version of Joan's replies when writing and editing their account.
6. That the notaries, prevented by fear, were expressly forbidden to insert in their account words pronounced by Joan which seemed in her favor. Instead, they were constrained to omit favorable remarks and insert statements held against her that she never said.
7. That because of these same fears and terrors nobody could be found to advise Joan, or conduct her case for her, or instruct her, or direct her, or protect her. Moreover those who sometimes put in some positive words for her suffered very great danger to their lives, for the English sought to throw them into the river as rebels, or deliver them to some other form of death.

8. That they kept Joan in a secular prison, her feet fettered with irons and chains; and that they forbade anyone to speak to her so that she might not be able to defend herself in any way, and that they even placed English guards over her.

9. That Joan was a girl of 19 or so, simple and ignorant of the law and judicial procedure; that alone, without direction or advice, she was not capable or clever enough to defend herself in such a difficult case.

10. That the English, desiring her death, went by night to her prison. Pretending to be inspired by some revelations, they exhorted her not to submit to the judgment of the Church if she wished to escape death.

11. That in order to trap her in her own words, the examiners plied her with difficult, insidious interrogations and questions, and that for the greater part of the time they interrogated her about things she did not in the least understand.

12. That they wore her out with their long interrogations and examinations, so that when she was finally exhausted they could seize on some unfortunate word in her replies.

13. That often, in court and elsewhere, Joan affirmed that she submitted herself and all her acts to the judgment of the Church and of our Holy Father the Pope; that if in anything in her words or deeds diverged from the faith she herself wished to retract it and to obey the judgment of the clerics.

14. That also, in court and elsewhere, Joan often affirmed that she submitted herself and all her acts to the judgment of the Church and of our Holy Father the Pope;... and that she would have been sorry if there had been anything in her that was in opposition to the Catholic faith.

15. That although her words of submission to the Church were often repeated to her both in the court and elsewhere, the English and those who favored their cause did not permit but rather forbade them to be inserted or written in the acts or in the record of the so-called trial. And that they caused them to be written down in another form, although this was a pervasion of the truth.

16. That if Joan ever affirmed that she would not submit to the judgment of our Holy Mother the Church, even the Church Militant [that is, the Church here on earth, in contrast to the Church Triumphant, the heavenly church], it was not proven by the previous article.

17. In any case in which it might appear that Joan said something implying her nonsubmission to the Church, the promoter says that she did not understand what the Church was, and that she did not understand by this term the community of the faithful, but believed and understood the Church of which her interrogators spoke to consist of those ecclesiastics there present, who had embraced the English cause.

18. That the alleged report, originally written in French, was translated into Latin with no great accuracy, many things having been suppressed that told in Joan's favor and even more having been added, in defiance of truth, that prejudiced her case, and therefore the said record disagrees with its original in numerous and substantial points.

19. That, the preceding truths having been recognized, the said trial and sentence does not deserve the name of a judgment and sentence, since there can be no real judgment when the judges, consultants, and assessors are too fearful to exercise judgment.

20. That, for the proceeding reasons, the alleged record is in many parts untrue, vitiated, and corrupt, and neither perfectly nor faithfully written; that it is also so defective that no faith can be put in it.

21. That the preceding and other points being weighed, the case and the sentence are both null and most unjust, since they were conducted and passed without the observance of legal formalities by judges who were not the rightful ones and who had no jurisdiction in such a case or over such a person.

22. That moreover, the said trial and sentence are both null and tainted with manifest injustice for the additional reason that on so grave a charge Joan was given no facilities for defending herself. Furthermore, that defense itself, which exits as a natural right, was totally denied her by manifold and insidious means.

23. That although it was abundantly apparent to the judges that Joan had submitted to the judgment and decisions of Our Holy Mother the Church, and that she was so faithful a Catholic that she was allowed to receive the body of Our Lord, nevertheless, out of their excessive zeal for the English, or not wishing to extricate themselves out of fear and pressure, they most unjustly condemned her as a heretic to the pains of the fire.

24. That without any further sentences from the secular judge, the English, inspired by rage against her, immediately led her to the stake under a large escort of armed men.

25. That Joan continuously, and notably at the moment of her death, behaved in a saintly and Catholic manner, recommending her soul to God and invoking Jesus aloud even with her last breath in such a manner to draw from all those present, and even from her English enemies, effusions of tears.

26. That the English perpetrated and caused to be perpetrated against Joan each and all the preceding acts, in deed and against the law, by means of pressure, because they had a lively fear of Joan, who supported the party of the most Christian king of France. They hated her and pursued her with a mighty hatred so that the most Christian king might be discredited for having availed himself of the aid of a woman so utterly damned.

27. That each and all the preceding facts were and are of public fame and popular report, and that they are commonly said and known in the diocese of Rouen and throughout the kingdom of France.

Appendix V

The High Court of Chivalry

The High Court of Chivalry was a uniquely specialized English court dealing with military matters, such as heraldry, which fell outside the purview of the common law.[1] In the Middle Ages this court was the responsibility of two powerful men — the constable of England and the marshal of England. They probably did not sit in the court on a regular basis themselves but delegated their duties to surrogates, who judged on their behalf.

One of the main functions of this court was to adjudicate questions about armorial bearings. Between 1385 and 1390, for example, the court heard the case of Scrope v Grosvenor. This involved a dispute between the Scrope and Grosvenor families over which one had the right to bear the arms technically described as *asure a bend* (blue with a gold diagonal stripe), which both parties claimed. The court also took up a much wider range of cases, however.

The first reference to the High Court of Chivalry was Edward III's 1348 order that the turncoat William Le Counte, who had been captured in Normandy and made a prisoner of war, be tried before the king's constable and marshal to answer for his broken faith and other misdeeds. Later, the court handled a wide range of other issues. These included unjust detention of prisoners of war (1374); prisoner exchanges (1383); the theft at Chartres of the portmanteau (big suitcase) of an English cleric (1384); payment of ransom (1385); cases involving lies, forgery, or breach of pact (all these were in 1385); debt (1386); breach of faith (1389); and attempted murder (1400).

The High Court of Chivalry was so active that it was soon trespassing on the jurisdictions of other legal bodies. Thus in 1389, the Commons complained that the court was

> encroaching contracts, covenants, trespasses, debts, detinues [common law actions for the recovery of a personal chattel wrongfully detained or for payment of its value], and other actions pleadable at common law to the great prejudice of the king and his courts and the great grievance of the people.[2]

To bring the court back into line, in that same year Parliament limited its mandate to

> cognizance of contracts touching deeds or arms and of war out of the realm, and also of things that touch [arms or war] within the realm, which cannot be determined or discussed by the common law, with other usages and customs to the same matters pertaining, which other constables have duly and reasonably used in their time.[3]

The court could also order trial by battle to resolve disputes for which there was no remedy at common law. Treason and homicide committed abroad are the best examples here, although such a trial might also be used to settle an unspecified "deed or action of arms." The legal proceedings for trial by battle began with a petition to the king in council, containing the articles of complaint. This document was then forwarded to the High Court of Chivalry, which set the date and place for the fight. The king footed the bill for preparing the field of battle, arming the combatants and even, if necessary, training them. In 1446, for example, Henry VI paid for two appellants to have lessons in fighting.

If such a trial involved treason, the losing party was disarmed, dragged behind a horse to the place of execution, and then hanged or beheaded there. In a homicide trial, the losing party was led, rather than dragged, to the killing ground. If the appeal involved only a "deed or action of arms," the vanquished party was disarmed and led off the field in disgrace. The king, however, had the power to stop such trials by battle. For example, in a 1398 dispute between the duke of Hereford (who would become king Henry IV the following year) and the duke of Norfolk, the king not only prohibited them from fighting but also banished them.

After a long series of civil wars between the rival houses of York and Lancaster finally came to an end in 1485, the court found that it had very little to do. It was inactive by 1496, at the very end of the Middle Ages, and remained dormant for some time thereafter. It was not until 1622 that letters patent were issued to the earl marshal authorizing and commanding him to proceed "judicially and definitely" in all cases within the court of the constable and the marshal.

The High Court of Chivalry last met in 1955, when the city of Manchester sued a local theater, the Manchester Palace of Varieties, for using its coat of arms. The city won its case, as the following verdict shows (punctuation as in the original):

> We the said Bernard Marmaduke Duke of Norfolk with the counsel of those skilled in the law whom We have consulted in this behalf pronounce decree and declare that the Plaintiffs lawfully bear the arms crest motto and supporters in this cause libellate and that the defendants have displayed representations of the said arms crest motto and supporters in the manner in this case libellate and contrary to the will of the Plaintiffs and the laws and usages of arms and We inhibit and strictly enjoin the Defendants that they do not presume to display the said arms crest motto and supporters or any of them.[4]

Previous to this case, the court had not sat since 1737. Heraldry enthusiasts today, however, will be happy to know that, when and if the need ever arises, the court can be called back into existence at any time.

Appendix VI

Justices of the Peace in the United Kingdom Today

Except for the last section, which reflects the views of the author alone, the following account is drawn chiefly from information provided by the Magistrates Association (for comments on England and Wales) and by the District Courts Association (for comments on Scotland).[1]

ENGLAND AND WALES

Who are lay magistrates?

Magistrates are members of the local community appointed by the lord chancellor. No formal qualifications are required but magistrates need intelligence, common sense, integrity, the capacity to act fairly and must not have a criminal record. They normally exercise their duties as part of a bench of three. They will at all times have available to them the advice of a qualified court clerk. Magistrates are trained before sitting and continue to receive training throughout their service. Drawn from all walks of life, they are unpaid volunteers but may receive allowances to cover traveling expenses, subsistence and child care.

Criminal matters

Over 95 percent of all criminal cases in England and Wales are dealt with by magistrates, either in the adult court or in the youth court. Some crimes, such as theft or fraud, are referred to as "either-way" offenses because they may either be handled by magistrates themselves or can be referred by them to the Crown Court. A person charged with an either-way offense can choose where his or her case is to be heard but the most serious crimes are always referred to the Crown Court, after the magistrates have established that there is a case to be answered and have set bail.

Magistrates' duties in criminal cases involve, among other things, deciding on applications for bail, judging whether a defendant is guilty or not, and passing sentence. For a single criminal offense committed by an adult, magistrates' sentencing powers include the imposition of fines, community service orders, probation orders, or a prison term of not more than twelve months. Magistrates may also sit in the Crown Court with a judge to hear appeals from magistrates' courts against conviction or sentence, and proceedings on committal to the Crown Court for sentence.

Civil matters

Magistrates decide many civil matters, particularly in relation to family matters. Specially selected and trained members of the family court panels deal with a wide range of matters, most of which arise from the breakdown of marriage, e.g., making orders for the residence of and contact with children. Proceedings relating to the care and control of children are handled in family proceedings courts, too.

The civil jurisdiction involves the enforcement of financial penalties and orders such as those in respect of nonpayment of local taxes. Most magistrates also carry out some routine licensing work regarding the sale of alcohol and permits for betting and gambling establishments.

Scotland

The District Courts (Scotland) Act of 1975 made significant changes in the operation of lay summary justice in Scotland. City, police, and justice of the peace courts were amalgamated into District Courts, the districts having been formed under a reorganization of local government.

The District Court is a lay court where a justice of the peace, who is a lay person, sits with a legally qualified clerk (in some areas, justices sit in threes). Currently there are about thirty District Courts in Scotland. This court is the lowest rung of the court hierarchy and deals only with summary criminal matters. There are certain offenses — for example, an assault resulting in a broken bone — which cannot be heard in the District Court but must go directly to the Sheriff Court.

The District Court can imprison for up to 60 days and impose a fine of up to £2,500 (about $3,800). The most common types of offenses to be dealt with in the District Court are breach of the peace, assault, vandalism, theft (but not theft by housebreaking), speeding and other traffic offenses, electricity fraud, etc.

Justices of the Peace: some pros and cons

Serving as a justice of the peace is very time-consuming. In England and Wales the lord chancellor requires that a magistrate should sit for at least twenty-six half-days each year and endeavor to be available to sit for up to thirty-five half-days each year. Magistrates must be prepared to sit for a whole day if necessary. Indeed, this is the norm in most courts.

Critics of this system assert that because of these time demands, magistrates tend to be middle class, middle-aged men and women who have a good deal of free time, i.e., they are not employed, are working only part-time or are retired. According to critics, the system does not adequately represent society as a whole because it is drawn chiefly from this narrow social stratum. They also argue that since magistrates are likely to lack personal experience with certain common social problems (drug use, for example), they may either be too hard — or too easy — on offenders.

Supporters of the system, on the other hand, point out that it has served British and Scottish society tolerably well for more than 640 years. A serving magistrate says that "whilst what you say about magistrates having a lot of time is true in some cases, others nearly kill themselves fitting in courts in their time off."[2] Supporters also point out that three heads are better than one and that efforts are now being made to recruit magistrates from a wider social spectrum.

Appendix VII

Listing of Selected Cases and Laws Cited in the Text

Chapter 2: Justice in the Early Middle Ages
- A werewolf clause (c. 500)
- A barbarian king condemns perjurers (502)
- The Salic Law (c. 507–510)
- Restitution after a Frankish raid (mid–520s)
- Justinian codifies Roman law (527–533)
- St. Gregory of Tours: oath taking and peacekeeping (late sixth century)
- Abbot Ermenoald loses his case (c. 692)
- For the repose of Waltof's soul (806)
- An open-and-shut case? (828)
- Dealing with sorcerers and witches (ninth century)

Chapter 3: Canon (Ecclesiastical) Law and Its Variants
- Bishop Burchard lays down the law (1014)
- Burchard's *Corrector* (c. 1015)
- Gratian on marriage (c. 1144)
- Clerics are forbidden to take part in the ordeal (1215)
- "The most illustrious jurist of his time": Oldradus da Ponte (c. 1350)
- A marriage made under duress (c. 1350)
- Responsibility for the loss of a castle (c. 1350)
- A royal ordinance against blasphemers (1397)

Chapter 4: Feudalism and Justice in Medieval France
- Becoming a vassal (820s–830s)
- French abbots prevent a battle between their monks (1064)
- Giving a man fair warning (1091)
- Monks' champions fight a judicial duel over a marsh (1098)
- A judicial battle over mills along the Seine (c. 1100)
- Navigation at the port of Arles (1150)
- A great nobleman of France is tried for murder (1259)
- When an agreement should not be honored (1283)

- Jamys Fyscher v Thomas Whytehorne (1456)
- Legal struggles of the Paston family (fifteenth century)

Chapter 9: Medieval Crime
- The folk hero Hereward (1070–1071)
- A blind, iron-fingered murderer (c. 1115)
- Unjustly convicted, Bricstan is miraculously freed (1115 or 1116)
- Entrapment by a matron (c. 1170s?)
- A fatal dispute over one penny (early 1170s)
- Another historical outlaw: Eustache the Monk (1170–1217)
- Low-life Paris (c. 1205–1210)
- A face-saving settlement: Chamberlain v Herbert of Patsley (1207)
- A "perfect" rape (third quarter of the thirteenth century)
- Sir William Wallace: drawn and quartered (1305)
- Robin Hood v the "proud sheriff" of Nottingham (c. 1330s–1340s)
- The Statute of Westminster creates justices of the peace (1361)
- François Villon (d. after 1463): a life of criminal excess
- Sir Thomas Malory (d. 1471): a "knight-prisoner" writes one of the world's great romances

Chapter 10: Justice in Medieval Germany
- A capitulary of the emperor Charlemagne (802)
- Gundhart v an unnamed count (c. 814)
- Count Gero v the Saxon Waldo (979)
- *Landfrieden* (1103)
- The *Sachsenspiegel* (1224–1225)
- "The Hole": the dungeons of Nuremberg (1332)
- Machiavelli on conditions in Germany (late fifteenth century)

Chapter 11: Where Medieval Law and Politics Meet
- The first trial of Joan of Arc (1431)
- Joan's conviction and execution (1431)
- The second trial of Joan of Arc (1455–1456)

Notes

Preface

1. Cited by Musson, *Medieval Law*, p. 251.
2. Cited by Gauvard, "Justice et Paix," p. 592. Emphasis added.

Chapter 1—Why This Book?

1. See Goetz, *Life in the Middle Ages*, p. 238.
2. Bellomo, *Common Legal Past*, p. xii.
3. See Brundage, *Medieval Canon Law*, p. 1. He lists these records as including charters, registers, writs, contracts, wills, court rolls, tax records, ecclesiastical legal documents, property disputes, treaties, crimes, punishments, marriages, dowries, divorces, and the disposition of estates.
4. Chiffoleau, "Droit(s)," p. 302.
5. After Chiffoleau, "Droit(s)," pp. 301–302.
6. Palmer, *Whilton Dispute*, pp. 5, 8.
7. Cited by Bellomo, *Common Legal Past*, p. 196.
8. Cited by Bellomo, *Common Legal Past*, p. 196.
9. Brundage, *Medieval Canon Law*, p. 2.
10. Cited by Bloch, *Feudal Society II*, p. 112.
11. See Bloch, *Feudal Society II*, p. 359. Perhaps it should be mentioned here that while Bloch was undoubtedly one of the most important historians of the twentieth century, his work is now at the center of an intense scholarly debate. Revisionist critics assert that his familiar concept of "feudalism" lumps together a range of factors which may not in fact be related. These critics, however, have yet to make a fully persuasive case, so "feudalism" will be used in this book.
12. After Bellomo, *Common Legal Past*, p. 149.
13. Chiffoleau, "Droit(s)," p. 290.
14. Nelson, "Dispute settlement," p. 228.
15. Private communication from Dr. Paul Brand of 12 January 2002.
16. Morall, *Medieval Impact*, p. 105.
17. Private communication from Dr. Paul Brand of 8 April 2002.
18. Swanton, *The Anglo-Saxon Chronicles* [sic], p. ix.
19. Koenigsberger, *Medieval Europe*, p. 8.

Chapter 2—Justice in the Early Middle Ages

1. Cited by Chiffoleau, "Droit(s)," p. 296. Italics added.
2. Cited by Chiffoleau, "Droit(s)," p. 295.
3. After McKitterick, *Early Middle Ages*, p. 44.
4. After McKitterick, *Early Middle Ages*, p. 44.
5. After Holmes, *Oxford Illustrated History*, pp. 36–37.
6. Bloch, *Feudal Society*, p. 111.
7. Cited by Barzun, *Dawn*, p. 225.

8. After Bloch, *Feudal Society*, p. 111.

9. A *solidus*, plural *solidi*, was in the later days of the Roman Empire a gold coin weighing 1/72 of a pound. During the Middle Ages, its value varied so considerably that for our purposes here it is not worth trying to compute its purchasing power. For an example of the difficulties in estimating purchasing power, see Appendix II (What Was One Penny Worth in the Middle Ages?).

10. James, "Northern World," p. 83.

11. Cited by Lewis and Reinhold, *The Empire*, p. 512.

12. For insights into "irrational proofs," see McCall, *Medieval Underworld*, pp. 53–63; and Bartlett, *Trial by Fire and Water*. Both have been used in this section.

13. After Pennington, "Law," p. 502.

14. These oaths are cited by Regia, "Long Arm," p. 4.

15. Cited by Bartlett, *Trial by Fire and Water*, p. 26.

16. Cited by Bartlett, *Trial by Fire and Water*, p. 26.

17. After Bartlett, *Trial by Fire and Water*, p. 13.

18. Medieval Sourcebook, "Anglo-Saxon Dooms," pp. 24–25.

19. Medieval Sourcebook, "Anglo-Saxon Dooms," pp. 24–25.

20. Avalon, "Anglo-Saxon Law," p. 9.

21. McCall, *Medieval Underworld*, p. 56.

22. Cited by Medieval Sourcebook, "Ordeal Formulas," p. 1.

23. Cited by Traill and Mann, *Social England*, p. 414.

24. Cited by Bartlett, *Trial by Fire and Water*, pp. 15–16.

25. Cited by Traill and Mann, *Social England*, p. 414.

26. McCall, *Medieval Underworld*, p. 60.

27. This account is taken from Reznick, "Tools," p. 3; and McCall, *Medieval Underworld*, pp. 60–61.

28. Cited by Bartlett, *Trial by Fire and Water*, p. 108.

29. From a private communication from Dr. Paul Brand of 12 December 2001.

30. McCall, *Medieval Underworld*, p. 61.

31. After McCall, *Medieval Underworld*, p. 61.

32. After Bartlett, *Trial by Fire and Water*. The citation is from p. 113.

33. Cited by Bartlett, *Trial by Fire and Water*, p. 116.

34. Cited by Bartlett, *Trial by Fire and Water*, pp. 117–118.

35. Cited by Bartlett, *Trial by Fire and Water*, p. 122.

36. Cited by Wood, "Disputes," pp. 21–22. Emphasis has been added and the text has been lightly edited.

37. Cited by Wood, "Disputes," p. 16. The text has been lightly edited.

38. Excerpted and lightly edited from Avalon Project, "The Salic Law," pp. 1–13.

39. Cited by Wood, "Disputes," p. 13. The text has been lightly edited.

40. Medieval Sourcebook, "Corpus Iuris Civilis," p. 1.

41. After McCall, *Medieval Underworld*, pp. 53–54.

42. Gregory of Tours, *History of the Franks*, "Sichar & Chramnesind," p. 2.

43. After Fouracre, "'Placita'," pp. 27–28.

44. After Innes, *State and Society*, p. 69.

45. After Nelson, "Dispute settlement," pp. 48–51.

46. Cited by Nelson, "Dispute settlement," p. 48.

47. Cited by Nelson, "Dispute settlement," p. 49.

48. After Fouracre, commenting in Nelson, "Dispute settlement," p. 51.

49. Davies and Fouracre, *Settlement of Disputes*, p. 222. A fear of witches is deeply embedded in the human psyche. In 2002, the World Health Organization reported that about 500 elderly women are killed each year in Tanzania as witches.

50. Cited by Bartlett, *Trial by Fire and Water*, p. 24.

Chapter 3 — Canon (Ecclesiastical) Law and Its Variants

1. After Brundage, *Medieval Canon Law*. This is an excellent introduction to canon law and has been used heavily in this book.

2. Bloch, *Feudal Society II*, p. 361.

3. Cited by Genet, "Politics," p. 18.

4. Cited by Brundage, *Medieval Canon Law*, p. ix.

5. Matthew 23:23.

6. Matthew 5:17.

7. Brundage, *Medieval Canon Law*, pp. 20–21.

8. Brundage, *Medieval Canon Law*, p. 22.

9. Brundage, *Medieval Canon Law*, p. 26.

10. Russian Orthodox Cathedral, "Great Schism," p. 1.

11. Brundage, *Medieval Canon Law*, p. 26.

12. After Brundage, *Medieval Canon Law*, pp. 26–27.

13. Medieval Sourcebook, "Burchard," p. 7.

14. Medieval Sourcebook, "Burchard," p. 10.

15. After Brundage, *Medieval Canon Law*, pp. 32–33.

16. After Brundage, *Medieval Canon Law*, p. 120.

17. See Winroth, *Making of Gratian's Decretum*, pp. 162–168. The phrase "lamp of the law" is cited by Winroth on p, 158.

18. Cited by Vauchez, "Normalisation," p. 438.

19. After Bellomo, *Common Legal Past*, p. 160.

20. After Van Caenegem, *Introduction to Private Law*, p. 53.

21. After Brundage, *Medieval Canon Law*, p. 48.

22. After Bellomo, *Common Legal Past*, p. 163.

23. After Winroth, *Making of Gratian's Decretum*, p. 7.

24. For details on these two recensions, see Winroth, *Making of Gratian's Decretum*, pp. 122–145.

25. Adapted from a text cited by Winroth, *Making of Gratian's Decretum*, pp. 7–8.

26. Adapted from a text cited by Winroth, *Making of Gratian's Decretum*, pp. 7–8.

27. Cited by Pennington, "Due Process," p. 8.

28. Cited by Bloch, *Feudal Society II*, p. 369.

29. After Pennington, "Due Process," p. 2.

30. Much of this section is drawn from Brundage, *Medieval Canon Law*, "Canonical Jurisprudence," pp. 154–173.

31. Brundage, *Medieval Canon Law*, p. 166.

32. After Bellomo, *Common Legal Past*, p. 72.

33. After Bellomo, *Common Legal Past*, p. 71.

34. Medieval Sourcebook, "Burchard," p. 2.

35. Medieval Sourcebook, "Burchard," p. 5. This has been lightly edited.

36. Koziol, "Burchard," pp. 1–2.

37. Koziol, "Burchard," p. 2.

38. Brundage, *Medieval Canon Law*, p. 190.

39. Medieval Sourcebook, "Gratian: On Marriage," p. 1.

40. Brundage, *Medieval Canon Law*, p. 142.

41. Cited by Medieval Sourcebook, "Lateran IV," p. 1. Emphasis added.

42. Brundage, *Medieval Canon Law*," p. 222.

43. Adapted from Medieval Sourcebook, "Oldradus da Ponte, No. 35 (Consillium)," pp. 2–3.

44. Adapted from Medieval Sourcebook, "Oldradus da Ponte, No. 92 (Questio)," pp. 2–7.

45. Medieval society was inherently unequal. The nobility had a special place in medieval justice. Bloch tells us that "Everywhere... — earlier in one place, later in another — we find evidence that the noble was specially protected in his person against the non-noble; that he was subject to an exceptional penal law, with heavier fines,... than those exacted from the common people; that recourse to private vengeance... tended to be reserved for him; that the sumptuary laws [laws regulating what kind of clothing a person could wear] assigned to him a place apart." See *Feudal Society II*, p. 328.

46. Adapted from *Livre des sources médiévales*, "Blasphemateurs," p. 1.

Chapter 4 — Feudalism and Justice in Medieval France

1. Cited by Hay, *Early Middle Ages*, p. 217.

2. Cited by Bloch, *Feudal Society II*, p. 411.

3. Painter, *Middle Ages*, p. 104.

4. A more detailed definition of feudalism is Marc Bloch's classic statement: "A subject peasantry; widespread use of the service tenement (i.e., the fief) instead of a salary, which was out of the question; the supremacy of a class of specialized warriors; ties of obedience and protection which bind man to man and, within the warrior class, assume the distinctive form called vassalage; fragmentation of authority — inevitably leading to disorder; and, in the midst of all this, the survival of other forms of association, family and State, of which the latter, in the second feudal age [after the twelfth century], was to acquire renewed strength — such then seem to be the fundamental features of European feudalism." (*Feudal Society*, Vol. II, p. 446.)

5. Private communication from Dr. Paul Brand of 8 April 2002.

6. After Morrall, *Medieval Imprint*, p. 105; Bloch, *Feudal Society II*, p. 372; and Koenigsberger, *Medieval Europe*, p. 201. Koenigsberger qualifies the statement that France was the center of European intellectual life by explaining that French cultural influences affected Norman England, Germany and Italy.

7. Cited by Le Goff, *Dictionnaire Raisonné*, p. 749.

8. "Glanvill," p. 7.

9. "Villein" is not a term that lends itself to precise definition. In general, a villein was a person who was attached to the manor, performed servile work for the lord and was in some respects considered to be the lord's property. Various kinds of villeinage existed, however. In some cases, the labor the villein had to do for the lord was specified; in others, he had to do whatever the lord wanted him to do. See Electronic Library, "villein," p. 1.

10. After Bloch, *Feudal Society II*, p. 329.

11. Morrall, *Medieval Imprint*, p. 104.

12. After Morrall, *Medieval Imprint*, p. 104.

13. By the twelfth and thirteenth centuries, most of the remaining allodial land in France was confined to small peasant holdings in the southwest. As feudalism declined, land formerly under a lord's control passed to the jurisdiction of the king. All land in France became allodial after the French Revolution of 1789.

14. Encyclopaedia Britannica Online. "Fief," p. 1.

15. Painter, *Middle Ages*, p. 122.

16. After Bloch, *Feudal Society II, p. 373.*

17. After Ganshof, *Feudalism*, p. 156; and Bloch, *Feudal Society II*, p. 372.

18. Bloch, *Feudal Society II*, p. 372.

19. Cited by Ganshof, *Feudalism*, pp. 157–158.

20. Cited by Ganshof, *Feudalism*, p. 156.

21. After Bellomo, *Common Legal Past*, p. 102. For a more detailed analysis, see his pp. 101–106.

22. After Bellomo, *Common Legal Past*, p. 103.

23. After Chiffoleau, "Droit(s)," p. 305.

24. After Ganshof, *Feudalism*, p. 158.

25. In a private communication of 11 January 2002, Dr. Paul Brand explained the reason why French kings were in control of so small an area. This was due to the previous status of the Capetians as local and not very powerful counts in the same region, who were lucky enough to be related to the Carolingians.

26. Petit Guide, *Le moyen âge*, p. 6.

27. Cited by Ganshof, *Feudalism*, p. 162.

28. Cited by Koenigsberger, *Medieval Europe*, p. 272.

29. "Charte des coutumes de Monflanquin," p. 2.

30. Cited by "La Cour d'appel de Paris," p. 2.

31. Medieval Sourcebook, "Hundred Years War," p. 1.

32. Machiavelli, *The Prince*, p. 61.

33. Letters patent (from the Latin *patere*, "to open") are open official letters, formally addressed "To All and Singular to whom these Presents shall Come." The opposite of letters patent are letters close, which are personal communications closed with a seal.

34. Cited by Ganshof, *Feudalism*, p. 27.

35. Cited by Ganshof, *Feudalism*, p. 26.

36. Cited by Medieval Sourcebook, "Charter of Homage and Fealty," pp. 1–2.

37. Cited by Medieval Sourcebook, "Judicial Duels," pp. 2–3.

38. Cited by Medieval Sourcebook, "Judicial Duels," p. 3.
39. Cited by Painter, *Middle Ages*, p. 120.
40. Cited by Medieval Sourcebook, "Judicial Duels," pp. 5.
41. Cited by Medieval Sourcebook, "Judicial Duels," p. 2.
42. Medieval Sourcebook, "Arles," pp. 1–2.
43. Both the Coucy battle cry and motto are cited by Tuchman, *Distant Mirror*, p. 4.
44. Cited by Tuchman, *Distant Mirror*, p. xv
45. Cited by Medieval Sourcebook, "The Trial of Enguerrand IV de Coucy," pp. 1–2.
46. Tuchman, *Distant Mirror*, p. 13.
47. These three citations are from Schenck, "Oral Customs," pp. 5–6.
48. Cited by Reznick, "Wager of Battle," p. 2.
49. Cited by Medieval Sourcebook, "Hundred Years War," pp. 4–5.
50. Cited by Medieval Sourcebook, "Hundred Years War," p. 5.
51. Cited by Medieval Sourcebook, "Hundred Years War," p. 6.
52. Cited by Medieval Sourcebook, "Hundred Years War," p. 6.
53. Medieval Sourcebook, "Hundred Years War," p. 6.

Chapter 5 — Anglo-Norman Justice in England before the Common Law

1. After Encyclopaedia Britannica Online, "Anglo-Saxon Law," pp. 1–2.
2. After Wickham, "Society," p. 77.
3. Stenton, *Anglo-Saxon England*, p. 60.
4. Cited by Avalon Project, "Anglo-Saxon Law," p. 1.
5. These examples are cited by Wormald in *Legal Culture*, pp. 269–275.
6. Stenton, *Anglo-Saxon England*, p. 429.
7. A few scholars believe that Asser's work was a later forgery, but this view has not gained widespread support.
8. Cited by Keynes, "Royal government," p. 230. This has been lightly edited.
9. Cited by Medieval Sourcebook, "Anglo-Saxon Chronicle," p. 2.
10. Cited by Medieval Sourcebook, "Anglo-Saxon Chronicle," p. 2.
11. Stenton, *Anglo-Saxon England*, p. 618.
12. Cited by Swanton, *Angle-Saxon Chronicles*, p. 216.
13. Stenton, *Anglo-Saxon England*, p. 652.
14. Many of the following comments on the Anglo-Saxon court system come from a private communication from Dr. Paul Brand of 24 January 2002.
15. Hudson, *Formation*, p. 35.
16. Hudson, *Formation*, p. 37
17. After Skyrme, *Justices of the Peace*, p. 26.
18. Avalon Project, "Anglo-Saxon Law," p. 8.
19. Medieval Sourcebook, "Anglo-Saxon Dooms," pp. 1–4; and Hay, *Early Middle Ages*, pp. 205–206.
20. Medieval Sourcebook, "Anglo-Saxon Dooms," pp. 7, 10.
21. Medieval Sourcebook, "Anglo-Saxon Dooms," p. 15.
22. This account is taken from Hadley, *Northern Danelaw*," p. 67.
23. Medieval Sourcebook, "Æthelred Unrædy," pp. 1–2.
24. Cited by Wormald, *Legal Culture*, p. 350.
25. Cited by Avalon Project, "Anglo-Saxon Law," pp. 13–14.
26. The following comments are drawn from Stenton, *Anglo-Saxon England*, pp. 494–498.
27. Cited by Hudson, *Formation*, p. 24.

Chapter 6 — Henry II and the Rise of the English Common Law

1. "Blackstone's Commentaries," p. 4.
2. Except for the first point, this discussion is drawn from Brand, *Common Law*, pp. 101–102.
3. Cited by Hudson, *Formation*, p. 185.
4. Cited by Medieval Sourcebook, "Assize of Clarendon," p. 1. The text has been lightly edited and the emphasis added.

5. Cited by Medieval Sourcebook, "Assize of Clarendon," p. 1.
6. Cited by Medieval Sourcebook, "Assize of Clarendon," p. 2.
7. Cited by Sandquist, "Justices, Itinerant," p. 184.
8. Brand, *Making of the Common Law*, p. 84.
9. Brand, *Making of the Common Law*, p. 83.
10. Cited by Sandquist, "Justices," p. 185.
11. After Skyrme, *Justices of the Peace*, p. 7.
12. Sandquist, "Justices," p. 184.
13. Adapted from citation by Sandquist, "Justices," p. 185.
14. Sandquist, "Justices," p. 184.
15. After Brand, *Making of the Common Law*, p. 85–86.
16. After Painter, *Middle Ages*, p. 9.
17. Cited by Sandquist, "Justices," p. 184.
18. After "Glanvill," p. 4.
19. *Bracton*, "Novel Disseisin," p.1.
20. Brand, *Making of the Common Law*, p. 86; and private communication of 19 February 2002.
21. Brand, *Making of the Common Law*, p. 5.
22. Cited by Dean, "Middle Temple Hall," p. 22.
23. Cited by Lilley, *Urban Life*, p. 28.
24. Private communication from Dr. Paul Brand of 7 May 2002.
25. Adapted from Thorne, *Inns of Court*, p. clv
26. Cited by Thorne, *Inns of Court*, pp. clv
27. After private communications from Dr. Paul Brand of 7 May 2002 and 29 January 2003
28. After Brand, *Making of the Common Law*, p. 77.
29. After Brand, *Making of the Common Law*, p. 135.
30. After Brand, *Making of the Common Law*, pp. 1–2.
31. Private communication from Dr. Paul Brand of 19 February 2002.
32. See Nevill Coghill's notes to Eliot, *Murder in the Cathedral*, p. 142.
33. Gervase of Canterbury, pp. 1–2. I have lightly edited this text.
34. Cited by Hudson, *Formation*, p. 76.
35. Brand, *Making of the Common Law*, p. x.
36. Cited by Brand, *Making of the Common Law*, p. 79.
37. Cited by "Glanvill," p. 1.
38. After "Glanvill," pp. 1–2.
39. Cited in "Glanvill," p. 3.
40. Cited in "Glanvill," p. 3.
41. Cited in "Glanvill," pp. 3–4.
42. Cited in "Glanvill," pp. 3–4.
43. "Women and the Law," p. 1.
44. Cited by Medieval Sourcebook, "Magna Carta 1215," pp. 2–3, 5, 6.
45. The abbey church was founded in 793 by king Offa of Mercia at the tomb of St. Alban, the first Christian martyr in England, who was executed by the Romans in about 230. Pilgrimages there were first mentioned by bishop Germanus of Auxerre in 429.
46. After Armstrong, "William Marshal," pp. 1, 3–4.
47. Armstrong, "William Marshal," p. 4.
48. These three points are cited in *Bracton*, supct.law.cornell, p. 1.
49. Maitland is quoted in bracton.law.cornell, p. 1.
50. Cited in *Bracton*, "Thorne Edition," p. 1.

Chapter 7 — Medieval Inquisitors

1. After Burr, "Inquisition," p. 1.
2. This discussion follows Peters, *Inquisition*, pp. 12–13, 17.
3. After Peters, *Inquisition*, pp. 68, 122.
4. Peters, *Inquisition*, p. 67.
5. Peters, *Inquisition*, p. 67.
6. Brundage, *Medieval Canon Law*, p. 153.

7. O'Shea, *Perfect Heresy*, p. 13.
8. "Albigensian Crusades," p. 14.
9. After Ladurie, *Montaillou*, p. xiii.
10. Cited by Ladurie, *Montaillou*, p. xiii.
11. Cited by Ladurie, *Montaillou*, p. 282.
12. Cited by Ladurie, *Montaillou*, p. 283.
13. Ladurie, *Montaillou*, p. 287.
14. Cited by Ladurie, *Inquisition*, p. 176.
15. Cited by Ladurie, *Inquisition*, p. 156.
16. After Burr, "Inquisition," p. 2.
17. Burr, "Inquisition," p. 3.
18. Cited by Medieval Sourcebook, "Gui," pp. 1–3. The account used here has been lightly edited.
19. After Ladurie, *Montaillou*, pp. xv, xvii.
20. After Ladurie, *Montaillou*, pp. xiv, xvii.
21. Ladurie, *Montaillou*, p. 42.
22. Ladurie, *Montaillou*, p. 152.
23. Cited by Stork, "Inquisition Record (Confession of Navarre, wife of Pons Bru of Pamiers)," p. 2.
24. Cited by Stork, "Inquisition Record (Confession of Navarre, wife of Pons Bru of Pamiers)," p. 2.
25. Cited by Stork, "Inquisition Record (Confession of Agnes Francou)," p. 1.
26. Cited by Stork, "Inquisition Record (Confession of Agnes Francou)," p. 4.
27. Cited by Stork, "Inquisition Record (Confession of Baruch, once a Jew, then baptized and now returned to Judaism)," pp. 9–10.
28. Cited by Stork, "Inquisition Record (Confession of Grazide, widow of Pierre Lizier of Montaillou)," p. 1.
29. Cited by Stork, "Inquisition Record (Confession of Grazide, widow of Pierre Lizier of Montaillou)," p. 5.
30. Cited by Stork, "Inquisition Record (Confession of Barthélemy Amilhac, priest, concerning his complicity in and concealment of heresy)," p. 1.
31. Peters, *Inquisition*, pp. 66–67.
32. Cited by Stork, "Inquisition Record (Jacqueline den Carot of Ax)," p. 1.
33. Cited by Stork, "Inquisition Record (Jacqueline den Carot of Ax)," p. 5.
34. Cited by Stork, "Inquisition Record (Jacqueline den Carot of Ax)," p. 6.
35. Cited by Medieval Sourcebook, "Na Prous," pp. 1, 10, 11.

Chapter 8 — A Sampler of Medieval Cases

1. Cited by Bartlett, *Trial by Fire and Water*, p. 111.
2. "Usamah ibn Munqidh," p. 2.
3. After *Medieval Sourcebook*, "Thomas of Elderfield," pp. 1–7.
4. Cited in Medieval Sourcebook, "Thomas of Elderfield," p. 3.
5. Cited in Medieval Sourcebook, "Thomas of Elderfield," pp. 3–4.
6. Cited in Medieval Sourcebook, "Thomas of Elderfield," p. 6.
7. After Clanchy, "Highway robbery," pp. 37–41.
8. After Jones, *Balliol College*, p. 2.
9. Oxford City Guide, p. 24.
10. After Brand, "Oldcotes v d'Arcy," pp. 64–92
11. After Brand, *Making of the Common Law*, pp. 113–133.
12. After Fryde, "Medieval robber baron," pp. 199–207.
13. Fryde, "Medieval robber baron," p. 207.
14. After Post, "Ladbroke manor dispute," p. 290.
15. Cited by Seaman, "Lawyers in Chaucer's time," p. 2.
16. After Brand, *Making of the Common Law*, pp. 6–7.
17. Adapted from Chaucer, *Canterbury Tales*, p. 16.
18. Cited by Seaman, "Lawyers in Chaucer's time," p. 8.
19. Cohen, *Peaceable domain*, pp. 9–10.

20. *Registre criminel,* p. 1.
21. *Registre criminel,* p. 1.
22. *Registre criminel,* p. 2.
23. Medieval Sourcebook, "Rykener," p. 1.
24. Cited by Medieval Sourcebook, "Rykener," pp. 2–3.
25. After Tuchman, *Distant Mirror,* p. 514, and Cohen, *Crossroads,* pp. 184–185.
26. Cited by Cohen, *Crossroads,* p. 185.
27. *Chronique du Religieux,* "Duel," p. 1.
28. *Chronique du Religieux,* "Duel," p. 1.
29. *Chronique du Religieux,* "Duel," p. 1.
30. *Chronique du Religieux,* "Duel," p. 2.
31. *Chronique du Religieux,* "Duel," p. 2.
32. Cited in "Punishment of the Pillory and Whetstone," p. 1.
33. Cited in "Punishment of the Pillory and Whetstone," p. 1.
34. After McCall, *Medieval Underworld,* pp. 59–60.
35. Cited by McCall, *Medieval Underworld,* p. 60.
36. A short but excellent introduction to the Paston family is "The Pastons and Chaucer," the first essay in Virginia's Woolf's *The Common Reader* (1925).
37. After Ibeji, "Paston Family Letters," pp. 1–6.
38. Cited by Ibeji, "Paston Family Letters," p. 5.
39. Cited by Woolf, *Common Reader,* p. 8.

Chapter 9 — Medieval Crime

1. Gauvard, "Violence," p. 1205.
2. Bloch, *Feudal Society II,* p. 411.
3. Cited by Salzman, *English Life,* p. 218.
4. Skyrme, *Justices of the Peace,* p. 2.
5. Skyrme, *Justices of the Peace,* p. 2, citing G.M Trevelyan's *History of England* (1929), p. 104.
6. Weatherford, *Crime and Punishment,* p. 5.
7. Morris, *Medieval Sheriff,* p. 276. Much of the other discussion on the sheriff's income is derived from this source, too (pp. 276–283).
8. Private communication from Dr. Paul Brand of 2 May 2002.
9. Medieval Sourcebook, "Inquest of Sheriffs," p. 1.
10. After Morris, *Medieval Sheriff,* p. 282.
11. After Skyrme, *Justices of the Peace,* p. 9.
12. Cited by Skyrme, *Justices of the Peace,* p. 16.
13. After Harding, "Early trailbaston proceedings," p. 144.
14. Cited by Revard, "The Outlaw's Song," p. 103.
15. After Brundage, *Medieval Canon Law,* pp. 147–151.
16. Brundage, *Medieval Canon Law,* p. 151.
17. McCall, *Medieval Underworld,* p. 56.
18. Painter, *Middle Ages,* pp. 265–266.
19. In a private communication of 28 May 2002, Dr. Paul Brand noted that *peine forte et dure* began as *prisone forte et dure.* This punishment was specifically authorized by statute in 1275. Prisoners were to be given dry bread and water only on alternate days. It is one of the small puzzles of legal history how within a generation this had turned into *peine forte et dure.*
20. After Brewer, *Dictionary,* no page number given.
21. After Verdon, *Loisirs,* pp. 128–152.
22. Cited by Verdon, *Loisirs,* p. 142.
23. Verdon, *Loisirs,* p. 148.
24. After Verdon, *Loisirs,* p. 151.
25. After Swanton, "Deeds of Hereward," pp. 12–13.
26. Swanton, "Deeds of Hereward," p. 12.
27. Cited by Swanton, "Deeds of Hereward," pp. 41–42.
28. After Hudson, *Formation,* pp. 58–59.
29. Cited by Hudson, *Formation,* p. 59.

30. After Hudson, *Formation*, p. 55.
31. Cited by Hudson, *Formation*, pp. 53–54.
32. Cited by Hudson, *Formation*, pp. 54–55.
33. It is possible that Bricstan was not quite as innocent as the good bishop would have us believe. Another account claims that when Bricstan grew up, he "was caught up more and more in the wickedness of the world, to the point where he obtained his livelihood from unhappy usury and nothing else." Cited by Hudson, *Formation*, p. 55.
34. Cited by Hudson, *Formation*, pp. 59–60.
35. After Hudson, *Formation*, pp. 159–160.
36. Cited by Hudson, *Formation*, p. 159.
37. Cited by Hudson, *Formation*, p. 160.
38. After Kelly, "Eustache the Monk," pp. 61–62.
39. Cited by Kelly, "Eustache the Monk," p. 71.
40. Cited by Bellomo, *Common Legal Past*, p. 115.
41. After Hyams, "Tales of Justice," p. 5.
42. Cited by Phillips, "Written on the Body" in Menuge, *Medieval Women*, p. 134.
43. Cited by Phillips, "Written on the Body" in Menuge, *Medieval Women*, pp. 134–135.
44. Much of this account is drawn from Scheps, "William Wallace," pp. 254–256.
45. Cited by Scheps, "William Wallace," p. 256.
46. Cited by Scheps, "William Wallace," pp. 262–263.
47. Cited by Scheps, "William Wallace," p. 255.
48. "The Trial of William Wallace," p. 2.
49. After Ohlgren, "Gest," pp. 216–217.
50. Cited by Ohlgren, "Gest," pp. 221, 233–234.
51. Cited by Skyrme, *Justices of the Peace*, pp. 31–33.
52. Cited by Laws, *Dance of the Hanging Men*, pp. 22–23; lightly edited.
53. Cited in "François Villon," p. 2.
54. Cited by Laws, *Dance of the Hanging Men*, p. 77; lightly edited.
55. Cited by Laws, *Dance of the Hanging Men*, p. 101; lightly edited.
56. The epic qualities of the Arthurian legend are well-known but this great work has some exceptionally moving passages as well. What is arguably the best one comes towards the end of the book, when Sir Launcelot and Queen Guenever part for the last time. He tells her:

> For I take record of God, in you I have had mine earthly joy; and if I had founden you now so disposed [to come away with me], I had cast me to have had you into mine own realm. But sithen I find you thus disposed [not to join me], I ensure you faithfully, that I will ever take me to penance, and pray while my life lasteth, if that I may find any hermit, either grey or white, that will receive me. Wherefore, madam, I pray you kiss me and never no more.
>
> "Nay," said the queen, "that shall I never do, but abstain you from such works." And they departed. But there was never so hard an hearted man but he would have wept to see the doulour that they had made; for there was lamentation as they had been stungen with spears.... And Sir Launcelot awoke, and went and took his horse, and rode all that day and all night in a forest, weeping. (Malory, *Le Morte d'Arthur*, vol. II, p. 524.)

57. Details of Malory's misdeeds are taken from an untitled biography of Malory published by the Sir Thomas Malory Society (see bibliography), pp. 1–2.

Chapter 10—Justice in Medieval Germany

1. Three *Encyclopaedia Britannica* articles, totaling 53 pages and covering medieval Germany between 476 and 1493, contain only a few passing references to legal matters. See "Germany. *Encyclopaedia Britannica*" in the bibliography.
2. Private communication of 27 June 2002 from Professor Benjamin Arnold.
3. Private communication of 27 June 2002 from Professor Benjamin Arnold.
4. Bellomo, *Common Legal Past*, pp. 106–107.
5. Arnold, *Medieval Germany*, p. 148.
6. After Arnold, *Medieval Germany*, p. 148.

7. After Arnold, *Medieval Germany*, p. 146.
8. Whitton, "Society of Northern Europe," p. 149.
9. Painter, *Middle Ages*, p. 288.
10. Morral, *Medieval Imprint*, p. 106.
11. Cited by Myers, "Law, German," p. 479.
12. After Myers, "Law, German," p. 479.
13. Pennington, "Law," p. 504.
14. Cited by Medieval Sourcebook, "Golden Bull," pp. 2–3.
15. Cited by Medieval Sourcebook, "Golden Bull," p. 1.
16. After "fehmic court," p. 1.
17. After Bellomo, *Common Legal Past*, pp. 217–220.
18. Cited by Bellomo, *Common Legal Past*, p. 220.
19. Bellomo, *Common Legal Past*, p. 222.
20. Cited by "Capitulary of Charlemagne," p. 1.
21. After Innes, *State and Society*, pp. 129–130.
22. After Arnold, *Medieval Germany*, p. 147.
23. After Arnold, *Medieval Germany*, p. 151.
24. Cited by Arnold, *Medieval Germany*, p. 154.
25. Cited by Myers, "Law, German," p. 480.
26. "Sachsenspiegel Lawbook," p. 1.
27. Bellomo, *Common Legal Past*, p. 109.
28. Cited by Myers, "Law, German," p. 480.
29. Cited by Dobozy, *Saxon Mirror*, p. 75.
30. "Medieval Dungeons," pp. 1–2.
31. Machiavelli, *The Prince*, p. 35.

Chapter 11 — Where Medieval Law and Politics Meet

1. Musson, *Medieval Law*, p. 217.
2. Harriss, "Formation of Parliament," p. 44.
3. Private communication from Dr. Paul Brand of 20 June 2002.
4. Private communication from Dr. Paul Brand of 20 June 2002.
5. Cited by Dunham, "Parliament, English," pp. 423–424.
6. Cited by Dunham, "Parliament, English," p. 424.
7. Cited by Dunham, "Parliament, English," p. 425.
8. Cited by Musson, *Medieval Law*, p. 186.
9. Harriss, "Formation of Parliament," p. 44.
10. Some of the points made in this section are drawn from Musson, *Medieval Law*, pp. 232–234.
11. Musson, *Medieval Law*, pp. 233–234.
12. Pennington, *Prince and the Law*, pp. 171, 183.
13. The following comments on *Saepe* are drawn from Pennington, "Due Process," p. 17.
14. This discussion is drawn from a private communication from Dr. Paul Brand of 8 April 2002.
15. Cited by Pennington, "Due Process," p. 17.
16. Shaw, *Saint Joan*, pp. 3–4.
17. Cited by Purcell, "Sowing Terror in Gascony," p. 3.
18. Vale, "Civilization," p. 323.
19. This account is drawn from Lanhers and Vale, "Joan of Arc, pp. 1–10.
20. Cited by Pernoud, *Joan of Arc*, p. 87.
21. Medieval Sourcebook, "Trial of Joan of Arc," pp. 1–4.
22. Cited by Pernoud, *Joan of Arc*, p. 133.
23. Cited by Pernoud, *Joan of Arc*, p. 133.
24. Cited by Pernoud, *Joan of Arc*, p. 136.
25. Pernoud, *Joan of Arc*, p. 152.
26. See Peters, *Inquisition*, p. 69.
27. Cited by Pernoud, *Joan of Arc*, p. 108.
28. From the introduction to the Medieval Sourcebook article, "Trial of Joan of Arc," p. 1.
29. Verger, "Université," p. 1166.

30. After Le Goff and Schmitt, *Dictionnaire raisonné*, p. vii.
31. Brand, *Origins*, p. 145.
32. Cited by Pennington, "Law," pp. 504–505.
33. Bellomo, *Common Legal Past*, p. xiii.
34. Helmholz, *Ius Commune*, pp. 3–5.
35. Brand, "Formation," p. 121.
36. Private communication from Dr. Paul Brand of 18 June 2002.
37. Brundage, *Medieval Canon Law*, p. 3.
38. After Brundage, *Medieval Canon Law*, pp. 59, 119, 218.
39. After Pennington, "Law," p. 505.
40. Faure, "Anges," p. 42.

Appendix I — A Brief Overview of the Inquisition

1. Many of the facts in this section are taken from the Catholic Encyclopedia's long article, "Inquisition," which was written before 1910. Although this article is both dated and sectarian, it is still useful because it contains a wealth of detail not found in more modern histories of the inquisition, e.g., Peters, *Inquisition* (1989).
2. Cited by Peters, *Inquisition*, p. 47.
3. Peters, *Inquisition*, p. 48.
4. Cited by Peters, *Inquisition*, p. 49.
5. Brundage, *Medieval Canon Law*, p. 92.
6. Cited by Peters, *Inquisition*, p. 63.
7. Cited by Catholic Encyclopedia, "Inquisition," p. 16.
8. Cited by Catholic Encyclopedia, "Inquisition," p. 8.
9. The process of inquisition did not, of course, end in 1498. The Spanish Inquisition was introduced into Sicily in 1517 and into the Netherlands in 1522. Pope Paul III established the Roman Inquisition (also known as the Roman Congregation of the Inquisition and as the Holy Office) in 1542. Under the direction of Pope Paul IV, in 1559 the Roman Inquisition drew up the first Index of Forbidden Books. In 1633, Galileo was tried for his heretical proposition that the sun is immobile and at the center of the solar system, and that the earth moves around it. Suppressed in Spain by Joseph Bonaparte in 1808, the Spanish Inquisition was restored by Ferdinand VII in 1814. It was suppressed again in 1820, restored again in 1823, and finally permanently suppressed in 1834. In 1908, pope Pius X dropped the term "Inquisition" and the institution formally charged with maintaining the purity of the faith subsequently became known as the Congregation of the Holy Office. Finally, in 1965 Pope Paul VI reorganized this body along more democratic lines, renaming it as the Congregation for the Doctrine of the Faith.

Appendix II — What Was One Penny Worth in the Middle Ages?

1. This appendix is a lightly edited version of a private communication of 6 June 2002 from J.L. Bolton, Senior Research Fellow, History Department, University of London.

Appendix III — Medieval and Later Laws Concerning Swans

1. After "The Annual Taking Up," pp. 1–2, and from a private e-mail of 25 April 2002 from University of Oxford Professor Christopher Perrins, the Queen's Swan Warden.
2. Cited by "The Annual Taking Up," p. 3.

Appendix IV — Joan of Arc: The Twenty-Seven Articles

1. After Pernoud, *Joan of Arc*, pp. 152–155.

Appendix V — The High Court of Chivalry

1. Most of the information in this section comes from Squibb, *High Court of Chivalry*, pp. xxv–28.
2. Cited by Squibb, *High Court of Chivalry*, p. 18.

3. Cited by Squibb, *High Court of Chivalry*, pp. 18–19.
4. Cited by Squibb, *High Court of Chivalry*, p. 127.

Appendix VI — Justices of the Peace in the United Kingdom Today

1. In the bibliography, for England and Wales, see "Who are Lay Magistrates" and "Duties and Responsibilities of Lay Magistrates." For Scotland, see "About the District Court" and "History of the District Courts Association."
2. Private communication of 5 July 2002 from Dr. Sue Dale Tunnicliffe.

Bibliography

"About the District Court." http://www.district-courts.org.uk/whatis.htm. Accessed 4 July 2002.

"Albigensian Crusades (1209–1255)." http://xenophongroup.com/montjoie/albigens.htm. Accessed 23 February 2002.

"The Annual Taking Up and Marking of Thames Swans." http://www.thamesweb.co.uk/swans/upping2.html. Accessed 24 April 2002.

Armstrong, Catherine. "William Marshal, Earl of Pembroke." http://www.castleswales.com/marshall.html. Accessed 3 May 2002.

Arnold, Benjamin. *Medieval Germany, 500–1300: A Political Interpretation.* Basingstoke (UK): Macmillan, 1997.

Avalon Project at the Yale Law School. "Anglo-Saxon Law — Extracts from Early Laws of the English." http:// www.yale.edu/lawweb/avalon/medieval/saxlaw.htm. Accessed 6 January 2002.

_____. "Capitulary of Charlemagne Issued in the Year 802." http://www.yale.edu/lawweb/avalon/medieval/capitula.htm. Accessed 16 June 2002.

_____. "The Salic Law." http://www.yale.edu/lawweb/avalon/medieval/salic.htm. Accessed 12 April 2001.

Bartlett, Robert. *Trial by Fire and Water: The Medieval Judicial Ordeal.* Oxford: Clarendon, 1999.

Barzun, Jacques. *From Dawn to Decadence: 1500 to the Present.* New York: HarperCollins, 2000.

Bellomo, Manlio. *The Common Legal Past of Europe, 1000–1800.* (Trans. Lydia G. Cochrane). Washington, D.C.: Catholic University of America Press, 1995.

"Blackstone's Commentaries on the Laws of England." http://web.2.uvcs.uvic.ca/courses/lawdemo/DOCS/BLACKSTN/B6367_73.HTM. Accessed 12 February 2002.

Bloch, Marc. *Feudal Society.* Vol. I. "The Growth of Ties of Dependence." Chicago: University of Chicago Press, 1961.

_____. *Feudal Society.* Vol. II. "Social Classes and Political Organization." (Trans. L.A. Manyon). London: Routledge, 1995.

Bracton. "De Legibus Et Consuetudinibus Angliae." http://bracton.law.cornell.edu/bracton/Common/index.html. Accessed 26 March 2001.

_____. "Introduction." http://supct.law.cornell.edu/bracton/Framed/English/va/19.htm. Accessed 2 February 2002.

_____. "On the Assize of Novel Disseisin." supct.law.cornell.edu/bracton/Unframed/English/v3/18.htm. Accessed 18 January 2002.

_____. "Thorne Edition." http://bracton.law.cornell.edu/bracton/Unframed/English/v2/341.htm. Accessed 15 January 2002.

Brand, Paul. "Oldcotes v d'Arcy" in Hunnisett, R.F., and J.B. Post (eds.) *Medieval Legal Records, edited in memory of C.A.F. Meekings.* London: Her Majesty's Stationery Office, 1978, pp. 63–113.

_____. "The Formation of the English Legal System, 1150–1400" in Padoa-Schioppa, Antonio (ed.) *Legislation and Justice.* New York: Oxford University Press, 1997, pp. 103–121.

_____. *The Making of the Common Law.* London: Hambledon, 1992.

_____. *The Origins of the English Legal Profession.* Oxford: Blackwell, 1992.

Brewer, E. Cobham. *Dictionary of Phrase and Fable.* "Peine Forte et Dure." http://www.bartleby.com/81/12959.html. Accessed 22 March 2002.

Brundage, James A. *Feudal Society II: Social Classes and Political Organization.* Trans. L.A. Manyon. London: Routledge & Kegan Paul, 1989.

_____. *Medieval Canon Law*. London and New York: Longman, 1996.

Burr, David. "Inquisition: Introduction." http://www.fordham.edu/halsall/source/inquisition1.html. Accessed 18 February 2002.

_____. "Na Prous Bonnet (Boneta)." http://www.fordham.edu/halsall/source/naprous.html. Accessed 18 February 2002.

"La Cour d'appel de Paris." http://www.ca-paris.justice/fr/cour/fr/visite/fr/page/c_histoire_royal.html. Accessed 5 April 2002.

Catholic Encyclopedia. "Inquisition." http://www.newadvent.org/cathen/08026a.htm. Accessed 13 February 2002.

"Chartre des coutumes de Monflanquin." http://patrimoinemonflanquin.ifrance.com/patrimoinemon flanquin/favorite.htm?. Accessed 10 July 2002.

Chaucer, Geoffrey. *The Canterbury Tales: A Selection*. London: Penguin, 1996.

Chiffoleau, Jacques. "Droit(s)," in Le Goff, Jacques, and Schmitt, Jean-Claude. *Dictionnaire Raisonné de l'Occident Médiéval*. Poitiers: Fayard, 1999, pp. 290–307.

Chronique du Religieux de Saint-Denys, "An Account of the Duel between Jean to Carrouges and Jacques le Gris in the Chronicle of the Monk of St. Denis." http://www.nipissingu.ca/department/history/muhlberger/froissart/RELIG3E.HTM. Accessed 2 April 2002.

Clanchy, M.T. (ed.) "Highway robbery and trial by battle in the Hampshire eyre of 1249" in Hunnisett, R.F., and J.B. Post (eds.) *Medieval Legal Records, edited in memory of C.A.F. Meekings*. London: Her Majesty's Stationery Office, 1978, pp. 25–61.

Cohen, Esther. *The Crossroads of Justice: Law and Culture in Late Medieval France*. Leiden: Brill, 1993.

_____. *Peaceable domain, certain justice*. Hilversum: Verloren, 1996.

"*Curia regis*." http://www.lectlaw.com/def/c155.htm. Accessed 19 January 2002.

Davies, R.G., and J.H. Denton, (eds.) *The English Parliament in the Middle Ages*. Manchester: Manchester University Press, 1999.

Davies, Wendy, and Paul Fouracre (eds.). *Property and Power in the Early Middle Ages*. Cambridge: Cambridge University Press, 1995.

_____. *The Settlement of Disputes in Early Medieval Europe*. Cambridge: Cambridge University Press, 1986.

Dean, Joseph. "Middle Temple Hall: Four Centuries of History." London: Honourable Society of the Middle Temple, 2000.

Dean, Trevor. *Crime in Medieval Europe, 1200–1500*. London: Pearson, 2001.

Dobbs, Michael. "French 'Sheriff' is on the case," *International Herald Tribune*, 24–25 November 2001, pp. 1, 3.

Dobozy, Maria. (trans.) *The Saxon Mirror: A* Sachsenspiegel *of the Fourteenth Century*. Philadelphia: University of Pennsylvania Press, 1999.

Dubourg, Jacques. *Histoire des Bastides d'Aquitaine*. Bordeaux: Editions Sud-Ouest, 1991.

Dunbabin, Jean. *Captivity and Imprisonment in Medieval Europe, 1000–1300*. New York: Palgrave Macmillan, 2002.

Dunham, William Huse, Jr. "Parliament, English" in Strayer, Joseph R. *Dictionary of the Middle Ages*. Vol. 9. New York: Scribner's, 1987, pp. 422–434.

"Duties and Responsibilities of Lay Magistrates." http://www.magistrates-association.org.uk/all_about _magistrates/duties_and_responsibilities.htm. Accessed 4 July 2002.

Edwards, J.G. "'Justice' in Early English Parliaments" in Fryde, E.B., and Edward Miller. (eds.) *Historical Studies of the English Parliament*. 2 vols. Cambridge: University of Cambridge Press, 1970, pp. 279–297.

Electronic Library. "Villein." http://www.encyclopedia.com/printablenew/13487.html. Accessed 8 February 2002.

Eliot, T.S. (with Introduction and Notes by Nevill Coghill.) *Murder in the Cathedral*. London: Faber and Faber, 1965.

Encyclopedia Britannica Online. "Anglo-Saxon Law." http:// www.members.eb.com/bol/topic?eu= 7685&sctn=1. Accessed 4 January 2001.

_____. "Fehmic court." http://www.britannica.com/eb/article?eu=34517. Accessed 25 May 2002.

_____. "Fief." http://members.eb.com/bol/topic?eu=34806&sctn=1. Accessed 16 September 2001.

_____. "Law and legislation." htp://members.eb.com/bol/topics?eu=108597&sctn=17. Accessed 18 September 2001.

Faure, Philippe. "Anges" in Le Goff, Jacques, and Jean-Claude Schmitt, *Dictionnaire Raisonné de l'Occident Médiéval*. Poitiers: 1999, pp. 42–54.

Fouracre, Paul. "'*Placita*' and the settlement of disputes in later Merovingian Francia" in Davies, Wendy, and Paul Fouracre (eds.), *The Settlement of Disputes in Early Medieval Europe*. Cambridge: Cambridge University Press, 1986, pp. 23–43.

"François Villon." http://www.bohemiabooks.com.au/eblinks/spirboho/fringe/villon/villon.htm. Accessed 9 November 2001.

Fryde, Natalie. (ed.) "A medieval robber baron: Sir John Molyns of Stoke Poges, Buckinghamshire" in Hunnisett, R.F., and J.B. Post (eds.) *Medieval Legal Records, edited in memory of C.A.F. Meekings*. London: Her Majesty's Stationery Office, 1978, pp. 197–221.

Gansof, F.L. *Feudalism*. Third English edition. London: Longman, 1976.

Gauvard, Claude. "Justice et Paix" in Le Goff, Jacques and Jean-Claude Schmitt, *Dictionnaire Raisonné de l'Occident Médiéval*, Poitiers: 1999, pp. 587–594.

_____. "Violence" in Le Goff, Jacques and Jean-Claude Schmitt, *Dictionnaire Raisonné de l'Occident Médiéval*, Poitiers: 1999, pp. 1201–1209.

Geary, Patrick J. *Living with the Dead in the Middle Ages*. Ithaca: Cornell University Press, 1994.

"General Prologue: Notes." http://www.sogang.ac.kr/~anthony/Chaucer/GenProlNotes.htm. Accessed 13 September 2002.

Genet, Jean-Philippe. "Politics: Theory and Practice" in Allmand, Christopher. *The New Cambridge Medieval History*. Vol. VII, c. 1415–c. 1500. Cambridge: Cambridge University Press, 1998, pp. 3–28.

"Germany *Encyclopaedia Britannica*." [three articles] http://www.britannica.com/eb/print?eu=109153, 109154, and 109155.

Gervase of Canterbury. "Thomas Becket's Death." http://www.loyno.edu/~letchie/becket/texts/gervase2.htm. Accessed 4 February 2002.

"Glanvill." http://vi.uh.edu/pages/bob/ehone/glanvill.html. Accessed 15 January 2002.

Goetz, Hans-Werner. *Life in the Middle Ages: From the Seventh to the Thirteenth Century*. Notre Dame: University of Notre Dame, 1993.

Gregory of Tours. *History of the Franks*, "Sichar & Chramnesind." http:// teaching.arts.usyd.edu.au /history/1025/sect2/sicharchramnesind.html. Accessed 24 November 2001.

Gross, Charles. (ed.). *Select Cases Concerning the Law Merchant, A.D. 1270–1638*. Vol. I (Local Courts). London: Quaritch, 1908.

Gui, Bernard. "Inquisitor's Manual." http://www.fordham.edu/halsall/source/bernardgui-inq.html. Accessed 18 February 2002.

Guillot O., A. Rigaudière and Y. Sassier *Pouvoirs et institutions dans la France médiévale — Des origines à l'époque féodale*. Vol. 1. Paris: Colin, 1994.

Hadley, D.M. *The Northern Danelaw: Its Social Structure, c. 800–1000*. London: Leicester University Press, 2000.

Harding, Alan. "Early trailbaston proceedings from the Lincoln roll of 1305" in Hunnisett, R.F., and J.B. Post (eds.) *Medieval Legal Records, edited in memory of C.A.F. Meekings*. London: Her Majesty's Stationary Office, 1978, pp. 144–168.

Harriss, G.L. "The Formation of Parliament, 1272–1377" in Davies, R.G., and J.H. Denton. *The English Parliament in the Middle Ages*. Manchester: Manchester University Press, 1999, pp. 29–60.

Hay, Jeff. *The Early Middle Ages*. San Diego: Greenhaven, 2001.

Hay, Malcolm. *Westminster Hall and the Medieval Kings*. London: British Museum Press, 1995.

Helmholz, Richard H. *The Ius Commune in England: Four Studies*. Oxford: Oxford University Press, 2001.

"History of the District Courts Association." http://www.district-courts.org.uk/history.htm. Accessed 4 July 2002.

Holmes, George. *The Oxford Illustrated History of Medieval Europe*. Oxford: Oxford University Press, 2001.

Hudson, John. *The Formation of the English Common Law: Law and Society in England from the Norman Conquest to Magna Carta*. London and New York: Longman, 1999.

Hunnisett, R.F., and J.B. Post (eds.). *Medieval Legal Records, edited in memory of C.A.F. Meekings*. London: Her Majesty's Stationery Office, 1978.

Hyams, Paul. "Tales of Justice and Vengeance." http://falcon.arts.cornell.edu/prh3/bktales.html. Accessed 25 March 2001.

Ibeji, Mike. "Paston Family Letters." http://www.bbc.co.uk/cgi-bin/history/renderplain.pl?file=/history/society_economy/society/.... Accessed 8 October 2001.

Innes, Matthew. *State and Society in the Early Middle Age: The Middle Rhine Valley, 400–1000*. Cambridge: Cambridge University Press, 2000.

James, Edward. "The Northern World in the Dark Ages, 400–900," in Holmes, George (ed.). *The Oxford Illustrated History of Medieval Europe*. Oxford: Oxford University Press, 2001, pp. 63–114.

Jones, John. *Balliol College: A History*. 2nd ed. Oxford: Oxford University Press, 1997.

Kelly, Thomas E. "Eustache the Monk" in Ohlgren, Thomas H. (ed.) *A Book of Medieval Outlaws: Ten Tales in Modern English*. Stroud (UK): Sutton, 2000, pp. 61–98.

Keynes, Simon. "Royal government and the written word in late Anglo-Saxon England," in McKitterick, Rosamond (ed.), *The Uses of Literacy in Early Medieval Europe*. Cambridge: Cambridge University Press, 1990, pp. 226–25.

Koenigsberger, H.G. *Medieval Europe, 400–1500*. Harlow: Longman, 1998.

Koziol, Geoffrey G. (trans.). "Selections from Burchard of Worms, *Decretum*, Book XIX." http://ishi.lib.berkeley.edu/history155/translations/burchard.html. Accessed 1 December 2001.

Ladurie, Emmanuel Le Roy. (Trans. Barbara Bray). *Montaillou: Cathars and Catholics in a French village, 1294–1324*. London: Penguin, 1990.

Langley, Andrew. *Vivre au Moyen Âge*. Paris: Gallimard, 1996.

Lanhers, Yvonne, and Malcom G.A. Vale. "Joan of Arc, Saint." http://www.britannica.com/eb/print?=eu109563. Accessed 11 June 2002.

Laws, Robert Anthony. *Dance of the Hanging Men: The Story of François Villon, killer, thief and poet*. West Bridgford (UK): Pauper's Press, 1993.

Le Goff, Jacques. *The Medieval Imagination*. (Trans. Arthur Goldhammer). Chicago and London: University of Chicago Press, 1992.

_____ and Jean-Claude Schmitt. *Dictionnaire Raisonné de l'Occident Médiéval*. Poitiers: Fayard, 1999.

Lewis, Naphtali and Meyer Reinhold. (eds.) *The Empire: Selected Readings*. 3rd ed. New York: Columbia University Press, 1990.

Lilley, Keith D. *Urban Life in the Middle Ages, 1000–1450*. Houndsmill (UK): Palgrave, 2002.

Livre des sources médiévales. "Droit Féodal." http://www.fordham.edu/halsall/french/feod.htm. Accessed 23 December 2001.

_____. "Ordonnance Royal Contre Les Blasphemateurs (1397)." http://www.fordham.edu/halsall/french/blasfeme.htm. Accessed 23 September 2001.

Machiavelli, Niccolò. (Trans. George Bull). *The Prince*. London: Penguin, 1999.

"The Magistrate in England and Wales." http://www.muffit.binternet.co.uk/myleval.htm. Accessed 18 September 2001.

"Magna Carta." http://vi/uh/edu/pages/bob/elhone/Magna.html. Accessed 26 April 2002.

Malory, Sir Thomas. *Le Morte d'Arthur*. 2 vols. Harmondsworth: Penguin, 1986.

McCall, Andrew. *The Medieval Underworld*. London: Hamish Hamilton, 1979

McKitterick, Rosamond. *The Carolingians and the Written Word*. Cambridge: Cambridge University Press, 1989.

_____.*The Uses of Literacy in Early Medieval Europe*. Cambridge: Cambridge University Press, 1990.

"Medieval Dungeons." http://www.museen.nuerenberg.de/english/lochgefaengnis-e/pages/geschichte_e.html and http://www.museen.nurenberg.de/english/lochgefaengnis_e/pages/justitia_e.html. Accessed 17 September 2002.

Medieval Sourcebook. "Æthelred Unrædy: The Laws of London, 978" http://www.fordham/edu/halsall/source/978ethelred-londonlaws.html. Accessed 7 January 2002.

_____. "The Anglo-Saxon Dooms, 560–975." http://www.fordham.edu/halsall/560–975dooms.html. Accessed 26 November 2001.

_____. "Assize of Clarendon, 1166." http://www.fordham.edu/halsall/source/aclarendon.html. Accessed 17 January 2002.

_____. "Bernard Gui: Inquisitorial Technique (c. 1307–1323)." http://www.fordham.edu/halsall/source/heresy2.html. Accessed 18 February 2002.

_____. "Burchard of Worms: Lex Familie Wormatiensis." http://www.fordham.edu/halsall/source/lex-worms.html. Accessed 1 December 2001.

_____. "Charter of Homage and Fealty, 1110." http://www.fordham/edu/halsall/source/atton1.html. Accessed 11 January 2002.

_____. "Charters relating to Judicial Duels, 11th-12 Century." http://www.fordham.edu/halsall/source/12Cduels.html. Accessed 23 December 2001.

_____. "Corpus Iuris Civilis, 6th Century." http://www.fordham.edu/halsall/source/corpus1.html. Accessed 23 November 2001.

_____. "The Domesday Book, 1086." http:// www.fordham.edu/halsall/source/1186ASChron-Domesday.html. Accessed 6 January 2001.

_____. "The Golden Bull of Charles IV, 1356." http://www.fordham.edu/halsall/source/goldenbull.htm. Accessed 2 June 2002.

_____. "Gregory of Tours." http:// www.fordham.edu.halsall/basis/gregory-hist.html. Accessed 24 November 2001.

_____. "Gratian: On Marriage (dictum post C.32.2.2). http://www.fordham/edu/halsall/source/gratian1.html. Accessed 4 December 2001.

_____. "The Hundred Years War in the High Court of Parlement." http://www.fordham.edu/halsall/source/100yrs.html. Accessed 26 December 2001.

_____. "Inquest of Sheriffs, 1170." http:// http://www.fordham.edu/halsall/source/isheriffs.html. Accessed 21 September 2001.

_____. "The Life of Burchard Bishop of Worms, 1025." http://www.fordham.edu/halsall/source/1025burchard-vita.html. Accessed 1 December 2001.

_____. "Magna Carta 1215." http://www.fordham.edu/halsall/source/mcarta.html. Accessed 5 February 2002.

_____. "Oldradus da Ponte, No. 35 (Consilium)." http://MCMANUS/RESEARCH/NO35.HTM,. Accessed 5 July 2001.

_____. "Oldradus da Ponte, No. 92 (Questio)." http://MCMANUS/RESEARCH/NO35.HTM. Accessed 5 July 2001.

_____. "Port of Arles: The Navigation Code, 1150." http://www.fordham/edu/halsall/source/1150portcode-arles.html. Accessed 25 December 2001.

_____. "The Questioning of John Rykener, a Male Cross-Dressing Prostitute, 1395." http://www.fordham.edu/halsall/source/1395rykener.html. Accessed 5 July 2001.

_____. "The Strange Story of Thomas of Elderfield." http://www.fordham.edu/halsall/source/wulftrans.html. Accessed 22 March 2002.

_____. "The Trial of Enguerrand IV de Coucy Before Louis IX, 1259." http://www.fordham.edu/halsall/source/1259coucy.html. Accessed 25 July 2002.

_____. "The Trial of Joan of Arc, 1431." http://www.fordham.edu/halsall/source/1431joantrial.html. Accessed 4 September 2001.

_____. "Twelfth Ecumenical Council: Lateran IV, 1215." http://www.fordham.edu/halsall/basis/lateran4.html. Accessed 6 January 2001.

Merdrignac, Bernard and Mérienne Patrick. *Le Moyen Âge dans le Monde.* Rennes: Éditions Ouest-France, 1999.

Morall, John B. *The Medieval Imprint: The Founding of the Western Tradition.* Harmondsworth: Penguin, 1970.

Morris, William Alfred. *The Medieval Sheriff (to 1300).* Manchester: University of Manchester Press, 1927.

Musson, Anthony. *Medieval Law in Context: The growth of legal consciousness from Magna Carta to the Peasants' Revolt.* Manchester: Manchester University Press, 2001.

Myers, Henry A. "Law, German: Post-Carolingian" in Strayer, Joseph R. (ed.) *Dictionary of the Middle Ages.* Vol. 7. New York: Scribner's, 1986, pp. 479–483.

Nelson, Janet L. "Dispute settlement in Carolingian West Francia," in Davies, Wendy, and Paul Fouracre (eds.). *The Settlement of Disputes in Early Medieval Europe.* Cambridge: Cambridge University Press, 1986, pp. 45–64.

Ohlgren, Thomas H. (ed.) *A Book of Medieval Outlaws: Ten Tales in Modern English.* Stroud: Sutton, 2000.

_____. *"A Gest of Robin Hood"* in Ohlgren, Thomas H. (ed.) *A Book of Medieval Outlaws: Ten Tales in Modern English.* Stroud (UK): Sutton, 2000, pp. 216–238.

O'Shea, Stephen. *The Perfect Heresy: The Revolutionary Life and Death of the Medieval Cathars.* London: Profile, 2000.

Oxford City Guide. *Oxford.* Andover: Pitkin, 2000.

Painter, Sidney. *A History of the Middle Ages, 284–1500.* London: McMillan, 1975.

Palmer, Robert C. *The Whilton Dispute, 1264–1380: A Social-Legal Study of Dispute Settlement in Medieval England.* Princeton: Princeton University Press, 1984.

Pennington, Kenneth. "Due Process, Community, and the Prince in the Evolution of the *Ordo iudiciarius.*" http:// classes.maxwell.syr.edu/his381/procedure.htm. Accessed 25 March 2001.

_____. "Law, Procedure of, 1000–1500," in Strayer, Joseph R. (ed.). *The Dictionary of the Middle Ages,* vol. 7, New York: Scribner's, 1986, pp. 502–506.

_____. "Learned Law, Droit Savant, Gelehrtes Recht: The Tyranny of a Concept." http://www.maxwell.syr.edu/maxpages/faculty/penningk/learned.htm. Accessed 11 April 2002.

_____. *The Prince and the Law, 1200–1600: Sovereignty and Rights in the Western Legal Tradition.* Berkeley: University of California Press, 1993.

Pernoud, Régine and Marie-Véronique Clin. (Jeremy duQuesnay Adams trans.) *Joan of Arc: Her Story.* London: Phoenix, 2000.

Peters, Edward. *Inquisition.* Berkeley and Los Angeles: University of California Press, 1989.

Petit Guide. *Le château fort.* Vichy. Aedis, 1998.

_____. *Le moyen âge: chronologie.* Vichy: Aedis, 1999.

Phillips, Kim M. "Written on the Body: Reading Rape from the Twelfth to Fifteenth Centuries" in Menuge, Noël James (ed.) *Medieval Women and the Law.* Woodbridge (UK): Boydell, 2000, pp. 125–144.

Post, J.B. "Courts, councils and arbitrators in the Ladbroke manor dispute, 1382–140" in Hunnisett, R.F., and J.B. Post, (eds.) *Medieval Legal Records, edited in memory of C.A.F. Meekings.* London: Her Majesty's Stationery Office, 1978, pp. 289–399.

"Punishment of the Pillory and Whetstone, for pretending to be a Hermit." http://www.courses.fas.harvard/edu/~chaucer/special/varia/pilgrimage/falsepil.html. Accessed 30 July 2000.

Purcell, Nanda, and Hunt Janin. "Sowing Terror in Gascony: The Black Prince and the Hundred Years War." Unpublished ms. dated 11 June 1999.

Regina Anglorum Publications. "The Long Arm of the Law." http://www.regia.org/law.htm. Accessed 6 January 2002.

"Registre criminel du Châtelet de Paris du 6 septembre 1389 au 18 mai 1392." (Trans. Jeay and Garay). Paris: Lahure, 1861, t. 1, 327–38. http://mw.mcmaster.ca/scriptorium/chat. Accessed 6 June 2001.

Revard, Carter. "The Outlaw's Song of Trailbaston" in Ohlgren, Thomas H. *A Book of Medieval Outlaws: Ten Tales in Modern English.* Stroud (UK): Sutton, 2000, pp. 99–105.

Reznick, Martin. "Iudicio et Ferro: the Tools of the Wager of Battle." http://www.ahfi.org/news/v2n2/newsletter6.htm. Accessed 23 December 2001.

Russian Orthodox Cathedral of St John the Baptist, Washington, D.C. "The Great Schism of 1054." http:// www.sjohndc.org/Homilies/9606a.htm. Accessed 1 December 2001.

"The Sachsenspiegel Lawbook." http://www.library.tufts.edu/Archives/Exhibits/Law/books/tulips.html. Accessed 26 Marcy 2002.

Salzman, L.F. *English Life in the Middle Ages.* Oxford: Oxford University Press, 1926.

Sandquist, T.A. "Justices, Itinerant" in Strayer, Joseph R. (ed.) *Dictionary of the Middle Ages.* New York: Scribner's, 1986, pp. 183–186.

Schenck, Mary Jane. "Oral Customs and Written Cases in the *Coutoumes de Beauvaisis* of Philippe de Beaumanoir." http://tell.fll.purdue.edu/RLA-Archive/1995/French-html/Schenck,MaryJane.htm. Accessed 17 February 2002.

Scheps, Walter. "From *The Acts and Deeds of Sir William Wallace*" in Ohlgren, Thomas H. (ed.) *A Book of Medieval Outlaws: Ten Tales in Modern English.* Stroud (UK): Sutton, 2000, pp. 253–287.

Seaman, Betsy. "Lawyers in Chaucer's Time." http://www.law.utexas.edu/lpop/etext/lsf/seaman6.htm. Accessed 13 September 2002.

Shaw, Bernard. *Saint Joan.* London: Constable, 1930.

Sir Thomas Malory Society. Untitled biography of Sir Thomas Malory. http://www.malory.net/pt1_txt.htm. Accessed 4 September 2002.

Skyrme, Sir Thomas. *History of the Justices of the Peace.* Vol. I. Chichester: Rose, 1991.

Squibb, G.D. *The High Court of Chivalry: A Study in the Civil Law of England.* Oxford: Clarendon, 1997.

Stenton, Frank. *Anglo-Saxon England.* 3rd edition. Oxford: Oxford University Press, 2001.

Stones, E.L.G., and Grant G. Simpson. *Edward I and the Throne of Scotland, 1290–1296: An edition of the record sources for the Great Cause.* 2 vols. Glasgow: Oxford University Press, 1978.

Stork, Nancy P. "The Inquisition Record of Jacques Fournier, Bishop of Pamiers 1318–1325." http://www.sjsu.edu/depts/english/Fournier/jfournhm.htm. Accessed 18 February 2002.

Swanton, Michael. (trans. and ed.). *The Anglo-Saxon Chronicles* [sic]. London: Phoenix, 2000.

_____. "The Deeds of Hereward" in Ohlgren, Thomas H. (ed.). *A Book of Medieval Outlaws: Ten Tales in Modern English*. Stroud (UK): Sutton, 2000, pp. 12–60.

Thorne, Samuel E., and J.H. Baker (eds.) *Readings and Moots at the Inns of Court in the Fifteenth Century*. Vol. II (Moots and Readers' Cases). London: Seldon Society, 1990.

Traill, H.D., and J.S. Mann. *Social England*. Vol. I. London: Cassell, 1901.

"The Trial of William Wallace." http://www.duhaime.org/uk-wal.htm. Accessed 9 July 2001.

Tuchman, Barbara W. *A Distant Mirror: The Calamitous 14th Century*. Harmondsworth: Penguin, 1987.

Tyack, Geoffrey. *The Bodleian Library, Oxford*. Oxford: Bodleian Library, 2000.

"Usama ibn Munqidh (1095–1188): *Autobiography*, excerpts on the Franks." http://faculty.juniata.edu/tuten/islamic/usama.html. Accessed 8 July 2003.

Vale, Malcolm. "The Civilization of Courts and Cities in the North, 1200–1500" in Holmes, George (ed.) *The Oxford Illustrated History of Medieval People*. Oxford: Oxford University Press, 2001, pp. 297–351, cited p. 323.

Van Caenegem, R.C. (Trans. J.E.L. Johnston). *An Historical Introduction to Private Law*. Cambridge: Cambridge University Press, 1992.

Vauchez, André. "A strict normalisation" in Fossier, Robert (ed.), *The Cambridge Illustrated History of the Middle Ages*. Vol. II (covering 950–1250). Cambridge: Cambridge University Press, 1997, pp. 396–443.

Verdon, Jean. *Les loisirs au Moyen Âge*. 2nd ed. Saint-Estève: Tallandier, 1996.

Verger, Jacques. "Université" in Le Goff, Jacques, and Jean-Claude Schmitt. *Dictionnaire Raisonée de l'Occident Médiéval*." Poitiers: Fayard, 1999, pp. 1166–1182.

Weatherford, John W. *Crime and Punishment in the England of Shakespeare and Milton, 1570–1640*. Jefferson and London: McFarland, 2001.

Wells, Colin. *The Roman Empire*. 2nd edition. Fontana: London, 1992.

Whitton, David. "The Society of Northern Europe in the High Middle Ages, 900–1200" in Holmes, George (ed.) *The Oxford Illustrated History of Medieval Europe*. Oxford: Oxford University Press, 2001, pp. 115–174.

"Who Are Lay Magistrates?" http://www.magistrates-association.org.uk/all_about_magistrates/who_are_lay_magistrates.htm. Accessed 4 July 2002.

Wickham, Chris. "Society," in McKitterick, Rosamond, *The Early Middle Ages*. Oxford: Oxford University Press, 2001, pp. 59–74.

Winroth, Anders. *The Making of Gratian's Decretum*. Cambridge: Cambridge University Press, 2000.

"Women and the Law; Rules of Law." http://vi.uh.edu/pages/bob/elhone/rules.html. Accessed 5 July 2001.

Wood, Ian. "Disputes in late fifth- and sixth-century Gaul: some problems," in Davies, Wendy, and Paul Fouracre (eds.). *The Settlement of Disputes in Early Medieval Europe*. Cambridge: Cambridge University Press, 1986, pp. 7–22.

Woolf, Virginia. *The Common Reader*. First Series. London: Hogarth, 1984.

Wormald, Patrick. *Legal Culture in the Early Medieval West: Law as Text, Image and Experience*. London: Hambledon, 1999.

_____. *The Making of the English Law: King Alfred to the Twelfth Century*. Vol. I: "Legislation and Its Limits." Oxford: Blackwell, 1999.

Index